The Practitioner Inquiry Series
Marilyn Cochran-Smith a

(continued)

TEACHING
through the
STORM

A Journal of Hope

KAREN HALE HANKINS

Foreword by JoBeth Allen

Teachers College, Columbia University
New York and London

Published by Teachers College Press, 1234 Amsterdam Avenue,
New York, NY 10027

Library of Congress Cataloging-in-Publication Data

Hankins, Karen Hale.
    Teaching through the storm : a journal of hope / Karen Hale
Hankins ; foreword by JoBeth Allen.
        p. cm. — (The practitioner inquiry series)
    Includes bibliographical references and index.
    ISBN 0-8077-4329-1 (cloth : alk. paper) —ISBN 0-8077-4328 (pbk. :
alk. paper)
        1. Elementary school teaching. 2. Teachers—Journals.
    3. Diaries—Authorship. 4. Education—Biographical methods.
    5. Narration (Rhetroic) I. Title. II. Series.
    LB1555 .H26 2003
    371.1102—dc21   2002040926

ISBN 0-8077-4328-3 (paper)
ISBN 0-8077-4329-1 (cloth)

Printed on acid-free paper
Manufactured in the United States of America

09 08 07 06 05 04 03 02   8 7 6 5 4 3 2 1

Dedicated to my husband, Brad,
"the Saint"

Contents

Foreword

Sylvia Plath, like Karen Hankins, kept a personal journal. In it she reflected, "Writing is a religious act: it is an ordering, a reforming, a relearning and reloving of people and the world as they are and as they might be" (1958/2001, p. 26).

In *Writing Through the Storm* Karen invites us into her narrative journal. Although she journals primarily for herself, to "construct reality, come to understand, make sense of my impressions," in this book she molds these narratives into the most startling and compelling of sculptures. She sculpts ebony kings and powerful preachers, gives voice to silenced pasts, "reloves" children as they are and crafts with them visions of who they might be. The clay is pliable enough for us as readers to shape the text with our own experiential readings. This gift, a closely examined year in Karen's first-grade classroom that made all the difference in the world to her students, may have as profound an impact on us as readers.

These life stories (and you will come to believe, almost against your will, that six-year-olds do have life stories) may change you as a teacher; the telling of them may change you as a researcher and writer; the shared living of them may change you as a human being, a so-journer in creating a community of compassion. Karen shared *Writing Through the Storm* with doctoral students in her course on narrative inquiry. The course, and the book, changed their views on what counts as data and about how we research our teaching lives. Jill Hermann-Wilmarth, who studies how prospective teachers' beliefs about religion and homosexuality shape responses to children's literature, wrote,

> The most significant part of reading Karen's book for me was the realization that my own process of teaching and thinking about that teaching *is* data. Her explanation of this process sent me to my computer, to begin a more intense teaching journal. I did not, until reading this book, know how to value that process in a way that can both expand my own understanding of my teaching (and my self, my own history and present) and make me a better teacher.

Dwayne Wright is an activist researcher, currently investigating the actions of a group of Black high school students following Martin Luther King's assassination. He wrote:

> Dr. Hankins book affected me as a teacher, researcher, activist, and human being. . . . Although [much] educational research focuses on those who are on the periphery of society, their actual voices are not present in the research. Hankins' narratives provide the vehicle for the historic voiceless to take part in the construction of the classroom.

Karen's narrative dissertation became, with few major revisions, the book you are reading now. Many doctoral students who read it felt, like Dwayne, "inspired and affirmed" in their desire to write research in ways that do what this book does so well: it engages the reader from the first page as well as any novel; it prompts the reader to become deeply involved in the lives of children—to become, as Karen did, their advocates; it calls upon educators to examine their own practices through the lenses of multiple narrative theories that Karen weaves so skillfully throughout the book.

Karen teaches in narrative. She uses children's narratives and her narrative reflections to help children articulate and re-vision their life stories, in the process reshaping their lives. She uses narrative to help us as teachers envision children and re-envision teaching-learning relationships. With her, we relearn and relove people and the world as they are and as they might be.

JoBeth Allen

REFERENCE

Plath, S. (1958/2001). And a cold voice says, "What have you done?": From the Journals of Sylvia Plath. In M. R. Waldman (Ed.), *The spirit of writing: Classic and contemporary essays celebrating the writing life*. New York: Tarcher/Putnam.

CHAPTER 1

The Year of El Niño

For we dream in narrative, daydream in narrative, remember,
anticipate, hope, despair, believe, count, plan, revise, criticize,
construct, gossip, learn, hate, and love by narrative
—Barbara Hardy, "Narrative as a Primary Act of Mind"

Much of my energy as a teacher is spent in wondering about the lives and dreams of the children I teach. I work at shaping and reshaping practice in ways that will address the unique promise each student holds. Challenges ubiquitous in teaching confuse me and drive my inquiry: time constraints, multiplicity of learning styles, incredible ranges in students' emotional and physical well-being, varied academic performance. The more I learn about the individuals I teach, the more I move between construction and revision as I plan for them. One of the ways I learn about them is through their initiations of conversation: "Mrs. Hankins, know what I remember?" "Know what I hope?" "Know what I hate most?"

Balancing their offerings of hope and despair, of love and hate, of joy and anticipation, with the knowledge that I have limited time to teach them and limited access into their lives creates a powerful disequilibrium. Sometimes it seems that there is almost no positive direction for me to take and at other times I feel so much validation that I wonder why the world doesn't rejoice with equal illumination.

I keep a teaching journal, which has become a place of reflection on and dissection of my own long-held perspectives on teaching, learning, and children. All my confusion, criticalness, and hope turn into narratives that help me to separate feeling from thinking and one event from another. I invite you inside my journal, inside the head and heart of a teacher-who-also-writes, into a difficult year. It was, to borrow a metaphor, the best of times and the worst of times . . .

1

A STORMY BEGINNING

Journal Entry (fall)

It was almost 6 o'clock on Thursday in the first week of the school year. I had stayed later than usual to meet with a new child's mother who insisted that she see me today, and no, it couldn't wait. I had not met her that morning; grandmother brought Charles to school. Just one day of school had revealed Charles's multifaceted academic needs. "Today is fine," I told myself; "good—really—but I am just so exhausted." As I waited in the front office behind its large glass wall I saw her come in the door of the school. Her size was imposing. Her walk, purposeful, though labored, put her in charge right away. I suggested we move into the conference room for privacy even though no one was in the outer office. I suppose I wanted to make a stab at asserting my professionalism, give a ring of authenticity to whatever I had to say in response to the storm in her deep brown face.

As we moved from the outer office into the inner one, I was a master of animated verbosity; an effort to buffer the weight of her silence. I was complimentary of her son's first day and tried to ac-knowledge her strength as a mother of three very young children. As we took our chairs side by side in that office we had a view of the almost empty parking lot.

I was somewhat distracted by the lateness of the hour, by wonder-ing about my own family, and by the depth of tiredness that always accompanies the opening of school. I slowed my banter, tried to make eye contact, and said, "Well . . . what specifically did you want to meet about today?"

She clinched her purse in her hands, continued to stare out the window, and nearly whispered, "Look . . . I never met you, I don't even know your name. But you are my enemy. I hate you and every-body connected to this school and any other school for what you are trying to do to my baby, my precious child."

Her anger was palpable, breathtaking. As she continued her accusations toward me and schools it was hard for me to know for certain whether my inability to breathe came from her consumption of the very air available in that room or from my holding my breath in a survival mode.

She was clutching her purse; clutch, release, pat, clutch, release, pat. I felt her anger growing at least as fast as my fear. I would not be able to talk to her as a teacher. I had to meet her mother to mother.

"You carry a lot of pain, don't you?" I said.

She nodded almost imperceptibly. The tears began to roll down her cheeks. They knew the path from going the same way so often. They fell without the aid of a sob, screwed face, or quivering voice. She didn't bother to wipe them away.

"When we wait 9 long months for our babies to be born we have no idea that some of them bring more pain than we have ever had to bear . . . right?" I needed to establish myself as friend instead of foe. I was afraid of this much pain in one room. Besides, I recognized this pain. It was the same anguished pain my own mother carried over my sister's education. This kind of pain would suck the very marrow out of your bones in order to stay alive to do the work it believes it must do.

For the next hour, she talked. I just made comments that basically affirmed that I was still listening. Charles, one of her twins, had been dropped as an infant. He had landed on his head and sustained brain damage.

> It is not his doing that he was dropped. They told me first he wouldn't live. When he did they told me he would never walk, or talk. Now, look at him running all over the place with more mouth than he know what to do with. Last year his school told me he needed special education. That's why I moved back home. It's the same story over and over. Nobody knows what he can do. Just like the doctors didn't. I say, give him time. He will surprise you. I didn't know 'til today they had made him repeat first grade. I came to tell *you*, teacher lady, he is never going to be in special education. I won't sign no papers putting him in special education. I tell you what I will do. I am going to watch every move you make with him. He better be doing what he can do and plenty of it. I do not want him sitting doing nothing; I want him learning. And just so you know, I don't care who I hurt to protect my child.

I remember that I reached out to touch her arm. "I promise I will not neglect him. I promise I will protect him and teach him where he is and take him as far as he can go with me. I also promise you that I will not refer him for any testing or special services. He is *your* child. Help me know what you want me to do; we will work together."

I told her about my sister and the pain that I recognized as belonging also to my own life. She listened as I talked about Kathy's struggles as a child with brain damage from birth, the multiple learning problems and the accompanying emotional distress it caused for her and for our entire family. I talked briefly about the pain of the unfixable. I saw her silent acknowledgment of my mother's pain as the briefest hint of softness passed her face. She nodded and stood up.

As we walked to the door together. I gave her my home number. She took it but did not put it in her purse, which she clutched less tightly now. She turned and said, "OK, then . . . I'll call you next week." Her voice seemed tired but there was no mistake in her message of watchfulness as she left.

I went back to the room and began digging through all my files for work for Charles. She wanted hard evidence of paper-and-pencil work, proof that he was not sitting idle. I had barely had a chance to assess him at all. I left school that night at 7:30, aching in body and spirit. I remember getting home and easing myself into a chair, feeling comforted by the sounds of home but overwhelmed with the task of the year ahead. The tears burned hot in my throat where I dammed them up, as if holding them in would prove I was strong enough for what this class would require of me.

So began what I will always refer to as the year of El Niño.

I remember the headlines about the El Niño weather pattern. Unpredictability and instability were the defining expectations of the weather, wreaking havoc with the ability to forecast. We knew to expect more frequent storms and that the storms we experienced would be extreme and intense. As in the weather pattern, unpredictability and intensity of storms became the standard for my classroom that year. The pattern was set and I would have to be alert, keep the watch and sometimes wait it out. How many of us spent nights in the basement that spring because we had learned to respect tornado warnings in ways we may not have before?

I met Charles's mother exactly one week, to the hour, after the Thursday evening welcome-back-to-school ice cream social. By the time I met her, I had also met most of the parents of the other 24 students. Before our meeting I knew that I had at least eight children with noteworthy special needs. I had four children in foster care, three children who had experienced early traumatic abuse, two children who struggled with English, and one child staffed half days in the behavior disorders program. Two children notorious for acting out in kindergarten were both placed in my class. Each of their parents contacted me for conferences before school even opened. A week into the year I knew that their legendary reputations were more accurate than rumor.

Charles's mother was not the only one "watching every move I made." Before our 5 o'clock meeting on Thursday, I had met with a group of parents who wanted to know how I planned to meet the accelerated academic needs of their children, especially in math. On Wednesday evening I had received a frantic call from a mother who was concerned that we didn't play outside long enough for her child to be healthy and another call with equal emotion from a mother who was concerned that we seemed to be playing too long and hoping the "extended play was just get-acquainted time for the beginning of the year." Parents were becoming more and more confused by the negative images of schools in the press. I felt their concern at the same time that I felt attacked by the insinuations of my inadequacies that their questions communicated. I began the year wondering if I had the stamina to teach this group. As the year progressed I had to admit that our coming together as students and teacher involved many moments of true displeasure with one another coupled with guilt, self-doubt, and even distrust from both sides.

El Niño had promised to bring weather extremes. The temperatures would be extreme, as would patterns of rain and drought. Feast or famine seemed an appropriate description of the weather and of my class as well. I had children who were reading anything they picked up and children who couldn't name the letters of the alphabet. I had children who were wealthy and children who were poverty stricken. I had children who acted out in the most bizarre ways and children who sat patiently waiting for the storm to pass. I had children who brought customized lunches in pretty boxes with special desserts and love notes from Mom, and children for whom I arranged extra portions of the free lunch and for whom I secretly placed peanut butter crackers and apples in backpacks for the weekends.

One fall afternoon I had a forced look at the disparate lifestyles of my children in the space of several minutes. Clarissa and Meg were working on a class mural. Clarissa was adding cotton balls to some sheep grazing in a pasture and Meg was painting flowers in a meadow. Before she began painting Meg had told me in her always exquisite, tiny voice, "I should take my shoes off before I paint so they won't get drippies on them. My gramma brought them to me from France." I admired the dainty soft leather slippers as I put them in her cubby for her so *I* could inspect them up close. When I came back to the mural, Clarissa held up two cotton balls and asked tentatively, "Can I have these to take home if they be left over?"

"I guess so," I answered. "Are you going to make something at home?"

"No, I'm going to put them in my ears at night to keep the roaches out when I be sleeping."

"Good thinking!" I said, praying that my face didn't betray the hard chill I felt from the thought of roaches crawling over a sleeping child.

Wondering and Writing

I wrote copiously for several days about those contrasting statements. The writings, sometimes sermonic, sometimes angry, often editorial, carried the same theme. They contained all that I would say if I were given the opportunity to cut in on the newscasts, editorials, and political speeches that reduce Meg and Clarrissa and me to shameful statistics on nonproduction. The journaling helps me assert that children who come to school are flesh and blood. They are not statistics, nor are they the anonymous children who are written about in the passive voice in the literature on schooling. They live and breathe both in and outside school. I feel compelled to write about them as the real children who remain unknown in the reports on test scores and demographic breakdown. This teacher is flesh and blood as well—one who works to absorb the obvious "savage inequality" (Kozol, 1991) of the living conditions represented in a single classroom; one who deals with the image of myself as teacher and the ways I react in the heat of a moment of chaos, disobedience, or disrespect. In short, the "narratives help to fashion my professional identity" (Ochberg, 1994, p. 114).

During the year of El Niño, my writing served as much needed calm in the eye of the storm, a breathing space that helped me to find my bearings in the midst of a predictable tempest. I wrote what I saw, what I heard, and what I wondered about, things that were not so easily seen, heard, or understood until I was able to move them to a place of silent reflection, a place of both recollection and introspection (Piantanida & Garman, 1999). For me, that silent reflection time, both recollective and introspective, comes when I write.

I invited you into my narrative journal, but in reality this is more a narrative about the narratives. Initially, I wrote the narratives exclusively for myself. It is the way I construct reality, come to understand, make sense of, my impressions and responses (Bruner, 1986). That original purpose was served *as* the narratives were written. Now the stories are more than original data and personal method. They are a way to illustrate *how* I used the narratives, thereby making them a new level of both data and method. As you read, I ask you to remember that the stories about the children are included to help me position myself within narrative theory. That theory holds the realm of narrative, of story, as "one of two modes of cognitive functioning . . . providing a distinctive way of ordering experience and constructing reality" (Bruner, 1986).

Although the stories of children are unfolding as you read, the point becomes what happened to me because of the children's stories and what happened to them because of what I came to understand about them and myself. The stories confirm how constructing my own cohesive story about events or children helps me live through them and how, ultimately, writing the narratives transformed the way I think and therefore the way I act in order to teach.

Setting Up the Chapter

The intent of this chapter is to help clarify my reflective narrative process for you in terms of style, concept, and history. I discuss, briefly, the ways I understand and use narrative inquiry and its codefinition: interpretation, or the hermeneutic. I give a brief explanation of my triple focus on narrative as theory, data, and method. I address the philosophy of time and its relation to narrative. The many levels of time that play into even one narrative event fascinate me, and that fascination is evident in each of the chapters. Philosophies of time, hermeneutic method, and personal narrative are all components of memoir. Each narrative involves memoir at some level, and I will elaborate that later on. Since this particular writing is full of my own thoughts and feelings and memoir, I felt that it was only fair to give you some pertinent personal background in the first chapter in an effort to flesh out the voice you keep hearing. I also try to anticipate what you may want to know about our school and about the children who were there with me but not written about in this book. Finally, I introduce you to the seven focus children in a brief paragraph about each child.

NARRATIVE, HERMENEUTICS, AND IDEOLOGY

Simply stated, the science of interpretation is called hermeneutics (Feinberg & Soltis, 1992; Polkinghorne, 1988; Ricour, 1981; Widdershoven, 1993) and is often equated with narrative methods (LeCompte & Preissle, 1993). Like narrative, hermeneutics holds a concern for interpreting and meaning. The term *hermeneut* comes from the Greek word meaning "to translate." So, a hermeneut was an interpreter. The term is used to explain how narratives create the reality of the narrator and of those being narrated about.

I began this book with a piece of data, a journal entry about Charles's mother, not because I intend to tell a story about Charles or his mother, but because I wanted to illustrate how that datum, the journal entry, became a method for my growing understanding of him. I include it also to explain how past journals enabled my understanding and interpretation of that visit. Although the contact was with his parent rather than with him, it was still very much a part of the teaching of Charles. It should be clear, as well, that memoir played a part in the interpretation of that meeting, not only through the autobiographical work I had done in the past but even as the conference was happening. Although the event occurred after the school day proper, it was contextualized in the understanding of a school day. The meeting took place on a Thursday in 1997, but the only way either of us could interpret what was happening lay in our ability not only to retrieve our own pasts but also to delve into the pasts of each other. Our ability to communicate rested on mutual recognition of a dream blocked, a set of hopes dashed for a person each of us loved beyond measure.

It was in our shared past that I found significance for that event. That shared understanding began the hermeneutic, the sense making narrative, the storied event.

When teachers get together, stories emerge as easily as breathing. I know that I can be found in the middle of any group of teachers narrating classroom experiences. When we tell our teacher stories, we are engaging in interpretation and, to varying degrees, hermeneutics. I hope to emphasize the importance of acknowledging where those interpretations come from. My interpretations—the way I narrate the events—are based on my lived experience, the knowledge I have about teaching, and the themes of the research literature I am drawn to. The interpretations we make are forever entangled in our social, political, economic, and ideological perspectives.

I take an interpretivist/hermeneutic perspective in my research. The interpretivist view supports staying within the studied group to understand it, so my narratives begin and end in the group, child, or event. Hermeneutics as method involves a reading and interpretation of some kind of human text. In this context, think of *reading* as observations and *text* as a social activity. I "read" one class of children and their "texts" (school activities) throughout one year. School activities have a set of rules, norms, concepts, and roles. In this study I use hermeneutics to dissect my role as teacher and to question the rules and norms that drive my practice. Always at issue are my values, assumptions, and attitudes, especially as they affect the way I "read" a school event. There is no such thing as *the* one or *a* correct interpretation of an event (conversation, lesson, activity), only possible interpretations.

It is important, also, to note that interpretation begins at the moment an event is selected as a source of data, when the narrative is created or an event deemed significant enough to recount and revisit and revise (Polkinghorne, 1988; Riessman, 1993). The interpretive turn then is both consciously and subconsciously applied to the narrative data as we try to make meaning of an event. That meaning is always "fluid and contextual" (Riessman, 1993, p. 15). It is not a fixed meaning nor is it universally applicable. "Narratives then, like the lives they tell about are always open-ended, inconclusive and ambiguous, subject to multiple interpretations" (Denzin, 1989, p. 81). Each interpretation is "like an hypothesis, a sophisticated guess that things will turn out a certain way if tested. An interpretation is 'tested' against the fact of the social 'text,' and as more and more of the 'text' is read the interpretation becomes more or less validated" (Feinberg & Soltis, 1992, p. 97). Even though the hermeneutic interpretation can vary, there is a science about the hermeneutic that requires logic and contextualization.

A scholar of religion uses hermeneutics when interpreting sacred text. Legal scholars engage in hermeneutics when they try to clarify the intent of a certain law. Children follow a similar process as they try to understand and conform to the norms of a classroom (Feinberg & Soltis, 1992). Social scientists engage in hermeneutics as they try to comprehend the ways of a culture or the meaning of the stories that participants tell. I engage in hermeneutics as I make sense of events in the classroom, especially in regard to the things children say to me.

Teaching is the ultimate ongoing hermeneutic, it requires an immediacy of interpretation based on a retrievable, banked collection of insight. Teachers do interpret and we do tell our stories. A more deliberate engagement in hermeneutics would help to anchor and contextualize our interpretive penchant. Being deliberate involves selecting an event and reflecting on it, forming as many questions as possible. Questions usually send me writing. Writing an event into a fixed time and space turns that event into an experience upon which I reflect, and sometimes rewrite. Writing, telling, or both usually reveal holes in my first interpretation that send me to the literature or to colleagues or to my own memories for a sounding board. Soon we discover that all of who we are and what we do seems to have some bearing on an event.

Put simply, in this book I have capitalized and slowly deliberated on a natural teacher process. There is a rich precedent of interpretivist writing about schools (Cusick, 1973; Jackson, 1968; Peshkin, 1978). These writers have used a variety of ethnographic tools to interpret school socialization and the relation of each of its parts to the others. My study does not look at macro norms but at the one-on-one relationship I establish with students and how that relationship ultimately shapes the curriculum and the community that is unique to one set of children in one year. This adds to the rich body of work by other teachers who are also writers, hermeneuts of the teacher and of teaching: Sylvia

Ashton-Warner, John Holt, Karen Gallas, Vivian Paley, and Betty Shockley, among others.

Each of us interprets the teacher's world in unique ways, but we have in common the need of the interpretive power of narrative to construct an understanding of our world. Writing those narratives is the way we shape our social self and important relationships (Dyson & Genishi, 1994). Indeed, narratives are the means by which we gradually import meaning into our own (teaching) lives (Greene, 1995).

Sometimes the meaning I come to is surprising, and certainly unexpected. The most jarring insights are those that challenge my beliefs, that shake the foundations of my ideological perspective. I discover through a conversation about myself, with myself, that sometimes my actions don't match what I say I believe, that my behaviors reveal values different from those I preach and that my plans have little to do with my dreams. Much of my writing addresses such jarring and unsettling challenges to my ideology. In other words, my values, beliefs, attitudes, and assumptions in regard to the families of "those other kids," or poverty, or standardized testing, or religious metaphor, or race and ethnicity, are exposed for the barriers I have allowed them to become.

Our ideological perspectives, the often invisible etchings in the soul that make us tick, shape our responses to others and form the way we interpret events. They are as individual as we are but are also as identifying at times as the groups we belong to and the bumper stickers on our car. It is often easier for us to detect the shape of another person's ideology than it is to discover our own. When I write about dissecting or dismantling my own ideology, I refer to the process of applying what I read, observe, write about, and hear my children say that causes me to shift my thinking, my beliefs, my attitude, or my assumptions. I make an effort to read myself in the way Taxel (1988) suggests teachers read literature: to bring "what is concealed and obscured, often below the surface, to the surface so that [I] can reflect on [it]" (p. 227). Teachers, myself included, must always work to keep the ways we perceive children, race, ethnicity, and gender painfully raw enough to need attention, and buoyant enough to rise to the surface. The important task before me was to read the story I wrote about others through the story I wrote about myself and vice versa. Always I retraced the event, the writing, the reflection, to discover what I had left out earlier. As Pierre Machery says, "A work is tied to ideology not so much by what it says as by what it does not say" (quoted in Nodleman, 1996, p. 120).

It is not nearly as important that I spell out for you the shifts in my ideology as it is for you to know that those examinations and shifts were necessary in order for me to build and cross bridges successfully with my students. However, the narratives do include reflections that reveal shifts and changes.

NARRATIVE AS THEORY, DATA, AND METHOD

The scholarly focus of this study is on narrative as method in teacher research, whether that research is formal (for other readers) or informal (for that teacher only). Narrative theory will be discussed within the data, which are the set of narratives contained in my journal. The structure of this study is unique in its triple focus on narrative: theory, data, and method. I use narrative as theory, narrative as data, and narrative as method to highlight the significant individual and cultural functions of narrative (Barthes cited in Polkinghorne, 1988).

I use the narratives as an individual function to enable me to construct what and who I am in the context of school. I draw from my personal experience, both immediate and as memoir, to understand my relationship to the lives of those I teach. At a cultural level, the narratives help me trace our classroom's shared history, our cohesiveness and attempts at building community.

At both levels I am able to see individuals within that classroom culture as representatives of world cultures and community cultures. The narratives then help me to acknowledge, value, and build on the personal experiences of individual students. Dewey believed that the direct personal experiences children bring to school are the greatest asset in their possession (Dewey, 1904, p. 153). The data, my narratives, are collected as method, but it is in theory of narrative that I find support for the idea that narrative thought is data and method even before it is written down (Bruner, 1986; Emerson, Fretz, & Shaw, 1995).

While narrative is recognized, discussed, and acknowledged as a mode of thought in all social sciences, there is considerable disagreement about the meaning of the term. Many begin with a definition that springs from the philosophy of Aristotle (Polkinghorne, 1988)—that only a story with a beginning, middle, and end qualifies as narrative—and they define narrative as a chronologically sequenced story about a past event (Cronon, 1992; Labov, 1972; Polanyi, 1985). I work from a definition with its origins in the philosophy of Augustine (Polkinghorne, 1988); this describes a story as but one kind of narrative and holds that even what constitutes story is open to interpretation and cultural variation (Britton, 1993; Delpit, 1995; Emerson et al., 1995; Heath, 1996;

Michaels, 1981; Smitherman, 1994). Other kinds of narratives that teachers see at school include conversations with others, recountings of events for show and tell, and running commentaries of children as they play. Karen Gallas (1994) expands the definition of narrative to encompass dance, painting, drama, and music.

Narrative as Theory

We can begin to talk a bit about narrative theory at the outset of this study, but the theory for the most part makes better sense if it is contextualized in the individual narratives, because that is where it interacted with my questions. I work from the narrative up, or out, really, rather than from the theory down. To begin with theory hoping to find a place into which it fits is an attempt to force one mode of cognition onto another, an attempt at a fusion that is unlikely, according to Bruner (1986).

Narrative thought is a mode of inquiry that is well suited to answer questions about the relation of thoughts to action (Vygotsky, 1986). Theories of narrative suggest to me that when teachers find themselves harried by activity and classroom confusion, the mode of attack that seems most impossible, taking time to reflect, is in fact the best prescription for a balance. My data, the written narratives, did provide that time in narrative thought and writing and granted some equilibrium in the day.

Narrative as Data

The data in this study are threefold. There are (1) the narratives that take place during the events (a conversation, a story that a child told, an exchange between children, a piece of writing, or an explanation of a piece of artwork). Next, there are (2) the interpretive narratives about the event or the recording of the way I viewed the event. That first recording may be in the form of an oral rehearsal, a journal entry, a quick jotted note stuck in my pocket, to be fleshed out later. However, the (3) narrative thought that drove the selection of the event from the multitude of classroom events in a day drive both (1) and (2). The data on one event may be threefold (recorded in three different time periods, for example), but that data generally are, or become, one narrative that has been rewritten a number of times. Each time I reread, I edit and reflect again.

I draw significant parallels between my journaling and the field note data produced by ethnographers. The written narratives (2) are direct observations of classroom events (1) (Hubbard & Power, 1993) and are created in the same way in which ethnographers observe and record. They make a case that ethnographers keep many entries that are never considered part of the data collection process and remain hidden or at least unaddressed.

Teaching journals are also hidden, rarely offered for public reading. I kept one for years before anyone ever saw any of the entries. The journal, in its "invisibleness" (Emerson et al., 1995) to anyone other than myself, then, is much the same as the "often hidden early notes of ethnographers" (p. ix). People sometimes question whether the whole messy journal should remain private in this study. Yet most researchers, especially those in the field of ethnography, record conjectures, interpretations, and emotions that do not belong in an ethnographic write-up. About this invisibleness, Emerson et al. wrote, "Indeed this often invisible work—*writing field notes*—is the primordial textualization that creates a world on the page and ultimately shapes the final published text" (p. 16, emphasis added). For this book the earliest writings, the earliest events I focused on, may have been discarded, or they have been rewritten so many times that the originals remain private, hidden forever. Yet I agree with Emerson that in the end, those jotted notes were significant in creating the world of El Niño on the page. Further discussion in *Writing Ethnographic Fieldnotes* (Emerson et al., 1995) calls some writing done after the time of observation "headnotes" (p. 18). *Headnote* describes well the interpretive process of listening and responding to children in the course of the day with the intention of writing about it later. I have referred to interpretation in earlier writing as "heartnotes" (Hankins, 1998, p. 83). Heartnotes as opposed to headnotes are the reflective and pointedly interpretive time spent writing an event.

The deliberate interpretive stance I take differs from case study and ethnography and even pure narrative analysis of interview data. Rather than claiming thick description that elicits the reader's interpretation, I select out write-up and rewrite reflectively, always claiming the personally interpretive stance. The term *heartnotes* adjacent to *headnotes* suggests that I always acknowledge the personal biases that are evident in the hermeneutic.

My narrative journal contains the basic data; the jots and musings leading to the fleshed-out full narratives are all kept in that collective teaching journal. (I use the word *collective* because I write in several different notebooks and in a file on the computer, not forgetting the box that holds writings on the backs of napkins, church bulletins, concert programs, and scratch pads.) The journal houses in written form the way

I think about the day. It holds the events I selected to focus on and the narratives of children that confused or validated me. It also holds—because of—constant rewriting, the revisitation of certain events, reinterpretations based on new knowledge, from the safety of distance.

This process of collecting the data is one level of writing. The writing that comes after the initial data collection requires a different level of reflection. The line between data and method is thin and hazy, and some would suggest that there is no line at all (Wolcott, 1990). In my case, it became evident that what I was "doing" in the classroom every day with the children was not fully separable from the "writing" I did about them after class. I felt confirmed by Emerson, Fretz, and Shaw (1995), who wrote that "doing and writing should not be seen as separate and distinct activities but as dialectically related and interdependent activities" (p. 15). I write selectively about the "doings" in the classroom. Those doings, or events, become data. However, once selected and written about, they become method (Denzin, 1989; Polkinghorne, 1988; Riessman, 1993).

Narrative as Method

The writing, the reflection, the record itself are all narrative method. This is the hermeneutic process I discussed earlier. Agar (1980) described the process and lent support to the inseparability of data and interpretive method, explaining, "You learn something ('collect some data'), then you try to make sense out of it ('analysis'), then you go back and see if the interpretation makes sense in light of new experience ('more analysis'), and so on. The process is dialectic not linear" (p. 9).

Narrative method includes narrative analysis that takes as its object of analysis the event or story itself. I narrate an event I find confusing or significant. The narration begins to draw from our immediate history to dispel some of the confusion. Revisiting the narrative against readings often adjusts my view of it, reshapes my understanding. Other times I see it differently because of the distance of time. The recursive nature of narrative method teaches me to reserve judgment, to exercise patience, and to believe that I will find something rational in the confusion that so often has been the first impetus for writing about an event.

Dealing with numbers of students in a given day, with multiple teaching events, and with complex interactions has a disquieting effect, to say the least. Teaching is always movement from the confusing to the merely uncertain. In a given moment we are called on to make powerful decisions that may appear mundane on the surface yet carry powerful messages. I believe sounder decisions will be a by-product of habitually using the narrative method we are quite naturally drawn to in our profession. Narrative thought can be strengthened, however, through deliberate practice. I practice through my written reflective narratives.

Narrative method requires me to contextualize each narrative within the history of the classroom, within my own knowledge of the participant's pasts, within narrative theory, and within pedagogical considerations. As I reflect on confusing discourses or behaviors that interfere with communication, I open myself to new knowledge. Narrative data holds the confusions, but the narrative methodology dissects it.

Method, Data, and Theory Together

Remember Charles's mom? My ability to read her anger as pain and to feel it myself came out of previous work. Six years prior to that meeting, my little sister's disabilities became a source of buried pain that I slowly uncovered when I attempted to make connections with three child victims of in-utero substance abuse (Hankins, 1998). I saw Charles's mom through that now unearthed lens of the past. When I reached out to touch her arm, I did so with the confidence that I would not be rebuffed, even by her anger. It took less than 15 minutes for my own defenses to be dissolved and for me to listen to her, to open up to *her* pain. Six years ago, however, it took me months to reach across the table, literally and figuratively. It took months to realize that my own family sat in front of me in the faces of three children and their disheartened parents. It took a year before I gave them permission to distrust me. At the time, I was just learning to write interpretively, to read with eyes full of questions about my students and myself. I had just learned to open myself to the possibility that I did not have the answers, that the truth did not lie in either one of us but somewhere in between.

Remember Clarrissa and Meg? Not too many years ago, I would have thought more judgmentally about their divergent statements. In my first shiver of recoil I would have deemed the child of the roach-filled nights as less able, or would not have paused to consider which child in fact had told me most about her creative thinking. I would not have considered my part in perpetuating poverty. I would have believed that imported shoes also signaled a wealth of emotional stability and a home devoid of economic struggle and enforced career changes.

The girls' comments were an indication that they both responded to the mural-related event through a lens from a past. The ensuing conversation required a dip of understanding into each of our pasts. At the end of the year, none of the students in the class remembered the mural on her own. When I reminded them of it they offered memories of wearing big shirts over their clothes and that Alex didn't get to do it because he was sick for 2 weeks and that a "big kid" leaned on it when we displayed it in the hall, and that was "disrespect!" Like me, they found that the mural itself was not as important in the end as the lives that had stepped up to it.

Going back to those previously recorded events gives you a small sample of the way that narratives must be contextualized in the event itself and situated in the established understanding of time and place in which the event occurs, as well as reveals evidence of the layers of time involved in the interpretation of any event by its participants.

TIME AND NARRATIVE

Journal Entry (mid-October)

Life in a classroom is schedule shackled. Teachers mark off the day in segments even when the curriculum is integrated. There is the morning report that must be done when the most natural thing would be to greet the children and to listen to the things each wants to share with me. Lunchtime is relentless, invariable, regardless of what meaty topic the class has just delved into. Other scheduled events are just as invariable (except on the day that you really need that music class . . . then count on it that the music teacher is sick!).

I am so scheduled, in fact, that I tend to pass judgment on the day based on the ability to stick to the schedule and to the accomplishment of things I set down in my written plans. Our plans often take on a life of their own. Some of my infinitely detailed plans have been the worst lessons because I listened to the plan, to my own driven connections, and only realized at the end that the children had made every effort to figure out what I was aiming at but had made none of my expected connections. They had been lost in the communication equation because I failed to listen to them. I look into a sea of 24 faces and hear the necessity of order, listen to the scope and sequence of the subject at hand and move to a now internalized march of the clock. I am on! I am teacher! I am in power and control . . . a master of it. Sometimes about 4 o'clock I sit down, aching from the physical stress of maintaining that picture above and find a note on my desk or a double-glued-still-wet-cut-and-paste note that says, "to Mz Hankis . . . luv" and realize just how little interaction time I actually had with the note sender that day. Marking off chronological events seems a little ridiculous then, a bit irreverent, even. It always sends me writing, like today. I can't write about Clarrissa's "luv" note without seeing in my mind's eye her way-too-big woman's coat, the way she eyed the snack Hunter had, her shoes always on the wrong feet! I hope writing about her today will help me connect better tomorrow.

When I write about a child or an event, I raise the level of time experience from the linear succession of events. I write remembered interactions, remembered comments, and the relationship patterns I see. The next time I see that child, I feel that we have spent special time together. And the time I spend off the chronological measure of the day prepares me to listen better and contributes to the way that we build relationships. The writing time spent in reflection on a past event expands the present moment, embroidering it with what matters most.

Finding Writing Time

The question I am asked most often by people who read my work is, When do you find time to write? They ask because it is true that we all have time constraints. The clock ticks just as incessantly for each of us.

My answer may seem somewhat deflective. I respond that the *time* I take to write is not as important as the *times* I take into account when I do write. Of course, I have to find minutes and hours in which to write, but as I write I am compelled to take note of the overlapping weave of the past of each person who is involved in that narrative. I am aware of the multiple "takes" that are possible on the way that each of us has lived the same event. In writing my own take, my interpretation, I do so always with the hope that while the writing illuminates my understanding of the event, it will also shape the way I understand similar events that will occur in the future. Past, present, and future are contained in any moment that we are fully aware of living; it is never only "now." "People simply do not experience time as a succession of instants" (Polkinghorne, 1988, p. 127). We experience time as events, memories, dreams, and relationships.

The completed narratives lie outside the daily now of following a schedule, grading the papers, washing the paintbrushes, filling out the reports. The narratives provide deeper levels of understanding of problematic behavior and confusing events, so that I become able to respond more effectively to them. I am, ironically, enabling the enactment of day-to-day, get-the-job-done activities by spending time in deliberate narrative reflection outside that realm.

To return to the question about finding time: The answer is that I do write daily. I set a kitchen timer just after school lets out and write for 10 minutes. I carry my journal everywhere, often making notes during a concert or during a lecture. I write sometimes in restaurants or waiting while my daughter tries on clothes at the mall. I have on occasion written during faculty meetings or even during church. I once got out a tiny flashlight to record a thought during a play at the Fox Theater in Atlanta. My husband has learned that I didn't do this out of boredom or disrespect or because of my ignorance of the price of sitting in that seat for only 2 hours. It seems that my thoughts about teaching, and about the children I serve, come when I am most inspired—by the genius of a playwright, the soul of a musician, the creativity of an artist, the sacred moment of collective prayer. Whenever the human spirit seems most indomitable, most creative, I think of my calling to teach and of the children I am learning from. Teaching deserves to be thought of in juxtaposition to the highest moments I experience.

I compose in my sleep, in the car, on a walk, folding laundry. I have learned to keep journals everywhere. I call my house and leave myself messages on the answering machine, sometimes complete with references and a caution to my family: "Do not erase!" My students and my teaching also need to be thought of during the routines of the day. The day-to-day gathering of thoughts, the comforting proof that life unfolds in the ordinary existence of our lives, provides a balance when I reel from the unexpected or the extraordinary.

I also compose after family gatherings. I have a large family and would never run out of story material, believe me. The layers of my family have expanded in the past 5 years to include sons-in-law, step-grandchildren, and my first biological grandchild. So I write from the perspectives of daughter, mother, wife, child, grandchild, grandmother, cousin, niece, sister, and aunt. I have 23 first cousins whom I knew well as I was growing up, and now I know their offspring too. There are yearly reunions of the extended family, whose members live for the most part a state away, and I have at least weekly contact with my parents and married children, who all live in the same town. I think my pupils deserve to be thought of in the context of my large, loving family. In addition to the warmth it generates, it reminds me that unconditional love can surround the bumps and warts of our existence and can survive whatever public "novel" one of my family decides to live out. We have lived more than our share, I admit. When the stories of my family are in the same journal as the complaints I lodge against others, it helps me to keep things in perspective. I hope always to look at the lives of those I teach with the mercy I covet for my own family's trespasses.

Wherever and whenever I write, reflection on the past is required. I live an event but I write about it later, revise it even later, and reflect on it time and time again, sometimes even when I am unaware of doing so. The meaningfulness, the interpretive turn, comes as that experience enters confluently into other experiences, to serve as a change agent for my thinking and therefore my behavior.

NARRATIVE AND MEMOIR

My earlier work has spoken to the power of memoir in research (Hankins, 1998). As I mentioned earlier in regard to Charles's mother, we come to understand an event or one another when our pasts subconsciously overlap. As I have a conversation with someone there stands between us a third party, our pasts. It is in the intersection of our common pasts that we build rapport, erect barriers, or cross bridges. Memoir has the impressive ability of making the past present. I am still in the process of becoming, as are the children I teach. But there is truth in the old saying that we'll never know where we are going unless we know from whence we came.

From Whence I Came

A theater friend of the protagonist in *Divine Secrets of the Ya-Ya Sisterhood* (Wells, 1997) told her, "Use everything in your life to create your art" (p. 182). Everything in our lives does measure into our work and our relationships. Many of us go through life without recognizing those powerful connections. Others, however, like Siddalee, a Ya-Ya daughter, intentionally delve into the amalgamation of life events to create their art. Teaching is art to the degree that I acknowledge how everything in my life figures into the decisions I make and plays a part in the belief and value systems from which I operate. I think often of the beauty that emerges from a paint-spattered, jumbled mess of an artist's studio and feel better about seeing my life as a studio and my teaching as the art that springs forth from the jumble.

I write as a middle-aged, southern, White woman, which sounds a cautionary bell in the minds of most who will read this. Add Baptist to that mix and the cautionary bell may begin to sound more like a warning siren. (Let me hasten to add that there are vast theological and ideological differences between Southern Baptists and Baptists. I guess I am just a Baptist from the South—although now I am Episcopalian.)

I concede some of the stereotypical qualities that such a label evokes, others I dispute. My early childhood, with its Dick-and-Jane days, was lived in a segregated town, where I never saw a "colored" child; I even wondered whether they existed—and if so, whether they were brown underneath their shirts, too (Hankins, 1998). I used the word *colored* to talk about African Americans, a southern "nicety" at that time. I didn't hear the word *nigger* until I was 7 or 8 years old and did not know then that it referred to "colored people." Although I played with children who were cared for by what some seem to think was the ubiquitous southern black "nurse," I never had one. There were times during those early years when my parents employed a young African American teenager named Mary Ethel to iron for us. One night, she babysat for my little brother and me, but after dark she became so afraid that her mother and daddy came to pick her up. Her father took her home and her mother stayed with us until my parents arrived. For years I thought that Mary Ethel simply had a fear of the dark, even after my father, a high school principal, banned the Key Club in his school. He did so upon learning that after-meeting amusement for club members involved "nigger knocking," the practice of riding through that part of town where I never went and tormenting people who were walking down the road. The club members held bats and sticks out of the car window, whooping as they "got one!" I heard the *n* word in the whispered conversations surrounding that incident. My father's decision was not a popular one. I was too young to contemplate the possible ramifications of his action in that little town in the mid-1950s. I did know that a cross had burned on the lawn of a White doctor (who, I came to learn, treated people regardless of skin color). The cross burning didn't seem connected to the Key Club incident then, but the fear in adult voices sounded the same in conversations about both events.

My parents taught me above all to honor God and talk nice. It's true I didn't know the word *nigger*, but I also didn't know the word *fart* until I was 13. By then I had memorized voluminous amounts of scripture and most of the hymns in the Baptist hymnal and was the sword drill champion (a Bible-verse-finding game) of any church group. I could find obscure Bible passages, such as Habakkuk 3:2, in 8 seconds flat!

By the time I was 13, my family had moved three times, my father had earned a Ph.D., and my baby sister had been born. She brought a set of questions into the middle of our picture-perfect family that changed the trajectory of my life. We had lived the American Dream.

My parents had escaped the mill village without "owing their souls to the company store," become educated, attained the two-kids-two-cars-and-a-little-wooden-house-complete-with-a-redwood-fence-around-the-property image. They had done everything right—until Kathy was born. My perfectly beautiful little sister suffered brain damage at birth—and though it was evident in many ways from the start, we could not grasp its permanence in our lives for years. She follows me to school in one child's face or another year after year (Hankins, 1996, 1998).

Maybe all the unspoken questions about Kathy caused us to question our god openly. Family conversations around the table, in the car, and in our family room centered for the most part on theological issues and also on the issue of race, especially as it applied to school integration. My friends saw my parents as having been born before their time. Although my parents never fell into the trap of being one of the gang, they were determined to help us think. They took active roles in the youth department of our church, turning all of us into young "Christian agnostics," believers who question (Weatherhead, 1965).

I had no idea that our family's conversations were out of the ordinary until adults—a schoolteacher, a church youth leader, and a parent of a friend—asked me if my parents *knew* I talked the way I did. The teacher called me into the hall and said, "Look, your parents may be raising you to think the way you do but you have to learn to keep your mouth shut! People have gotten killed for less."

It was not tolerated in any circle for me to say that given a choice, I would marry a Black man who loved me and treated me well before I would marry a White man who treated me badly. The worst confrontation I had was with an aunt who ordered me out of the room at a family dinner after a comment to that effect. "We don't talk nasty in this house!" Her eyes bulged as she spit the words out. I left in tears. But I cried them silently while, mentally, I piously remonstrated with her and the whole silent table, expressing all I wished I had said: "*Bless*-ed are ye [meaning me, of course] when men shall re-*vile* you and *per*-secute you and say *all* manner of evil against you falsely . . . for so persecuted they the *prophets* which were before you" (Matt. 5:12). Prophets? Apparently, I had suffered no real blow to my ego.

I prided myself on being liberal, open minded, the antithesis of Archie Bunker. It is easy to be open-minded when you believe that you hold the key to world harmony. It is a sick kind of privilege to be able to believe that your tolerance, your acceptance, holds the invitation for another person to exist. It is a blind bigotry, really, that operated in the late 1960s and 1970s. Those of us who saw ourselves as the pivotal piece in the race problem thought that color was the whole puzzle. We represented the TV mentality that once *we* ignored *their* color, they would be just like us—which we assumed all along was what *they* wanted.

So, I grew from a blind child—I just didn't see them—into an ignorant teen: I knew what they wanted and needed. Then, I carried my oddly yoked moral conservatism and political and theological liberalism to college, burned a few peace candles, wore a sorority pin that meant very little to me, and waited impatiently to become a teacher. A teacher who would teach Red, Yellow, Black, and White children to *"smile on [their] brothers, everybody get together, got to love one another right now"* (Valenti & Cullen, 1967).

I got married; lived for a year in Korea, where I taught conversational English in a Korean girls school; and within 4 months of my wedding had adopted a Korean baby girl with the brightest smile God made that year.

The following year we were back stateside and I began my teaching career, confused by being so ill accepted as the only White teacher in an all-Black school in Louisville, Kentucky. I was hurt by the faculty's silence. I was bewildered by their unwillingness to answer even simple questions about securing supplies or turning in reports. I was humiliated by the behind-the-hand snickering when I told a group that I didn't know how to fill out my attendance because more than half the children on the roll had not shown up yet but at least that many extra children had come. (I didn't know then that for some children, the names by which they were known in school didn't match the names by which they were called in their neighborhoods.) I was afraid when rocks were hurled through the window while I was making out lesson plans in the afternoons. I quit the day two young men came in to retrieve the rock that they had thrown through the window and were in no hurry to leave the room. (This was also the day a doctor's call indicated that my nausea was called pregnancy.) I had not realized when I took the job that I was part of a token integration plan in Louisville. I must have represented a token smack in the face to that community as well. It was the first time I had come up against the reality that race was more than color and that 3 centuries of hatred would not be erased by one 23-year-old blond teacher's smile.

For the following 20 years, I juggled the roles of teacher, wife, and mother. After several moves, four children, a bitter divorce, a sojourn as a single mother, and meeting and marrying "Saint" Brad, I entered graduate school, in 1995.

My Graduate School Focus

During my doctoral study, I designed my courses to allow me as much as possible to delve into African American voices. I read Geneva Smitherman (1977, 1981) on the legitimacy of all dialects and her charge that too often students with nonstandard dialects are presumed by the largely White, middle-class teaching force to be incapable of learning. I was surprised to discover the early date of her writing. The message I took from that discovery was twofold: (a) As a teacher I had not considered searching the literature for answers to my questions about African American students and learning; and (b) during the more than 15 years that had passed since Smitherman's work had been published, we should have seen at least some infusion of her research into the knowledge base of the practitioner. In a course on women and minorities in literature, I read texts that were completely new to me but had been written in the 1970s, specifically the books of Mildred Taylor. I was delighted by the stellar contributions to children's literature by African American illustrators whose names I'd not known: Jerry Pinkney, James Ransom, Donald Crews. Why had I passed over those books before they were handed to me in a syllabus? For some reason, I had not noticed them. The question, of course, lies in the phrase *for some reason*. The most eye-opening course I took was from Dr. Dolan Hubbard, professor of both African American studies and English, who taught a course on African American autobiography. It was 1996 and I was 47 years old, reading the autobiographies of Frederick Douglass, Richard Wright, and Zora Neal Hurston. I had had only cursory knowledge of them before. I also read Maya Angelou's, Malcolm X's, and Langston Hughes's autobiographies; their names and claims to fame I did know, though nothing of their real struggles. I was amazed that I could have gone through my entire undergraduate education before reading a collection of African American authors whose publications appeared from the 1800s to the early 1970s. It was not easy to see inside the mind of a protagonist who fought so hard for self-worth against an enemy who looked very much like myself. I became ill that particular quarter. It was a "stress-produced illness," according to physicians. I did not want to be the enemy; I did not want to accept the place I took in history, and I had to work hard to find some objective distance from the readings as well as a realistic and workable vocabulary about White America's repression of the voices of people of color. For me, the most powerful images in each of the writings centered on the authors' remembered childhoods and on their self-perceptions, in contrast to the views of those who saw them as less capable, indeed less human, than their White counterparts. I made a promise to remember their stories, and especially those from their childhoods, every time I looked into the face of an African American child I taught. In large part, the impetus of this book lies in the complicated nature of keeping that promise.

Where It Brought Me

It has taken just a matter of pages for me to tell you enough of who I am to help you read this text. I have revealed the issues I can identify that influence this set of narratives most. I am concerned about children who are labeled and written off; it happened to my sister. I am concerned that color and culture still negatively permeate the dialogue about schools today. I am concerned that the composition of the teaching force of our schools is still largely White in an increasingly Black and Brown student population. Most of all I am disturbed that we live in denial of the shaping influence of our lived experiences with race and with the impact it has on our teaching.

I have spoken briefly about my church background; it is impossible to pretend that my sense of story and my narrative style are not shaped by it. The sermons I heard all those years are evident in the way I write and the way I think. The ease with which I interpret from readings to life and from an event to an interpretation has its genesis in the way those early preachers were taught to exegete scripture and prepare homilies. Many used the diamond-sermon model, which holds a scripture reading or an event up like a diamond to natural light. Each turn reveals new reflections to contemplate, thereby charging a student of scripture to examine carefully the context of an interpretation (K. Anglin, 1999, personal communication). It is a narrative style I accepted early in childhood as imparting important, indeed life-giving, information. I would be dishonest not to consider that my earliest brushes with hermeneutics came from those days when I sat swinging my patent leather–shod feet from the third row, left side, of the First Baptist Church in Gaffney, South Carolina.

SCHOOL AND STUDENT PROFILE

I teach in a university community in a suburban school. About 35% of our students come to us from the surrounding neighborhood and the others are bused from all over the city. The student population is about 70% African American; 25% European American; and 5% a combination of other ethnicities, including those of the international students. The board of education instituted a school choice plan that had the stated intention of reducing the burden of forced busing that is born by poor communities of color. In truth, however, the system is so complicated that it continues to keep families of poverty marginalized. The plan reduced the possibility of shared school experiences in poor neighborhoods. Sometimes five families on the same street had children attending five different schools. No longer were families able to ride to school with a neighbor who had a car. The choice plan required parents to come to the board office in person and fill out an application indicating several school choices. Many poor parents were unable to come to the office, for one reason or another, and as a result, their children were placed in leftover spots. Sometimes several children in the same family were placed in several different schools. This plan that was meant to reduce the burden that had been placed on children of poverty actually added to their problems. Our school is located outside the city limits and therefore has only minimal access to public transportation, making school visits next to impossible for parents who do not have their own transportation.

The faculty, more than 80% White, come largely from the neighborhoods close to the school. Most have been there since the school opened 10 years ago. I have always called us "that hyperactive faculty." The faculty as a whole puts in longer hours and does more creative planning than any collective staff I have ever worked with. Our halls are resplendent with children's writing and art projects, class graphs, and photographs of class projects.

We are in a time of transition in regard to our school population, however, with a growing number of children living a ghetto existence. Questions reverberate from a staff in increasing culture shock: Does it seem we are working harder and accomplishing less? Why are we having to do so much more for children's physical care? Why are we confronted with the worst social ills on a daily basis now, when 10 years ago we saw so few of these?

The Children

That first year back in the classroom, after my graduate school leave, I became increasingly impressed with the wide range of emotional, physical, and academic needs in my classroom. Our school was part of a 3-year university research study intended to identify at an early stage children who showed signs of school failure as a result of behavior and to set up proactive interventions for them. The ACT Early Project

(Kamphouse, 1997) provided us with a number of behavior checklists for each of our children and led data analysis classes to help us discern the information we received from the scales and checklists. The lists categorized each child into one of seven behavioral typologies (Childs, 1999). My classroom was the only one out of those in three participating schools in which all seven typologies were represented. The typologies were labeled well adapted, average, mildly disruptive, disruptive behavior disorder, learning disorder, physical complaints/worry, and severe psychopathology (Kamphouse, 1997). This confirmed what I had already suspected and had recorded in my journal.

Journal Entry (fall)

Teaching is a lonely profession and especially so when the systems we all believe in and honor (human service agencies, families, churches, school social workers) leave us to hold the fragile pieces of children's lives in our hands without even offering us workable glue. The emotional needs of the children I teach this year far exceed those of any group I've ever dealt with, in terms of both severity and numbers. How will I teach them? How do I identify the strength that we do possess? Something stronger is holding this fragility intact; how do I build on it? How do I come to grips with time factors that render some of my smallest dreams impotent? How do I deal with my loneliness when by all appearances I seem in need of solitude, a rest from the crowded press of needy children? How do I hold reading up as the beacon of life to children who struggle with issues big enough to swallow us all alive?

Selecting the Narratives

All those questions drove the selection of the narratives for this book. It wasn't as hard as you might expect to choose which children to include, for the stories had a way of sharpening into a focus that seemed magnetic. Still, you may wonder, Why those 7 children and not 7 others or all 23?

The choice wasn't made because of lack of material for reflection from other children. There was the boy, threadbare and beaten, whom I brought home to stay with us. He stayed for 2 weeks and then was taken into police custody, to be eventually placed in an alternative educational setting in another city with experts available to handle his pathology. The two boys who needed constant parent-teacher interaction were quite a story as well. I met every Friday at 5 o'clock to confer with one set of parents and every Monday during lunch break with the other. Those were tough meetings at times, but we developed several creative plans that worked—as well as many that did not. Why not include Charles's whole narrative? What did I do with the facts he presented in his own repetitive banter, contrasted with the memory of the way his mama clutched her purse at our first meeting?

"Don't touch my mama pocketbook. She gots her gun in there!

"Don't touch *your* mama pocketbook. She gots her gun in there!

"Don't touch *any* mama pocketbook. They gots *gu-u-u-n-s* in there!"

What about the little girl who wrote about her absent father day after day as if he would come see her, though he never did? Or Tybee, who went into marked depression when his father, not long back from the gulf war, was sent on tour to Korea? What about brilliant, quiet Sean, who shook when he talked but wrote long, beautiful stories about his father's childhood, stories that held a Patricia Polacco kind of magic? And there was Raji, who wrote long Indian fairy tales, getting various children to play parts in them, and whose grandmother, visiting from India, surprised me with a pointed question in her beautifully articulated accent: "Have you accepted Jesus as your personal lord and savior? I want Raji to have a *Christian* American teacher." There was Matthew, with his constant stories—of possum and squirrel hunting, of his "almost-Daddy" going to "chicken fights," of his mother wanting to name him Elvis—that seemed a throwback to a novel out of Butcher Hollar. His stories elicited passionate responses from me, and my journal is full of them. Then there was Rosalee, who was born in Mexico but came to us via California and Alaska and whose constant adornment of white lace anklets added just the right balance to the lacy black ringlets spread about her shoulders. She delighted the class when she understood everything the intern Spanish teacher said, even when the teacher was reading aloud. All of a sudden, being bilingual had real meaning for our class, and Rosalee was perceived as a champion communicator instead of a limited one. The biggest thing in her life was the "new bebé coming soon . . . soon." The new bebé turned out to be twins! "Now we both hold bebé, don't have to share!" There was Meg, whose illustrations were usually about the size of a postage stamp and who often gave me gifts of nature. Once she made ladybugs out of hand-painted gravel. Another time she gave me a walnut shell, carefully halved and emptied of its nut, painted gold, and its halves held together again with a satin ribbon. On the inside was a long, folded piece of paper on which she had drawn tiny angels and stars. She wanted to learn to read more fervently than any child I have ever met. It came laboriously to her but her tenacity paid off early.

So often that year, one of our specials (art, music, or physical education) teachers would tell me, "Hankins, you have the class from hell!"

"Maybe," I'd reply, "But they've got one foot in heaven, too!"

In fact, the students were a miraculous mixture of extremely needy children who possessed the ability to respond deeply out of their own suffering counterbalanced by more comfortable yet thoughtful children who were able and willing to articulate their thoughts.

I have hundreds of pages of writings about that year. Every child I taught is represented in those writings. (All names are pseudonyms with the exception of Santana's and those of the members of my own family. Santana's grandmother gave me permission to use her name; which I requested, since the name itself figures heavily in the narrative.) The narratives I have chosen for this collection have several things in common, aside from revealing the overarching goal of demonstrating the way I use narrative reflection to shape my teacher craft:

1. The most well developed narratives center on children who fit the description of "the children we worry about most" (Allen, Shockley, & Michaelove, 1993).

2. Each of the children is African American. Although it wasn't my intention from the start, the selection of those children is, I believe, representative of my lifelong quest to understand racism and prejudice as it applies to the way I operate in the world. I understand the risk I take in writing about children of color from a White perspective, and I ask you to understand that I write first for myself. I ask questions about how I can learn to make, and cross, cultural bridges in the boundedness of the school day. I genuinely covet helpful responses and instruction from African American readers.

3. Each of the narratives contains a response from that focus child, to literature or to their fit into our literacy community. This component, combined with the focus on African American students, allows me to reflect on the fundamental angst that sent me to graduate study. I was discouraged by the unavoidable evidence that half the children I taught each year were consistently performing below the other half. More disturbing, our performance indicators divided my class along racial and economic lines. I thought I treated all my children the same. I spent the bulk of my graduate studies moving from a defense of my practice to a dissection of it.

4. Each of the narratives explores the reciprocal nature of time and narrative. My personal identity is inexhaustibly tied to the school identities of those I teach; therefore the layers of time and experience that have shaped my identity also frame how I interpret events.

The linear march of time cannot erase how the "narrative of any one life is part of an interlocking set of narratives" (MacIntyre, 1981, p. 203). We come to meaning as we move in and out of our memory banks. Each of the narratives has a component of my memoir in it and reveals a determined search into the lives of my children before I met them and of the ways they spent their time outside school.

I discovered at the very end of the writing that I had arranged the narratives from the shortest to the longest. They can be viewed in a widening spiral. They move from "The Preacher," which is about an event; to "A King and Would-Be Professor," which is the narrative of one child; to "The Firth of Forth," a narrative that takes in two children; and finally to a triple narrative called "Singing Songs of Silence."

Randel. The first narrative is about Randel, a little boy who called himself a preacher. It spins off of an event that taught me how important it is to hear the narrative styles of other cultures. In this case, a child used the call-and-response narrative style, which reflects an African American worldview (Smitherman, 1977), to lead our class in a response to a song-poem, within the context of a nationwide celebration of Martin Luther King, Jr. The power of that day lay in the risk I took to let him lead us, to step aside as teacher, to hear the call of a student over my need to be in control and in the seat of power over lesson content. The research literature for this narrative centers on the importance of understanding diverse narrative styles, on the pervasiveness of narrative style in shaping our construct of what constitutes a story, and on time and narrative.

Kenny. The second narrative is about Kenny, a child who needed to see himself in a new way. It is about the agony I felt for his circumstances in contrast to the anger I felt when he threw tantrums and destroyed the learning and teaching environment. I began to respond to him differently when I tried to help him take a new view of himself. The narrative draws from the literature in psychology that centers around reworking our life stories, our own narratives. It deals with recognizing the defining power of the way others talk about us. Essentially, we become what others think and say we are, especially when we repeat those stories. Kenny had certainly become the negative story he told about himself and worked overtime to perpetuate it. I did not want to hold that mirror up to him in our class.

Tommy. The third narrative is about Tommy's journey into reading. It is also the story of how I almost prevented it from happening. It becomes a showcase for the power of memoir to shape an understanding of a child. The memoir from my father juxtaposed with the narratives about Tommy did uncover misperceptions I carried that were supported by still-viable prejudices. It revealed good intentions that served badly and interfered with high expectations for Tommy. It is a happy story in the end, however, one that reminds me of the necessity of bringing that which is concealed to the surface for examination in full light of direct observations. The literature influencing this particular work comes from the books I was reading during that year that dealt specifically with teaching African American children and that were written by African American writers, specifically Lisa Delpit (1995) and Michelle Foster (1997). I also draw heavily on my past work on the importance of memoirs in teacher research (Hankins, 1996, 1998, 1999).

Santana, Clarrissa, and Nickole. The last narrative is a combination of three different girls' narratives. I present them together because that way they create a picture of the chaotic and fragile hold I had on coming to understand who these little girls were. Their lives carried cruel similarities. I came to know them individually, but as I tried to find a cohesive story about them, one that made me able to bear the sorrow of what I knew, I began to see strong parallels in their lives. I wrote their narrative in sets of three to help me talk about the comparisons I drew. I needed to find a story line that helped me work things out for myself; I believe Isak Dineson, who said, "All sorrows can be borne if we put them into a story" (Riessman, 1993, p. 4). The literature for this set of narratives comes from writings that address the reciprocal nature of time and narrative. I learned how children understand time, and that narratives depend on the constructs we build about the nature of time. Frederick Beuchner's memoirs (1982, 1991, 1992) construct a metaphor of time and the development of a self-narrative that lent support to my understanding of Nickole, Clarrissa, and Santana. Hence, I include part of his metaphor "once-below-a-time" (Beuchner, 1982) in a section of that chapter. The girls' chapter contains the darkest of the narratives because it deals not only with trauma but also with the girls' continued sense of displacement. As I wrote about these girls, I was often haunted by the closing paragraph of the introduction to *I Know Why the Caged Bird Sings*: "If growing up is painful for the Southern Black girl, *being aware of her displacement* is the rust on the razor that threatens the throat. It is an unnecessary insult"

(Angelou, 1969, p. 3, emphasis added). So much of what happened to my girls were unnecessary insults. Through the storms of El Niño, I hoped to hear them sing from inside their caged memories. This narrative, in large part, deals with that hope next to the crushing reality that I could not fix things just because I saw and understood them.

Each of the narratives has the ability to stand alone and yet each is supported by reading the others. They are not in chronological order and do not build on one another as chapters in a book to tell a story. It was watching them all unfold together that helped me to understand the powerful hold that narratives have over each of us.

A Note About the Literature

The literature that is referenced in each narrative is by no means exhaustive of what I've read. The literature cited reflects what I was reading as that narrative was written and as I was particularly able to apply it. The citations serve to illustrate the ongoing connection to research literature that I believe the practitioner must have. The way the citations enter the narratives represent the limited amount of time that is available in a day in which to read the research, write, plan, teach, assess work from the children, attend meetings, and act on the agendas that grow out of those meetings. At times it appears that one author is overcited for a while and then not referred to again. Again that represents the reality of connections within or between the one or two texts I was reading as I wrote about a particular child. The quotes and notations I made in the journal refer me back to sections I had read or vice versa.

THE INVITATION

I ask you now to come into the year of El Niño, as I saw it, as I lived it, as I remember and record it. You will come knowing that you would have seen it, lived it, remembered it, and recorded it differently. However, your reading my interpretation of the year will allow you to look at the way I use narrative reflective writing to build stronger student-teacher relationships and to craft my teaching differently. This chapter has given me the opportunity to write myself more pointedly into the work for you. This process brings to mind what Denzin said of Montaigne, following his quoting of Montaigne's words: "'Painting myself for others, I have painted my inward self with colors clearer than my original ones. I have no more made my book than my book has made me'. So, [Montaigne] is not a biographical illusion, he is a biographical production" (Denzin, 1989, p. 63). I too am a kind of production, a teacher in process and hopefully in progress as I create my teaching self on the page. In a very real way I am made by my book.

I found one of narrative writing's great powers to be the enabling of my timid spirits and my bold spirits to come tentatively and tenaciously together, somewhat as in the meeting of cold and warm fronts that brings a turn in the weather, to sometimes stormy, sometimes calm. It is that tenacious bonding of our timid and our bold spirits that makes us both sensitive enough and brave enough to unravel the intricacies of that invisible (but no less real) space that teachers and students bridge between them. For it is in that invisible space that possible worlds, new patterns of thinking and knowing, begin to emerge, take shape, and explode into teaching and learning.

CHAPTER 2

The Preacher

I am that existence which includes what I have done, what I am doing and what I will do, and each moment is part of the whole that I am.
—Polkinghorne, *Narrative Knowing and the Human Sciences*

Journal Entry (winter)

It was cold, rainy, and gray as I drove to school. I was no more up than the sun and feeling somewhat out of control from a building migraine.

Days like that make me wonder what it must be like to have a job where you can tell a secretary to hold your calls for the first hour.

I knew that in the next half hour I would have to greet children with all the cheer and compassion I could muster, fill out a morning report, greet a parent or two, calm at least one unruly or unhappy child and begin the instructional part of the day. I remember thinking, "I am really not sure I am up to it today. I just want to be quiet and still . . . very, very, still.

"Where will we go on a day I don't feel like singing?" I wondered.

I couldn't even remember what I had planned for today. The radio brought me up to date. Martin Luther King's birthday.

Oh, now I remember, reading and writing about Martin Luther King. We would write chronological events of his life based on the song we had learned this week.

I got out of the car at school, carrying my coffee cup and my bags, trying to think my headache away before it became full-blown.

I began the lesson with a rather mechanistic singing of a song we'd learned about MLK's life. "*There was a boy,/a Georgia boy,/ named Martin Luther King./He learned in school the golden rule/ did Martin Luther King.*"

As we began to make a list of the events of his life, a puzzled child raised his hand.

"Mrs. Hankins, why you keep singing, 'There was a *boy* a Georgia *boy* named Martin Luther King,' when he already growed up and died?"

There they go again, I thought. Asking what I least expect, pushing this growing migraine to a different level. Be patient.

"Well . . ." I said, slowly enough to find an answer, "do you suppose that the children who were in Martin Luther King's first-grade class *knew* that he would grow up to be a famous preacher?"

They nodded in the affirmative.

"No-o-o-o." I shook my head in opposition. "They didn't know. How could they? He was just a little kid like the rest of them. Do you think the man at the store where Martin ran errands for his mama knew that the boy he was waiting on would grow up to lead marches and make speeches about freedom?"

"Yes!" they answered

"No," I countered. "How could a store owner know that this little boy buying sugar would grow up to be famous?

"Do you think his mama knew he'd grow up and preach in his daddy's church?" I ventured.

"No?" they questioned hesitantly.

"Exactly, because after all does your mama know what you'll grow up to be?"

"No," they answered in unison.

"Do you think his teacher knew what he'd grow up to be?"

"YES!"

"No. Do I know what any of you will grow up to be?"

Silence.

"Well, I don't. I don't and you don't. And, hey, always remember that you don't know who you are sitting beside . . . except for today. That person you are sitting beside today may become famous someday. They may become president, or, or a movie star [I did go to school with Kim Basinger, I was thinking . . . and we did make fun of her] or the teacher of your children or the preacher in your church or a famous artist or an author."

"Mrs. Hankins . . . Mrs. Hankins," I was being interrupted by Randel, a soft-spoken, smiling little boy. I touched his shoulder to acknowledge him but kept on talking.

"So when we sing, '*There was a boy, a Georgia boy, named Martin Luther King*,' we are remembering that he was once just like all of you, a child. Then, we sing about all he grew up to do and we remember that each of you will grow up too."

"Mrs. Hankins. But, Mrs. Hankins." Randel again. This time I acknowledged him by raising a finger and nodding, but I kept on talking.

"So, let's make a list of the things we sang about in the song," I urged them.

"Mrs. Hankins," now he just blurted out. "I'm going to be a preacher when I grow up."

"Great, Randel! Hey! Let's start with what Randel said." (I was trying to acknowledge his comment but *go on with the list!*) "S-o-o-o one thing we sang about was . . ."

"I already do . . . preach." Randel said.

I smiled. But didn't answer.

"What shall we put first?" (Hands were up.)

Since Randel had the floor, I called on him. "Randel, what will we list?"

"I preach sometimes . . . now . . . me and Jaleesa be playin' church. So I know I *will* be a preacher too."

I nodded but called on someone who was saying, "O-o, o-o, o-o I know! I know!" The little girl I called on sang, *"There was a man, a preacher man, over in A-la-ba-a-ma."*

As I recorded the sentence and told them to think of the next verse, Randel interrupted again. I was getting a little exasperated. After all, I was trying to keep to a controlled agenda, to do something that would look like instruction. You know: make a list, read it back, circle the words, write a response—all the *right* things.

Following an agenda of my own to list chronological events after the sermonic atmosphere I'd introduced is incongruous to me now and certainly was to Randel even then. I had laid a place wide open for this child. I had brought three arenas (home, school, and church) together without understanding it. His energy and persistence felt invasive in my currently unfolding plan to turn the song/story into an objective. I tried to turn the mood into method, but Randel had already picked up the call I had unwittingly issued. I kept noting the passing time and worrying that we'd strayed into not-teaching territory. I sought to reclaim "teaching" by making a list, sequencing chronological events. His constant interruptions were bothering me. I turned to him with a hint of challenge in my voice and said,

"Well, Randel, if you were going to preach today, what would you say?" I fully expected him to shrug his shoulders or give me a one-sentence answer. Instead, he slowly rose to his feet, then stood behind his chair, looking down at his hands for a moment as they gripped the back of it.

Then he squared his shoulders and raised his voice, hands and eyes in tandem saying, "Does anyone have a problem they'd like to *lift up* today."

The children came to attention, as I did, and he repeated the question. "I say! Does anyone have a problem they'd like to lift up today?" He had the intonation of every Black preacher I'd ever heard. Then he began to move, to walk rhythmically a little to the right and a little to the left, issuing the call. We were all responding to it at varying levels.

The first child who responded orally said, "Drugs. I'd like to lift up drugs."

And Randel called out with a wide, sweeping gesture that ended in a pointed finger directed at the boy. "DRUGS! So, are you gonna talk about it or you gonna *pra-a-y* about it. I say, I say, are you gonna talk about it or you gonna pr-a-ay about it?!"

Some of the children said "talk" and some said "pray." And I, well . . . I said nothing.

He asked again and again, "Does anyone else have a problem they'd like to lift up today?"

They began to call out: "guns," "divorce," "stealers," "bullies."

Every response from a child received a new call: "Are you gonna talk about it, or you gonna pra-a-ay about it?"

Then the children began answering the call with shouts of "preach it" and applause. The children (and their teacher) were all transformed, imbued with a unified and somewhat explosive feeling of excitement.

I realized after a few pointed "problems" that the children were "lifting up" the problems recorded on the bulletin board display of our responses to *Tar Beach* (Ringgold, 1991) from a week or so back. Reading *Tar Beach* solicited a shared question from most of the children. Why did she want to fly? As part of the answer, I read to them the African American folktale "The People Could Fly" (Hamilton, 1985). The two stories acted as a springboard for talking about and listing problems that are so big we'd like be able to fly over them. We had talked about the difference in complaining about a problem and working to solve it. We had talked about problems that we could solve alone and those that we would need a group of people to solve. Our individual responses were put together in a group mural about our community, made with collage, tempera paint, and markers. Over their mural of our town each child placed a flying self-portrait. Accompanying each flying child was a speech balloon spelling out a problem that that child thought about. The problems ranged from drugs and violence to children who broke school rules.

The most important aspects of that series of responses to *Tar Beach* (Ringgold, 1991) and "The People Could Fly" (Hamilton, 1985) seemed to come together in Randel's preaching performance.

Journal Entry (continued)

I read the scene with some apprehension. I remember thinking, "What if someone walks into this room? How will I explain this?" At the time, I did not understand that the moment was as curriculum based as any moment could be. I ventured into the waning momentum, saying, "Dr. King knew that the problems he faced were too big to solve without a whole lot of people working together. He wanted people to unite to solve the problems by talking and working and singing and, yes, Randel and our class praying together.

"There was a song," I told the children," that Dr. King sang sometimes when he marched or when he was in a meeting with lots of people."

As soon as I sang the first two words, *We shall,* I heard two little treble voices sing with me, *"O-ver-co-o-ome."*

One little girl said, "I know that song!"

Randel said, "Me too!"

They began to sing with me, and soon others were singing as Randel said, "We supposed to *all* join hands." We did.

His voice was raspy but strong and his little hand was warm and damp. I turned to the sound of his voice as he grabbed hold of my hand and I looked into his eyes and his smiling face. His sparkled when our eyes locked and he sang, *"Oh-h-h deep in my heart . . . I do believe/that we shall overcome someday."*

In his face and demeanor and in the words of his preaching style, I saw a promise. In our clasping of hands, mine clammy and his hot, I felt a stirring peace that somehow brought the past right into the very center of our circle. In our mutually raised voices, I felt the reality of a present unfolding into the future.

Now, I make no claim, no interpretation—I am simply reporting here—but as we finished the song and he dropped my hand, my headache was gone.

THREE LAYERS OF TIME

The philosopher Augustine suggests that the present is not a singular notion. Expanding on Augustine, Heidegger (1927/1962) suggests that we narrate time. Time is, in his schema, a threefold notion that includes a present about the future (expectation), a present about the past (memory), and a present about the present (attention).

During Randel's performance, he became our leader. He made his lesson and our past lessons immediately accessible in a present to which we gave complete attention. Then he led us through memories and expectations. He brought together what he had been thinking about over the past 2 weeks. He called each of us into his reiteration of all we should have come to understand from the stories and our collective responses. In his preaching, he asked us into the present-about-the-future. What did we expect to do with the problems named? He called us to the present-about-the-past. What could we do to blend the memories of Dr. King and memories of the literature? He called us to the present-about-the-present in the response he commanded from each of us. Randel made visible Augustine's philosophy that time is not a singular notion. The co-constructed narrative of that morning gives support to Heidegger's insight into the "symphony of multi-levels of awareness of time" (quoted in Polkinghorne, 1988, p. 130).

A Story of Our Own: Spanning Time

It is in the narrative record of the events, the telling about that day, that I find the teachable moment. The recursive nature of the process gives me the layering of time, the chance to participate in the symphony that Heidegger talked about. The-boy-who-can-preach as event held all the complexity of any drama. Narrating and *interpreting* that event helps us to make meaning of it as a part of our school life and a part of Randel's outside-school life. Individuals narrate their own reality (Bruner, 1986). Randel did just that as he insisted, "I already do . . . preach." Cultures also narrate a shared reality, through the stories they claim as their own and through unique narrative styles. There is wide credence given to the view that a person's thinking is shaped by the environment in which he or she develops. That view supports the notion that language is the primary mediator of learning (Bakhtin, 1981; Vygotsky, 1986; Wertsch, 1991). In most societies, language plays a crucial role in the ways people absorb their culture. "Simply stated in most cultures people learn how to think by listening to and participating in the way in which the people around them talk" (Marshall, Smagorinsky, & Smith, 1995, p. 7).

Randel's preaching event embodies the language he had learned through the culture of his church. It is a way of thinking, a means of using call and response, the expression of an ability to apply text to life and to make interpretive leaps from story to living. He was able to use the strategies of practiced preachers (Delpit, 1995). He was context specific and talked to individuals. He employed the "'para-linguistic' features that are crucial to communication in the black church: rhythm, intonation, gesture, emotion, audience participation which are but slightly modified reflections of secular black communication style" (p. 137).

Randel was not sophisticated enough to realize that the context created a mismatch. He assumed that if it made sense to him it would make sense to me and to the others. In fact, he was so masterful at what he was doing that it did make sense. He used the event to show me that he could preach and to practice a bit of the future he held out for himself in the middle of retelling a piece of history that he absorbed through home and church of Dr. King's life and dream.

He used "narrative to shape and reshape [his] life" (Dyson & Genishi, 1994, p. 2). He used narrative to give a new shape to our class as well, and to show me a way to shape my teaching and my attitude towards nonschool language.

Our classroom community had a story that was ours alone to understand. The story, narrated both collectively in the making and differently by the individuals involved, gives us both definition and cohesiveness. It was a shared history-making experience.

By using a narrative style learned in a place he loves, Randel pulled our curriculum together. His response to the literature was a deep and personal one that connected him back and forth to the places in which he first began thinking about problems. His willingness to bring an oral performance of call and response, which is unique to an African American worldview (Smitherman, 1994), into the classroom gave him a new designation in our class. Randel became known, for a while at least, as the preacher.

Journal Entry (January)

On Tuesday morning, after the long MLK weekend, the children's journals still held stories of Dr. King and the idea of harmony. Dylan wrote, "I want everybody to do Dr. King's dream. Everybody should believe that we can live in harmony. I know I do." However, the most telling event of the shaping influence of that morning on our class came when we were walking back from art today [about 2 weeks later]. A teacher stopped me and complained that a boy at the back of our line was making fun of a boy in her line and that it hurt her student's feelings and made him cry. Just as I was about to respond, one of the children said, "And didn't Randel just preach about that stuff too?!" Another child said, "We don't do that in our class, do we, Ms. Hankins!"

Temporality and Narrative

Ricour (1981) urges those who write about narrative to perceive the reciprocal relationship between temporality and narrative. As I write the narratives of the year of El Niño, I feel the sense-making power of the narrative relived, retold. I also write them fully aware that as I try to make sense of the events, time is of the utmost importance: the real time, the chronological-reading-on-the-clock time in which the event occurred, the time when the event gelled before I wrote it down, or retold it, or transcribed it. That time between the actual event and the recognition of the event as being significant has the power of a slow fire under a simmering stew. It is the experiences of past times we all brought to the experience that gave it significance for us.

The experience of celebrating Dr. King's birthday occurred as a multilayered slice of time. That experience became organized into strata analogous to several melodies in a symphony, each going on at the same time (see Hankins, 1998; Heidegger, 1927/1962; Polkinghorne, 1988). That morning, we had to bring our varied strata into common operation. How interesting that the solidifying common experience was led by a child. How validating that the children pulled together the literature, the responses, Dr. King's birthday, into an "integrated lesson." My format for the morning would have made an event separate from those of the prior week. My format would have made a mockery of the time the children had spent painting the mural and making the speech balloons. My format would have eventually asked the children to focus on decoding and phonetic spelling. Randel took us to a place where the spirit of dreaming and flying and working as a unit was a present possibility. Randel contextualized the song into the last 2 weeks of our classroom activities.

A classroom is bounded by the constraints of a year and of a day. Although that boundedness is recognized, the reality remains that we come with "cumulative records of our own pasts that generate expectations concerning the future" (Britton, 1993, p. 12), both common and unique. We must not allow ourselves to be bound by the constraints of a mutually lived set of classroom experiences. Randel proved that he would not be bound to the time inside the school.

HOME AND CHURCH TO SCHOOL

Journal Entry (home visit week: early October)
Randel was looking out the window when I got to his house. He was so excited that his mother apologized for his rambunctiousness. He lives with his mother and sister in a compact townhouse in federally subsidized housing. On four walls of the L-shaped living-eating area were alternating pictures of Jesus and Martin Luther King, Jr. Sitting on the sofa next to Randel's mother, with Randel

finally wedging in between us, I explained his report card to them. She beamed as I told her how hard he worked, what a good reader he was becoming.

Pointing to the wall, Randel asked his mother, "Am I like *him*, Mama, am I growing up good?" She hugged him to her, saying, "Yes, baby, you are. Mama's so proud. You are a fine and wonderful son. You just keep on learning your books and acting right. You'll go somewhere."

I don't know if he meant growing up like Jesus or like MLK, but clearly the social, political, and spiritual are not separate entities in this household. It appears also, as seen in the words of Randel's mother, that school is not separate from the spiritual either. Her expectations, wrapped around the icons in the living room, are that her child will grow up as a reader and a leader.

I wonder if this home is unlike many in that neighborhood; or is it somewhat similar? I notice that people lower their voices, almost whispering, when they speak the name of this community: "Well, you know, they live in . . . *Oakdale*." I wonder if we whisper the word *Oakdale* in an attempt to mask the negative attitude that is evident in our intonation. We fear what Oakdale kids bring to school from home, and worse, question whether they take anything back to Oakdale from school!

When we say, "It takes a village to raise a child," what do we do in our minds with the part of the village that the Oakdale children call home?

The lines between home and school are less marked for some of the children I teach than they are for Randel and other children in his neighborhood. The academic expectations are almost encoded on their birth certificates. In school, people talk in very particular ways. Much of the talk centers around the knowledge that teachers expect to be in place before a child can be successful.

I know that all children have to learn to read . . . get to learn to read . . . *must* learn to read. I know that I must do all I can to keep my expectations free from the biases inherent in my own narrative patterns. I must not hold a child in a place of low expectation because their narrative patterns don't match up to school discourse. I use phrases such as *have high expectations, believe* all *children can read, level the playing field for every child*. My own stated agenda is to find evidence that my using those phrases has paid off. How will I actualize those phrases in ways that enlarge the village to include Oakdale and similar communities? How can I do more than give lip service to phrases such as *more equitable access to the codes of power and learning agendas.* Those big, frightening words must stay right in the front of my head as I look into the faces of the 6-year-olds who hug me in the morning.

EXAMINING CHOICES

When I contemplate my classroom and see myself standing right there in the middle of it, I marvel that the phrases don't render me inoperative at times. There are so many perspectives to consider, so many infractions possible, so many ways I could subconsciously ignore the gifts that children are bringing into our classroom. I reflect on the children and on that day when a child outside my own culture offered gifts that brought us together for a morning, and I realize that the notion of cultural capital (Apple, 1990) has found a new operational toehold in my thinking. As I made a great effort to move that lesson in a way that "looked like instruction" I operated to preserve the "cultural capital— the symbolic property, that schools preserve and distribute" (p. 3).

As it would have been for many teachers, I suppose my first question, as I addressed the day, was curricular, not child centered. I didn't ask *whom* will I *meet* today, but *what* will I *do* that looks like the right thing? I was concerned with what Apple (1990) deems "the formal corpus of school knowledge we preserve in our curricula, and on [the] mode of teaching" so that in the end I could tell where we had been in an equally preserved "standard form of evaluation" (p. 8).

I have to ask myself if the rabid attack being made on schools today doesn't reflect the fear of a new emerging capital, from an unconscious concern that we cannot so easily advance what we understand school to be. Clearly Randel had cultural capital that day that many of the children also possessed. He had a sense of what needed to be advanced and preserved that surpassed my own. As I look into my teaching future at that school, I realize that more and more often I will be on the outside of a set of cultural knowledge, or capital, brought into that classroom. If the "knowledge that *now* gets into schools is already a choice from a much larger universe of possible social knowledge and principles" (Apple, 1990, p. 11), that larger universe seems bound to expand. Our choices must expand with it. Our choices will affect what sort of possible worlds we will create together. I hope always to be more excited about the possibilities than fearful of them.

The possible worlds that emerge or come together in one classroom will not be a clean fit. They will be full of what Maxine Greene (1994) called "ragged edges." The ragged edges have the potential to promote all the envy and greed necessary to destroy us unless we cast a wide net on what counts as story, what counts as response, what counts as discourse styles.

> We want our classrooms to be reflective and just; we want them to pulsate with a plurality of conceptions of what it is to be human and to be fully alive. We want them to be full of the sounds of articulate young people, with ongoing dialogues involving as many as possible, opening to each other, opening to the world. And we want them to care for one another, as we learn more and more about caring for them. (p. 25)

TEACHER-STUDENT-CURRICULUM RELATIONSHIPS

One of the ways that we teach children to care for and about one another is in our modeling tolerance and acceptance of varying narrative styles. Understanding the ways that children think about school and teaching, based on the things they are taught about school and what about school is valued in their homes and in their cultures at large, are important considerations for teachers in diversely populated classrooms.

Lisa Delpit (1995) talks about the Schulman-reported model of relationship between teacher, content, and student that pervades the middle-class agenda. Representing it graphically, she shows how the content shapes the way the teacher relates to students:

Teacher <—————> Content <—————> Student

Teachers show students how to interact with the content. A model purported to be definitive of effective teachers of poor children of color looks more like this:

Teacher_____ Student
‾‾‾‾‾‾‾‾‾ Content ‾‾‾‾‾‾‾

In this model, the strongest relationship is between the student and teacher, and the content is only one aspect of their relationship. Randel trusted our relationship. He trusted that because I had been in his home and his mother and I talked on occasion, we "knowed each other a lo-o-ong time." The day he brought church to school, he gave me the gift of trust, among others.

Research suggests that children of poverty and other pocket minorities often value the social aspect of school more than mainstream children do (Dandy, 1991; Delpit, 1995; Foster, 1997; Heath, 1996). They put an emphasis on feelings, acceptance, and emotional closeness. It is likely that the emotional experience of the content was the contextual center of Randel's preaching event. It was that emotional approach to the content at hand that brought the other children to affiliate with it at the same time they affiliated with him.

Randel had built a context for what the class had learned and what we were talking about. He demonstrated a firsthand understanding of the rhetoric involved in a preaching style that Dr. King employed to move a nation. Randel demonstrated that he was able to quickly apply the full meaning of a text (the song) to his life. Then in order to enlighten the rest of us, he brought his life to bear on the text of that song.

Connecting My Narrative Style to Randel's

Journal Entry (written in a lobby during the spring Children's Literature Conference at the University of Georgia).

I have just heard Patrica McKissack defend the dialect she uses in her stories. She read from *Flossie and the Fox*. Wow!

I have been thinking about Randel, about the comfort that he had bringing his narrative style to school. Of course it fits the day of a Martin Luther King celebration, but as I think of it, his inflection was not unlike that at other times when he had become passionate about something, especially over the mistreatment of people.

I think back to my own childhood. Our segregated living, along with the absence of the wide media infiltration of today, allowed those practiced cultural ways of storying to be, perhaps, more often repeated and therefore solidified.

I, like Randel, grew up in arenas where great points were made with small stories and sometimes small points were made with large stories. One thing for sure, there was honor in narrating our lives and greatest respect for multiple interpretations, especially surprising ones. The sense of life, the dreams of life, the best and worst of life—I came to acknowledge and understand these through deliberate and practiced narrative styles that bridged the schoolroom, the church, the backyard, and the grocery store. In a homogeneous world the loose borders between operating fields was accepted. Ironically, we still live inside our ideological heads in homogeneous worlds, but we bring our homogeneity into heterogeneous classrooms and forget that we might not understand one another. I did not understand how Randel made the leap so efficiently from Martin Luther King to preaching, then to bringing in the curriculum, but I recognized the overlap of arenas he assumed. I recognized my once-taken-for-granted understanding that what I was taught at church matched the expectations found at home, at school, in the Brownie Scouts, in the connecting backyards we all romped through, and at the corner grocery store, where my 6-year-old order to "charge it" was taken as seriously as my dad's.

INTERPRETATIONS, CONNECTIONS, AND LESSONS

Through Randel's preaching event, I received firsthand instruction in the lesson that we must not allow any child to come to school unable and not asked to contribute his or her narrative way of knowing to the community we attempt to build. Randel gave testimony to the adage that it "takes a whole village to educate a child" through his preaching. He brought the outside in through the learned narrative style of the preacher. When we went with him, we unloosed the boundedness of time and claimed our pasts. When we allowed a little boy to connect literature, history, and a narrative style he learned in his community, we became through his individuality more of a group.

What if I had been so content centered that I had told him to stop interrupting? What if I had let the moment pass? It would have been so easy to justify. We can't have church talk, God talk, in a public school. And yet we proudly display posters saying, "It takes a village to raise a child." In that moment when I widened the net to include Randel's whole village, I also expanded my own. I took the opportunity to do what I asked him to do every day, to interact in a narrative style that I did not bring with me to an experience. Consistently, we ask children from certain communities to speak two ways. Although I may not speak two ways, it would be a good thing to hear two ways, multiple ways.

Journal Entry (first week of school)
He has the biggest smile, completely engaging; but that is not the first thing I noticed. He was wearing a gold cross, very shiny, large, made for a much bigger person. It hung pointedly towards the logo on his colorful shirt, obviously new, that stated, "God don't make no junk." I haven't noticed that slogan around since the 1970s.

Odd that the first time I saw it was in an Episcopalian rector's office in Louisville, Kentucky—the city that was struggling so desperately against the idea of desegregation, the same city where I took my first real teaching job, the job I quit out of fear. I shiver thinking of those first teaching years, my arrogance, my mission to change children. I am glad to have grown beyond that . . . I mean, I have, haven't I?

At any rate, there is something bashful in his smile, something tentative about the sparkle in his eyes. But when we sing he becomes so fully energized that every ounce of him sings. I find myself choosing the songs that he likes most just so I can have the joy of watching him! His moves seem to compliment the song in ways that add in extra sets of unwritten words. Sometimes I wish I could hear it the way he must hear it. Then maybe I could sing it the way he sings it. Just where did he learn to do that; what makes him tick I wonder?

As I go back and read again the journal entries from the first weeks of school, I am often surprised by the way I first viewed a child, how wrong I may have been in my first assessment—but not so with Randel. As I read this one from the first week of the year, I am thrilled to find that I saw Randel's gifts from the start and that I had also recorded evidence that I was beginning to appreciate just how it is that narrative can be more than words, more than story, even more than patterns of speaking. Randel knew what it was to contribute to the "pulsating awareness of what it is to be fully human and fully alive" and to bring me into that pulse as well . . . over and over and over again.

CHAPTER 3

A King and Would-Be Professor

We tell stories in order to escape the stubbornness of identity.
—B. Hardy, "Narrative as a Primary Act of Mind"

I'll not forget the first time I met Kenny. I went into his kindergarten room to read a story. That year I was a roving teacher, hired to lower pupil-teacher ratios during direct instruction. As I read into the sea of new faces he caught my attention over and over with his breathless eagerness, as he intently attended and responded cue by cue and word by word to the story. I was impressed, drawn to notice his maturity. He was bright, quick, and cooperative in the small group I conducted next.

The kindergarten children, who were all so new to school, were trying to decide why *I* was there and told me repeatedly, in their words and actions, that I was not their teacher. They seemed to waver between distrust and ambiguity. Not Kenny. He was activity driven and asked me repeatedly, "Like this? Is this right?" I found I was planning activities based on his delighted response. He fed my addiction to teaching in a wonderful way.

AN ANGRY START

As fall got under way, Kenny began acting out. At first he just wasn't himself; soon the behaviors he exhibited were outside the norm for most kindergarten children. The developing behaviors were not only confusing but also hard to deal with. A perceived mistake on his part produced a dark veil over his eyes and shut him down. He began to be driven by an urge toward perfection instead of discovery. Sometimes he would refuse to continue an activity and could not be humored or argued out of his negative mood.

He began playing out odd acts of aggression. Once, he moved slightly into the work space of the child next to him, who simply moved over. He moved; she moved; this happened over and over until she was nearly off the table. She said, "Hey, move over!" He didn't comply. My

47

intervention resulted in Kenny's accusal that I liked her better than him—why didn't I tell *her* to move out of *his* way? He wouldn't move or make eye contact; he shut down completely. I left his teacher to deal with it, glad to be called by the clock to another class.

The following day, I observed Kenny and Kirsten, a popular class-mate, struggle over a bead that each wanted for a necklace. It was a plain round red bead like several others lying within easy reach. The teach-ing assistant suggested that they make a quick compromise if they wanted to have a necklace to wear, and besides, it was time for large group. The struggle persisted. Mr. Tyler, the teaching assistant, called them both by name—as a verbal reprimand. Kirsten dropped the bead, looked down at the floor, and moved, embarrassed, to the large group. Kenny slung himself on the floor then kicked at the box of beads. He tore off the necklace that he had made earlier and threw it. The aide told him to go sit by himself until he calmed down. Kenny ran to the side of the room, slumped onto the floor, and cried loudly. He rubbed his fists into his eyes fiercely, mumbling that people hated him, and named all manner of attacks he was going to wage on those of us who were within earshot. He alternately yelled and mumbled through his sobs.

It was hard to believe that this was the same child I had encoun-tered during the first weeks of school. The aide remarked, "Look at these two kids: same behavior, same consequence. One is already engaged in the next activity and this one has gone berserk! How do we deal with this and teach the others?" The lead teacher suggested that maybe I could talk to Kenny while she gave instructions to the group, but he would have nothing to do with that plan. It was clear that we couldn't have class with the tantrum going on. It was also clear that this little boy was reacting to much more than a bead.

Three teachers standing in a classroom and we couldn't conduct class because of one 5-year-old. We all agreed that we had seen behav-ior from him lately that was out of character but that this was a more radical departure. His loudness finally subsided enough for us to carry on. We had the good sense not to send him away from the room. Be-sides, if three adults couldn't handle him, what good could a fourth be? He was silent but refused to join a group for the following hour. He was close to the books, and after a while he chose one. He turned his back to the room and rested the top of his head on the wall, looking down at the book he had placed on the floor.

His teacher used her lunch time to make an emergency referral to our school counselor. During the afternoon, Kenny confirmed our unspoken fears to the counselor that something drastic had happened.

He was being sexually abused in his foster home. The school made a report and Child Protective Service removed him that day from that home.

Learning to Manipulate

Kenny learned above all that the adults at school could be trusted to hear and respond to the unbelievable events in his life, but he also learned that dramatic behavior got results. Can you blame him? I wish that our intervention had smoothed his life out. He did retrieve his higher moments, but the scars were there and his pain produced continued moments of shut-down and despair. The peaks and valleys we all demonstrate in our behavior were simply more dramatic with him. On reflection, I think it was that wide balance that kept him functioning.

I saw Kenny twice weekly in that kindergarten year, but in first grade he was all mine. During this year I saw the frequency of the tantrums and the acting out and experienced the anxiety of his building moods throughout the day instead of being able to walk out after a couple of hours. I was pivotal to his school success and was no longer afforded the luxury of having a participant observer status with Kenny. I was easily overwhelmed by his behavior and my attendant fears.

Kenny came to first grade excited to be back at school and to have a "teacher I already know." I saw the same bright active participation I'd seen in him before, but I also saw the troublesome mood change in response to kids around him who also wanted to participate. A child who said what Kenny was "fixin' to say" or sat in a chair Kenny was "just about to sit in" could cause a complete shut-down.

Kenny is imposing, taller than most children in his age group, and smart, even sly. His chief threat tactic was what the kids called "bucking up to me." He would stand very close to the person in front of him in line, his arms straight down by his sides, and bump into them with his chest. The whole time, he would have his chin out and his eyes focused beyond the child he was bucking up to. When the child would protest verbally or physically, Kenny would cry out that they had pushed him or shoved him or stepped on his foot. It took multiple eyes to discern finally what was actually happening. When we would confront Kenny with what we had seen, he would be unwilling to admit that he was the instigator. He would sling himself against the wall and sob loudly that we were picking on him. He would slump down onto the floor by stiffening his torso and letting his arms go straight down his body as he used his shoulder to drag himself down the wall, slowing his movement to the floor. When he would hit the floor, he would use his arms to cradle his face and lie straight out on the floor, in the very antithesis of a fetal position, and become silent. That was only the overture to the real show, which always unfolded slowly and interfered with the day on multiple planes.

I was almost always baffled by his response to the consequences of his behavior. Sometimes he withdrew; sometimes he threw himself face down on the floor and cried. Both were scenes that I came to dread. He was a master at building a warning, and I learned as other teachers did to be manipulated by his moods, his sudden glazing of the eye, and his clenched fists. I didn't notice for a while just how tense I would become as I worked with him, talking constantly, praising him too much for too little. I moved between anger and despair over his moods. The anger was caused by my inability to carry on as I had planned and the despair grew from what he was missing in the curriculum. There was fear as well, the big fear that I was part of this child's marginalization because I was ill equipped to deal with him. How many times have I read and concurred with the advice that we not accept excuses for poor academic performance, that we not let a child get by with underachievement because we pity the child for his or her life history? Still, Kenny is a real boy and I am a real teacher who knows that his very real pain does interfere with performance. It doesn't seem fair for either of us to become a statistic in the miseducation of this African American boy.

Gradually we worked into an understanding of each other. When I made a pact with myself to attend more to his academic prowess than to his poor behavior, I became less manipulated by his moods. I needed to view Kenny as the talented boy that he was, minus his tantrums, in order to teach him well. So it was that I began to write about the good things that happened between us and the powerful ability he demonstrated to lead others. As I reread the year's narratives of our relationship and the entries documenting Kenny's walk into academe, I find that they are almost all positive, perhaps to a misrepresentative fault.

As I revisit and rewrite the original narratives, I realize that Kenny and I had the same important task: the reframing of Kenny. I had to learn to focus on him differently. As I began to do that, I understood that in fact he had to learn to see himself differently, too. He was more stubborn about it than I was. He didn't like himself and was convinced that no one else did either.

I have had editors read my work in the past and remark, "But I didn't get it until the end." Neither did I. That is an important point of this work, which is centered on the process of narrative to inform my teaching. It serves as a model of the way I "got it" at the end.

This is the unfolding of a yearlong experience. Read it play by play, as I lived it. Struggle patiently, understanding that I struggled also to understand and to operate within a "retrospective revision that need[ed] to conclude and coincide with the known present" (Polkinghorne, 1988, p. 106). Through retrospective revision, all of us tell our lives. The struggle of this telling will feel hauntingly familiar . . . if you let it.

Showing Academic Strength

Journal Entry (October: first grade)
"Ms. Hankins, you don't have to write your numbers down to keep up wid 'em. You just can hold 'em in your head!"

Kenny's statement thrilled me! Even after all these years of primary classroom teaching, I find myself impatient watching children gain an understanding of conservation of number. For most it doesn't happen in first grade. They still have to count over and over just to prove that the five cubes that were there a minute ago are still there now.

"That's right, Kenny!" I exclaimed dramatically, hoping for the attention of some of the other children during this hands-on computation session.

"Good for you! Show us what you mean."

He moved his tub of counters away and became serious.

"Like, if you might be adding up numbers and you don't have enough fingers and all, you just can put one of the numbers up there." He points to his head and shuts his eyes tightly. "And the-e-e-n put the next number up there. Now look at it in your mind . . ." He moved his head slightly up and down as if he were really seeing something. Then he opened his eyes, straightened his shoulders, and held his arms outstretched, palms up, and said with delight, "Then, *bam*, there it is."

"Let's see if he can do it," I said to the children around him. I gave him a problem to add.

"OK . . . 6 in my head; now put 4 up there too . . . (head moving up and down) . . . 10! See? There it is!" He got his answer while the others were counting out their stacks of six and four counters.

Convinced that Kenny was counting something he could see but that they could not, his table partners were not impressed in the same way that I was. They wondered aloud how he could see what to count by closing his eyes.

"I think I see it now."

"Kenny, Kenny, is this right?"

So firm are we in our beliefs that at any given moment it is hard for any of us to frame the world except on our own terms and around our own set of experiences. I watched the children as they closed their eyes and counted, trying over and over again to "see" the counters in their heads. I was also busy convincing myself that amusement, rather than impatience, on my part was the kindest and most teacherly response toward them.

I watched Kenny for the longest mind-burning moment as he varied his approach at the table, sometimes using his method and then double checking with the counters, sometimes using counters and sometimes "just his head." The child beside him said, "Here, Kenny, do this one for me." He gladly did so. He was the picture of cooperation, of control, of decorum. What a teacher he appeared to be. But I sat knowing what raged inside him and wondered when this smoldering moment might ignite. For Kenny, it is as hard to reframe his emotional world as it seemingly was for the other children to reframe the concrete one.

A STUBBORN SELF-DESCRIPTION

The distance of a year of writing makes it no less difficult for me to imagine Kenny's plight at any real level. Watching his life unfold is akin to reading *Oliver Twist*, without the assurance that things *will* right themselves if only I read long enough. In less than a year, Kenny experienced a fire in his home and then life in a homeless shelter; his mother's incarceration for shoplifting, which separated him from his siblings, who were in different foster homes; sexual abuse by an older girl in his foster home; being sent to live with an older aunt; his mother's release from jail and much hopeful talk of getting the family back together; and his mother's reincarceration for theft on the job.

I learn these facts piecemeal. There is no thick folder containing this crucial information. There is only the little boy with the dark, dark skin and the sometimes dark, dark mood, one that coexists with his giftedness, gregariousness, resistance, withdrawal, and sense of persecution. Some things were revealed to me in his writings, in his voiced complaints, and from information that his aunt shared only late in the year, when she felt she could trust me. There is a bit from his kindergarten teacher who was as ill informed as I was. For the most part, I dealt with symptoms without a diagnosis. I managed his tantrums, his anger, and his withdrawal through a veil of uncertainty. The bits and pieces I learned made me attend especially well to anything I read about narrative as method in psychology and psychoanalysis. Kenny taught me about the power of story to aid his escape from what Barbara Hardy (1978) has called "the stubbornness of identity" (p. 12).

I came to know Kenny best in the solitude of writing, in that quiet time after school, when the light from the computer screen hypnotically sheds a soft glow around the events of the day. I write for the extended quality time it gives me with a child. It may seem odd to spend time with a child in absentia, but I found that this time of reflective writing held the power to transform the image of that child the next time we came to an unexpected battle. With Kenny the battles were usually unexpected and almost always asserted a direct challenge to me.

By interspersing revisited and rewritten journal entries with the bridges between the entries and the literature on narrative theory I try to create the picture of intertextuality that this narrative method hinges on. As I move between the texts of our lives and the texts of our stories and the literature on narrative theory, I narrate my growing understanding of the way I began to perceive and fight against the tenacious hold of Kenny's identity.

Attempt to Redescribe

Journal Entry (September: first grade)

September is so Georgia humid hot! The children begged to go out—and as soon as we got out, begged to come back in. I wanted to go back inside, too, but if we went inside it meant I had to be in charge, to come up with a game plan quickly! I decided to go ahead and read one of tomorrow's stories today. It seemed to be an appropriate choice on two counts. First, the book we were to read was set in Africa and made me think of Michelle [a friend of mine who was traveling there]. If she could survive the heat of Botswana, I could survive a playground in Georgia. The second reason is the obvious: I try to share stories that portray children from all over the world and especially to answer the charge from the African American community that they never saw themselves in the literature that was read and discussed at school. My class is more than half African American, so I make a concerted effort to bring in stories that show all kinds of African Americans, and Africans as well.

We came back into the building with our clothes sticking to us, feeling dehydrated after only 10 minutes. The children seemed to steam as they gathered on the rug. This time, there were no complaints that the air conditioner was blowing right on someone.

"I have a great story to share with you today. It is fun because it is a guessing story almost the whole way through. This book is set in Africa." I held up the book *Golimoto* (Williams, 1990).

Suddenly Kenny got up from the circle and moved to a table.

"Where are you going, Kenny?"

"I HATE Africa!"

"Why do you hate Africa? Have you ever been there? What do you know about Africa?" I used my most challenging but cajoling joke voice. "Now get yourself back over here and see if you don't think this is a good book! Have mercy, at least give it a chance."

Usually, he responds to that inflection in my voice with a slow smile. Not today. He got up slowly. He has this way of complying in a noncompliant way. He held on to the table as he walked all the way around it before moving away. Then he slumped down to the group with his back to us and his ears covered. I figured that this was the best I'd get, so I continued reading.

I fought the anger and confusion I feel when a child refuses to participate in a book activity or another experience that I have created expressly to draw them in. After a while, however, he began to listen and got somewhat caught up in the story. As soon as we began talking about the book, he pulled back into himself. I decided to ignore it this time. At least he hadn't left the group.

After the story ended, the children began moving about the room, selecting books to take home for their nighttime reading. I was standing with several of them, who were rummaging through baskets of books at a table when Kenny sauntered up to me. He began talking to me about his hatred of Africa as he picked up our book, *Golimoto*. I wondered if he was deciding to take it home for the evening.

He used his reverting-back-to-4-years-old whining voice to say, "The reason why I hate Africa is my cousin always calls me 'you ugly black African' and because that big girl at the bad house called me 'ugly black African.' Everybody calls me that."

"Who, Kenny? Here at school? People here at school call you that?" I asked.

"No, on the bus and at home. My cousins always be saying, 'Don't let him play. He too black. He might take you to Africa with him!'"

Witnessing his pain took the obnoxious edge off the whining voice for me. I realized that instead of attending to the obnoxious I should attend to the information he was giving me. This complaint/ explanation was really more like a gift. It may have been his way of saying, "I'm sorry I acted out in group time and I want to explain my

behavior." It was at least something to go on, a new set of thoughts
for me to have when he began his routine withdrawal. It may have
been the beginning of saying, "I trust you, Ms. Hankins, to understand. I want to be here. I do want to learn. I do not want you to give
up on me."

I didn't understand all that right then when we were standing at
the books, but I did know that he was measuring me. He kept flipping
the pages of that book, not really looking at them, as he talked to me.
He did not face me but stood beside me as he flipped and talked. I
stopped what I was doing and got down to ear level by sitting in a
chair beside him. I can still conjure up the electricity of the minutes
that followed.

"Oh, so they're jealous, are they?" I said casually, my voice
expressing a confidence that my heart did not feel. "They are so
jealous of you that they have to pick on something, so they pick on
your skin!"

"They not jealous. Seem like they hate me. They say it real
mean." He didn't buy that one easily. He still flipped the pages back
and forth and kept his head lowered.

"O-o-o-h, well now, that's how that works, don't you know. Sure,
they are jealous! Why, just look at you. You are tall, you're faster than
anyone in the class, and well, . . . let's face it, you are smart . . . real,
real smart! I bet none of the people who make fun of you are half as
smart as you are. If they were they wouldn't be saying all that stuff
to you!"

As I talked, he turned his body toward me and began at first to
just glance up into my face. Then he locked into my eyes with a fierce
hold. He sunk so deep into them that I wondered if I had enough of
what he needed. I plunged forward, having all the audience I needed
in the ear of one little boy to tell a story. I love it when kids do that.
His face had already moved from disbelief to hope.

I dropped my voice to a whisper and enunciated the words slowly.
"It is the king thing, Kenny. You see, your dark skin is the color of
ebony. Have you ever seen real ebony or obsidian? It is jewel dark,
black and shiny. It is so shiny, why, it's like a mirror. I have heard that
the closer your skin is to the color of those two jewels the closer you
are to royalty. Kenny, you are probably descended from a king. A
king, do you hear me? So . . . why wouldn't folk be jealous of that?
Now those kings don't have kingdoms today, maybe, but you still have
all the important parts of a king. Like tallness and handsomeness and
being smart and being fast. If we *had* a king, you'd be a good one.
Now look, the next time someone makes a remark about your black

skin, just smile and say, "Yes, I am very black thank you!" Because
when they talk about it, even if they don't understand why, exactly,
they have noticed that you are different! Kenny, you *are* different. You
be proud now, because one day, you will see, you are going to put all
this to work. You're going to do something great! I believe that."

His face was smiling, beaming. He took the book and walked back
to his table of friends, who were getting ready to go home. I became
distracted by the 23 other demands on my time in that 3-minute
interval before the bell rang for dismissal.

I never cease to be amazed that we get out the door and loaded
into the right cars and on to the right buses in the first month of
school. Just before he got on his bus, Kenny came running back and
hugged me.

"See you tomorrow, Ms. Hankins!"

It's the first day he's left with a smile.

Just think, it's only September, and I already have a relationship
that has the potential to go places.

Some Theory

How I wish that our conversation on that September day had solved
Kenny's problems, but this is not a movie. The relationship we had was
vastly more complicated than one story could solve.

One of my favorite books as a child was *A Little Princess* (Burnette,
1893/1987). I carry a continuing response to it even these many years
from the reading. Clearly, there is a parallel between Sara Crew, the
protagonist of the story, and me in the construction of our narratives.
If Sarah Crew could sustain the loss of her father, believing that she
was a princess and that all girls are princesses, then why not give Kenny
the same story? I did not meditate on the construction, nor on the substance, but I knew from the readings I do in narrative theory and autobiographical studies that Kenny was creating his life every time he
repeated the description of himself as an "ugly black African" (Bruner,
1994; Widdershoven, 1993). I knew that if he perseverated on the negative construction of himself, it would feed his anger and relegate any
mistake he made to a confirmation of his inferiority. "From infancy and
early childhood, children strive to overcome a real and an imagined
personal perception of inferiority" (Dagley, 1999, p. 6). He did not need
much more outside help to remind him of "every human being's striv-
ing for significance" (Adler, 1931/1980, p. 8). He fights for that significance on a daily basis. The harder he fights, the more negatively he is
perceived and shunned.

On that hot September day when Kenny was busy mentally reconstructing his life for me, the memories clung one to another. "My cousins call me names, the neighbors call me names, my chief violator calls me names . . ." coupled with the underlying angst that Mama is not around to help him. We learn about ourselves from the people around us, from the things they tell us about ourselves. "The narrated self is a relational self. . . . we define ourselves in relation to others" (Miller & Mehler, 1994, p. 47).

Kenny was giving me his story: "I am Black; therefore I'm ugly." No White child called him black, but the people of his own race did, the people he lived with and the children in his neighborhood. I know what to say about racial slurs between races, but I have had little direct observation of the colorism that is discussed by African American writers (Bell-Scott, 1994; Angelou, 1969). I was reminded of Pauli Murray (1956/1984), who wrote that skin color "has been a cruel weapon in the world at large but infinitely more cruel in the intimacy of family relationships" (p. 90).

I knew that my words might not have the impact of affirmation from one of his friends or relatives, but I did know that his story had to be reworked. I was his teacher and a part of his life at school and I had to be satisfied with the impact that one teacher could have. One of the reasons I enjoy teaching is that I believe I can make a difference. Jerome Bruner (1994) and several colleagues researched the ways in which people told the stories of their lives. He used the metaphor of sitting for a portrait, asking each of his subjects to tell his or her life story in one sitting, with a time limit. My story to Kenny was an effort to reframe the portrait story he told, to unsettle the stubbornness of identity, to attack his willingness to dwell on one way to tell the facts. "Mind is never free of precommitment. There is no innocent eye," writes Bruner (1994, p. 36). He believes that the ways we *narrate* our lives can become so habitual that they finally become the ways we *live* our lives. Those ways of telling become "recipes for laying down routes into memory, for guiding the life narrative to the present and for directing it into the future" (p. 37).

Psychologists' work with people often centers around reworking narratives from the past and projections of the future (Widdershoven, 1993). The narrative approach within psychology and psychotherapy can be seen "as a process of citation . . . of transferring texts to new contexts" (p. 18). In this case, the text is Kenny's story. The text is also his life as he sees it defined and confirmed in the stories he reiterates. My story for and about Kenny sought to provide a new context, a new frame, for his stated self-portrait: "I am very black." So, the story formed a different frame around an accurate picture. He is still black, very black, but instead of being ugly, he is a king. He is the color of a jewel and as reflective as a mirror. "Any story one may tell about life is better understood by considering other possible ways in which it can be told" (Bruner, 1994, p. 37). My goal was to give him another possible telling.

I am a teacher, not a psychologist. My goal perhaps was not pure. My goals are frequently refocused by the need to pull a child into the meat of the day. The meat of the day in a first-grade classroom is literature, reading, and writing. In order to completely trust what I understand to be true about immersing a child in print and story and text, I have to ensure that a child feels more than invited to the lesson. I have to know that he or she feels compelled to come to the lesson. I have to know that the child is "with us" most of the time. Unfortunately, Kenny used story circle time to retreat emotionally and physically over and over again. It is almost as if the emotions in a good story spawned another set of emotions in him. I was worried.

I believed that his refusal to participate in story and discussions would hinder his reading progress. I knew that feeling the hindrance would confirm what I was already hearing when things got difficult for him: "I can't, I can't." He stubbornly clung to the negative story he used to identify himself, "My cousin say Black folk can't read good as White can." So what is he supposed to do with the charge that he is blackest of all?

Bakhtin (1981) has argued that the stories we tell place us in the sociocultural landscape in particular ways. School was a landscape we were going to create together. For us to meet our academic goals for Kenny, he had to secure a positive place in our classroom landscape. He needed to repeat good things about himself inside our environment in order to change.

Kenny's "self development includes not only the moment-by-moment interpersonal encounters but also his participation in the iterative narrations of those encounters" (Miller & Mehler, 1994, p. 47). Every story we repeat reinforces the self.

A New Descriptor

Journal Entry (fall: first grade)

Today, I told the children we were going to create book nooks for ourselves, places to sit when we read alone, places to mark as individual territory. I showed them how we would be marking our places with clear contact paper on the wall or bookcase. They were really excited. They spent time selecting their books. I demonstrated how they were to sit and read in their special spot as I roamed the room visiting and listening to various children read. They all loved it . . . except Kenny. He felt a sudden drop in support, I suppose, and felt that he would not be able to read the books. I showed him once again how he could even bring into his book nook books that only had pictures. He could bring catalogs or magazines there. The point of book nook time was to hold the book you wanted to look at most and just read it how you knew best.

I told him I'd read with him first. He had chosen a small "easy-start" reader about a fire truck. He overattended to the text, as usual, ignoring the pictures and the context clues. This time, however, he seemed even more inflexible in his approach to the story. When his turn was up, I told him to spend time looking only at the pictures before he read the next story and see if it didn't help him to figure out the words sometimes. As I was reading with the next child I looked over to see Kenny just lying on his stomach, not reading.

As I moved to the next child he edged to another child's spot and began to look at the stack of books beside him. The child protested, "Don't touch my books, boy!"

"Stop calling me black!" Kenny whined.

"Kenny, I heard what he said; he didn't call you black," I said.

"He said I can't read."

"*No*, I didn't!" countered the other child.

"He didn't say that, Kenny. You know he didn't," I insisted.

He hears the name even when they don't say it! The child he accused of calling him black is an African American child himself.

I look at the composition of this group. It's true that Kenny is not the strongest of the readers. But he is not the weakest, either. This is a group that is on grade level or above. During this time each day, I have 13 children who are able to decode simple sentences and read the little leveled readers that accompany our literature series. I refuse to let Kenny's behavior relegate him to a group that needs more support than he does to get meaning from print.

I am not going to let him doom himself to the oft cited ill fate of African American males in today's schools: marked underachievement, high drop-out rates, and disproportionate representation in special education and behavior-disordered classrooms (Dandy, 1991; Delpit, 1995; Smitherman, 1981). With that thought, I am consumed with fear as I look at Kenny.

(December 3)

Today Kenny was so kind to read to Eric. I worry about Eric. He looks like Tom Terrific winding himself up like a spring. Eric's red head and Kenny's black were touching as they lay on their stomachs looking at the book that Kenny was reading to him. Eric's body stopped at Kenny's knees, so they looked like a big brother reading to a little brother, except for the stark difference in their physical characteristics. Eric just hasn't figured this reading thing out yet.

Kenny was so patient, and for that matter, so was Eric. Kenny stumbled over some words, and instead of forging ahead, each time he sent Eric with the book to find someone who would tell them the word.

We all came together to have book share on the rug. Eric raised his hand to share the book he had "read." He "read" his favorite part to the class and told a bit about the book. We asked the standard questions: What made you choose this book? Did you read it yourself or with a friend? Do you think you'd want to read it again? Did it remind you of another book? Etcetera. During the dialogue Eric said, "Kenny taught me how to read this page." He read it again with feeling, pointing to words that were written larger than the others: "GIVE ME MY BONE!"

I asked him what Kenny had told him to do. Eric repeated louder, "GIVE ME MY BONE."

Brandon covered his ears and yelled, "Yikes!"

Kenny interrupted then, explaining, "When the words are too bigger than the rest or if sometimes they be littler then you say it loud or soft." Not the most eloquent of descriptions, but his point was made.

"Kenny must have been a good teacher, then, because you sure did what he told you to do," I said.

Kenny smiled that proud-of-himself smile. He is always so surprised to find that he's done something well. I am so glad that I held back from redirecting his behavior with Eric. I wanted to comment on his sending Eric off for the word instead of using the clues we worked on so diligently. But this was free-choice reading, when you chose whether to read with a buddy, a small group, or alone. I weighed two things as I watched Eric and Kenny. First, going to find out a word gave Eric a way to help and a chance to move. Second, for Kenny, who is more word caller than meaning maker as he reads, getting the word from Eric gave him faster access to the story. Oh, let's face it—I was afraid I'd lose Danielle's attention (she was reading to me at the time) if I stopped them. There's always that balancing act: What is least disruptive? What is helpful? How much control do I need to have?

I'm glad that Kenny seemed on task today. I'm glad I've found a way to praise him that he accepts.

(December 4)

Today we had free-choice reading again and Kenny asked, "Can I help Tommy read today?"

Tommy is a small black version of Eric, who happens to be his best friend.

"You like to help people, don't you, Kenny?" He nodded yes.

"Does Tommy want some help?" He nodded yes.

"Tommy, do you want to read with Kenny?"

He nodded too and answered, "Yeah, I want to read that book he teached Eric how to read."

"Well great! Go to it, Professor!" They grinned. I hoped they would stick to business and read more than the loud page.

During book share, Tommy couldn't wait to read the loud page to the class! It went over as it had yesterday, with the kids being prepared to cover their ears and scream. I both love and hate moments like those! I also noticed during the reading time that Kenny sent Tommy only once to find out a word. Tommy went to Eric, who sent him to someone else. So the reading time turned out to be one of those reinforcing repeated readings for Kenny (Fountas & Pinell, 1996).

At lunch, Kenny asked me, "Ms. Hankins, what *is* a professor anyway?"

"It's a teacher, Kenny, a special teacher." I told him that my teachers at the university were professors. The children had met two of my teachers earlier in the fall.

I said, "I see you doing that someday, Kenny. You'd be a wonderful professor."

His reply? "I'm not no girl!" The only teachers of mine he had met were women.

"Oh no, Kenny, men are professors too. Men were professors before women were. I have male professors too; you just haven't met them. It's cool, Kenny, really!"

He believed me when Megan spoke up and said, "My daddy is a professor . . . *finally!*" (Sounds like tenure and promotion time were lived by that whole family!)

Confirming the Stories

(February 11)

We read a book today from our literature series, *I Am Eyes: Ni Macho* (Ward, 1978). It was set in Kenya, on the continent of Africa. Serendipity! We also got postcards from Botswana, from my friend

Michelle, on the same day. A teacher up the hall had on a piece of Kente cloth and I had a book called *Come With Me to Africa: A Photographic Journey* (Kreikemeier, 1993). Also on the table was the *Egyptian Cinderella* (Climo, 1989).

I was a little nervous about Kenny, although he had not objected much to the word Africa since early in the year. The table at the front of our "library" was full of African books and things about Africa. Dylan was perusing them and said excitedly, "Look, Ms. Hankins, you were wight [right], Kenny must be a king!"

Others gathered around the book Dylan was looking at and went to show Kenny the picture of the king. The king was very black and wore all manner of regalia. There was also a profile of a child in a photograph on the cover of the book, called *Africa*, that in all honesty could have been a photograph of Kenny. The child was beaded and serious looking.

I watched Kenny as he looked at those pictures. He heard the children's approving voices and didn't react negatively. I wonder what he was thinking.

When I look at Kenny, I see a bright child full of what it takes to grab hold of the responsibilities handed to him. He should see what I see. He would like that little guy.

It is difficult to see so many positives in a face in which others see so many negatives. I keep holding a positive mirror up in front of Kenny, but he seems to read his reflection as a backlash of other times.

I learned through Kenny that the real power of a life story may come from the shared voices in that story. Kenny began to get confirmation that the frame around "black African" could be changed when *other children* began to tell the same story. Instead of saying negative things, now children were reminding him that he just might be a king. Once again I am moved by the power evident in the voices of the children themselves.

Dagley (1999) supports the belief that children see themselves as others see them. He concurs with Bruner (1986) and others that a story has staying power. Children learn to view themselves based on the stories they hear and repeat about themselves. Cooley (1902/1956) calls this the looking glass self. "The looking glass self arises from an individual's perception of others' imagination of her or him: her or his imagination of their assessment; and her or his reaction or self-feeling" (p. 184). The looking glass self Kenny saw at home was out of my control. But the looking glass self he saw at school could be shaped, at least in part. If his sense of significance "would come from the level of contribution he made to the lives of others" (Adler, 1931/1980, p. 8), then he is most likely to see himself as powerful enough to offset the meanings he has attached to his experiences.

As I reread the narratives that I constructed around Kenny, I read a theme of empowerment. When the rest of the class bought into the theme, the story, the power was intensified. As his positive contributions were pointed out more often by other children, he became more courageous about offering himself as helper.

Two things happened on February 14 to add positive weight to the classroom stories about Kenny.

Journal Entry (February 14)

"Ms. Hankins, look how many valentines I got. I didn't think I'd get any!"

The children, all of them, seemed astonished as they opened valentine after valentine. Maybe they didn't remember last year's school observance of Valentine's Day.

I watched, both amused and full of warmth, the thrilled countenance of acceptance on face after face. They would sometimes ask me for confirmation of a child's name and then look absolutely stunned that they had got a card from that person. They looked at those cards for the longest time, studying every detail. I could see only three or four different kinds of little cards, based on the themes of Barbie, Space Jam, Mickey Mouse, and 101 Dalmatians. But as the children read and fingered and sorted them, each one in turn, I couldn't imagine these cards being any more appreciated than if they had been engraved in gold.

As we packed up to go home, the children held those red envelopes, bulging with cards and candy, to their chests, telling one another what they were going to do with them at home. I suggested we put them inside their book bags to keep the candy from spilling out. "Yeah, and the big kids might try to get our cards," several of them said. They all hurriedly unzipped their book bags—except Kenny, who answered, "I don't really need to put mines up, nobody won't touch mines."

"Believe me, they will if they see all that candy that I can see from here!" I said as I began unzipping his empty book bag.

With a big smile, no whining, he said, "They always be saying 'Don't touch his things they dirty. His ugly black self is all over it.' They won't sit with me either. So I get to sit all by myself and they be scared to take my food."

Not sure how to respond to his negative words and his smiling face, I just shook my head, thinking and stuffing his valentines.

Randel said, "Oh-h-h ho! You trickin' them boy. They don't know you a king."

Kenny just grinned and looked at me.

Maybe it was the preacher chiming in and the party mood of the day—I don't know what led me to it, but I began to take up the inflection and began to pace my speech as Randel had modeled for me.

I stood up straight and shook my head as I'd seen him do and said to the air while raising my hand for punctuation, "I tell you what Kenny! I wish . . . o-o-o-oh I wish I could be there when you get grown.

"I can almost picture it now. You'll be sitting on College Avenue downtown with some more of your professor friends drinking a cup of coffee and talking about stuff so smart I can't even understand it. You'll have on this nice set of cords and a Bill Cosby kind of sweater and those fine shoes. Some of those smart alecks will come struttin' by, their old do-nothin'-self lookin' all beat in from talkin' ugly for so long." At this point the children were feeding the tale and the telling. I got more into the code switch as they hooted their approval. They hooted and laughed and o-o-o-w-e-e-ed and clapped. I continued on and began acting as well now, demonstrating the way those do-nothin' guys would walk.

"Ye-e-e-ah, walking by and recognize you they do. One of 'em hit the other one on the shoulder and say, 'Now ain't that Kenny?' So he'll walk up to you and say, 'Hey Kenny!' And you so busy you don't hear it at first and then the other one say 'Kenny? It's not Kenny.' Then one of the folk you are talking to will say, 'Um excuse me Dr. Fuller but is that gentleman trying to get your attention?' So you'll look up and say [very distinctly, I modulated my voice], 'May I help you?' 'Hey, don't you remember us Kenny we used to ride your bus! You remember?'

"And you'll say, 'Not fondly.'"

The children slapped Kenny on the back and he grinned as we put the valentines in his book bag. Randel said, "I love it when you preach!" (When I preach? What could he mean?)

The children all wanted to hug me, so whatever happened must have been good. It's the first time I've ever seen quite that look on Megan's face. It was a look of delighted surprise.

MY NARRATIVE SHIFT DEFENDED

As I rewrote the preceding narrative, I was struck by two feelings. One came from hearing a reader say, "There goes the story again. She must think she is an actress or something." It sounds so sugary in the retelling. In fact, it was not. The truth is that sometimes you just have to break the resistance. I was talking a mile a minute and stuffing those valentines in his backpack even faster. The overarching agenda at the moment was keeping the party mood and getting out the door! How often have we heard that because we take the little kids home first then come back to run the older kids' routes, "one late classroom holds up the whole fleet of buses. If we're late the middle school is late; if the middle school is late the high school leaves late!" The responsibility can demand more than a moment. However, in the spirit of documenting things that worked for me with narrative and informed teaching and management, the children's response in that scene was reminiscent of their reaction in the scene with Randel. It felt as though we went somewhere together. There seems to be the attachment of authority in the inflections. I became, or the scene became, a reality.

I think I have learned how to use my body and a little bit about the power of using words creatively that Delpit talks about. Ochberg (1994) shifts the attention in his study of narrative "from a focus on the told to a focus on the telling" (p. 113). The power seems to have been in the inflection and phrasing of the telling. At least it was the place that the children responded to. Maybe that is what Randel had noticed and referred to when he said, "I love it when you preach, Ms. Hankins."

There are those who would wonder if I was mocking. What a strange world. How can I expect children to code switch when I am accused of mocking them if I code switch to their mother dialect and inflection? I wonder if it says that we still believe that the definition of *standard English* is "White talk" and "the best talk" and "the highest talk." If all dialects were perceived as holding the power to comfort and communicate, I would be allowed the opportunity to use that speech without being accused of demeaning behavior. I have worked in schools for so long that I am approaching fluency in the vernacular of the "other half" of my groups of children. I love the sound of it and the way it feels in my mouth; the call to the dramatic that it lends and the very specific message it sends that can only be sent their way.

What mattered today was Kenny and the stories that go on. To us, he is a king and would-be professor. When I look at the future Kenny, I see African American male professors whom I know. I have never meant to assert to him or to anyone else that teaching is the only profession acceptable for him. I know that hearing something one time is not enough for it to sink in. I may be the only person who ever tells Kenny that the University of Georgia, in his own hometown, is a viable professional opportunity for him. I want it to sink in deep, deep, deep.

PAIN AND PROMISE

Journal Entry (March 2)

My body goes white hot and then limp when I see the kind of pain Kenny showed today. Apparently he was misbehaving in the hall and the aide fussed at him. Kenny felt that he was unjustly accused and told her so. She didn't like his tone and "got in his face," and he folded. I walked up to them at about that time. It was evident to me that she was not the complete problem; his tears were too deep. He flung himself against the wall with his arm raised, covering his face, and sobbed. When I touched him he dropped to the floor and began wailing. At about that time, the school counselor walked out into the hall. I was too emotionally wound up in the scene to be helpful, I think. I seemed to be producing a greater flood of tears. I heard the counselor question the aide, and then the counselor came over and asked Kenny if he wanted to talk. I backed away and let her escort him to her office. He still had his face pressed into the crook of his elbow and was crying, but quietly now. The children watched in silence as he moved in front of the line. I was shaky, with sweat prickling the back of my neck, despite the very cold air that blew into the hall from the doorway.

(March 17)

It's the buried face that gets me the most, Kenny's attempt to hide from the rigors of school. The emotion of a shared story most often manifests itself in a physical turning away. The head goes down, then there is the rolling of the shoulders and back and the gradual slump that takes him all the way to the floor during circle time. I call his name, looking him in the eye, telling him that I expect him to sit up and give me his best. He responds for a while, then I watch him begin to disappear again. I have learned to give him a job that makes him stand up; Kenny, please write down these page numbers on the board. Kenny, please go bring me that blue book; or please go turn out the lights, I think I'd like a softer light—anything I can do to get him on his feet and put him in a contributor role. Then I have the opportunity to say thank you, and I keep him even longer that way. I am moved to action by stories told to Michelle Foster (1997) about good teachers refusing to accept less than a student was capable of. I wince at the charge that those "liberal White teachers coddle Black children, demanding less and less of them." I hope I am striking a balance between a demand for excellence and respecting Kenny's work.

Lately, I feel that I am losing ground. It seems we have come so far and then suddenly we are back to last year's behavior. Something is just not right. Maybe spring break will help Kenny. Maybe he is just tired.

As I reread the narratives surrounding Kenny and sense the positive power of the stories we told, I find myself hoping that the same kind of power will be sent in my direction. I hope that writing entries that remind me of the connections that Kenny and I made, both personally and to the curriculum, will have the effect of defining me as "the good teacher," the one who cares, the one who surely would never figure in negative press about schools. But like Kenny, I have trouble believing my own words. The successes retreat as each new wave of failure hits me full in the face. I lose my bearings, as though caught by surprise in the ocean, the water rushing around my ears, my eyes shut, and my hands and feet frantically reaching for the bottom, which seems to have dropped off completely. I hold my breath and try to stay calm, grabbing hold of faith from experience that I am being pushed toward shore, toward a firm footing and a clean breath.

More Facts

Journal Entry (April 7: spring parent/teacher conference)
Today I met with Kenny's aunt, who seemed more relaxed than at the other times I'd talked to her. Last time, she had smelled of alcohol. Today she had come straight from her job, her hair had been styled, and she really looked beautiful. As we talked about Kenny, she asked me if he had said anything about his mother getting out of jail and then going back to jail after about 2 weeks.

No, of course not. I am continually shocked by the prevalence of the parent-prisoner. Prison rarely enters the White middle-class consciousness. It is something distant, something from the movies. Yet it is so much a part of the lives of so many of my children. I listen, trying to keep my face from betraying my judgmental thoughts. At least the news gives me something with which to explain Kenny's recent behavior.

As she talked, she got to her real lament. "I am too old for these children. I told them I would take the baby, but then I got Kenny too. Taking Kenny was just for an emergency, but it's been over a year now and he still with me. I'm tired, no help, I raised my boys—they grown now. I thought this time the mama would get herself straight and get these children back together. Kenny seems like he need her most of all." As tired as she is, and as free as she wants to be of the children, she does not trust foster care.

I found myself in a comfortable silence with her as we both stared at some of his writing samples, knowing that we were probably thinking the same thing . . . Kenny was sexually violated after he was taken from her. I know that she feels some responsibility for that event. She is the one who said she could keep the younger brother but not Kenny. The aunt has never brought up his sexual abuse and I have not either.

Unfortunately, we cannot assume that a different placement will be an improvement when a child is removed from his or her home. We can always hope, and we can know that most people are good and have their hearts in the right place when they open themselves to foster care. Sometimes, even in the homes of relatives the sense of duty and loyalty is to the family name rather than to the particular child being served. Kenny needed something to take him from place to place. He needed to believe that he held some control over his existence and that the future was bright. He needed the power and courage that control and vision afford us.

Possibilities

With renewed effort toward Kenny's empowerment, I enlisted the help of two volunteers and reshaped my schedule. I asked a young African American male counseling student to visit with Kenny. He met with him a half dozen times at least. Kenny responded well to those visits and looked forward to them. I also asked someone to take Kenny to surf the Internet at school. He was interested in hearing the children talk about places they visit on the Web at home. He has no computer at home. I also began to take small groups of children during my planning time for extra reading support. Since he was going to be pulled from the classroom when those volunteers could come, I needed to make sure that he was not missing reading instruction. The special attention he received may have been nothing more than a mental break for him from the things he usually thought about and not a real catalyst for change, but I did see him move through that recent regressive rage. An interesting discussion was related to me by the volunteer who took Kenny to the computer.

Journal Entry (late April)
Today when Catherine came to get Kenny, I asked him if he would like to go to the media center and get on the computer and go

to the Web. His face lit up like a Christmas tree. He put his pencil down so fast, he almost threw it. He fell over two chairs and didn't even whine about it as he made his way to the door where Catherine was waiting.

After school she came to me and said, "Kenny said the cutest thing going up the hall.

"He asked me, 'Do you know what they call me in my class?' I said no, of course, and he got the biggest grin on his face and said, 'Professor . . . yep, they call me professor! Want to know why they call me that?'

"'Yes, why would somebody call a little kid a professor?'

"''Cause I might be one someday.'

"'Really?'

"'Yep. Professors all know how to do computers. I'm going to learn all about them too. You have to know all kinds of stuff like that you know.'"

It seems that our story had spread from me and Kenny to the class and now even to the outside.

As it turned out, Catherine mentioned that conversation to several other people, who then repeated the appellation to Kenny. Even the principal said one morning, "Oh, so this is the professor!" Kenny's smile couldn't be beat that day. We do shape ourselves by the things people say and repeat about us. We shape our images of who we are by the stories we repeat about ourselves. In many ways Kenny was showing evidence that he was seeing positive images of himself now.

Perplexities

In May, however, Kenny had another round of tantrums. It seemed that once again we had lost ground. It is easy to lose faith as a teacher when a tantrum strikes. This year I had the power of my writing to teach me through the storm. I went back to my journal and reread accounts and remembered the conference with his aunt. It takes me multiple revisits to journals to find the places where I have written about a particular child, because in the original version, the narrative is not constructed as it is in this present, edited form; rather, it is spread out and stacked next to entries for other children. As I read, it was tempting to see Kenny as a problem. On a daily basis it is tempting to say," Look, kid, I'm breaking my back to get you through and you keep folding on me. Why are you making my life so difficult?" It is too easy to make myself the victim instead of understanding the many ways I contribute to a child's victimization. It is more comfortable at times to be the one who is hurting, to be the one who seeks sympathy, instead of the one who is called on to act on behalf of the one who needs help.

Kenny's tantrum scenes involved cursing, slinging himself onto the floor, and threatening kids around him. They usually took place in art or physical education or in the hallway. I would be summoned and we'd spend time getting him out of the room and to a "place where he could have his tantrum," as I would tell him. Meanwhile, the class had been disrupted and the lesson stopped. It was as maddening as it was tragic.

However, in about a week, the tantrums stopped and we were somewhat back to our regular chaos. Kenny was able to come back to normal faster this time. While I celebrated his growing resilience, I still wondered what had triggered this fresh rage.

School Yard Sweetheart

Journal Entry (May)
Today on the playground I overheard some little girls playing with Keesha, one of the favorites of first grade. She is noted for both her beauty and her brains. She has a rather pixie expression, with her large black eyes, surrounded by the thickest set of eyelashes I have ever seen. Her chocolate-milk-colored face has two deep dimples, flanking a full, expressive mouth with pearly pink lips. She is a champion reader who is admired and looked up to by all the children.

Today, the "who do you go with" routine was big conversation on the playground. I watched the girls circle various groups of boys and invariably they would circle the places where Kenny was playing. He would charge at them and they would scream as they retreated.

One of the girls said, "Keesha, you know you want to go with Kenny!"

"You think I want to go with that black thing! I don't want to have anything to do with his old black self!" She called out loudly.

Kenny's response interrupted my ready-to-be-delivered admonition with, "So! Look how fast this black boy can run . . . and I know where the honeysuckles are."

He ran off, yelling, "Ninny, ninny boo boo!"

Then this loveliest of first graders put her hands on her hips, tossed her head, and looked at me. "I reckon I'm 'on have to chase that boy."

She sauntered saucily to the honeysuckle branches at the edge of the yard, where he stood grinning at her. They stood there for the longest time, working to get a tiny drop of sweetness from the blossoms. Then, predictably, she jerked at his shirt and the chase was on again, until she took refuge on the picnic table beside me. Kenny went to find others to play with.

That gave me the chance to say to her that I was surprised to hear her call such a good friend "out of his name."

"It hurts people to be called by their skin color," I told her. "Kenny especially is hurt when people call him black. You are so kind that I know you didn't mean anything by it, but just the same, it's something to think about," I told her.

We were both sitting on the table, looking across the playscape and not making eye contact. My delivery had been rather nonchalant.

She listened and then in typical 6-year-old fashion responded with a question that seemed unrelated: "Ms. Hankins, remember when we made those big ol' fish last year?"

"Yes."

"Me and Kenny shared the markers. Oh . . . here he comes I gotta go!" The chase continued.

She confirmed for me that indeed Kenny had always had friends and that she counted herself among them. Now he seemed to know it too. He showed me that he was seeing the picture "black" in a new frame, learning not from me this time but from a beautiful little girl. The friendship was more important to him than the descriptor this time. Besides, he had confirmation of his attractiveness, didn't he? After all, the prettiest girl in the first grade was chasing *him*, the "king."

A Revelation

The day before school was out, Kenny wrote and shared a powerful journal entry. It revealed to me why the tantrums had escalated again in May. It also speaks to the power of writing to hold our biggest issues. Kenny must have felt assured that his writing would be heard and that it would provide an opening to talk about a very personal event. He read:

I love my mom
becis she is nies. [Because she is nice.]
And she gaves me sawsag [sausage] it good.
    And she gave me some chican [chicken].
But she is gon now and I don't no were
She is. Maybe she will come back someday.
But I still miss her and Ill never stop loving her
good-by Mom.

I asked him what he meant by "she's gone now" and he told me that she was released from jail on May 1 while he was in school.

"She came to our house and brought two big bags of potato chips and told my auntie to give them to us. She said she was going away and that she would call us sometime, but she ain't."

He went on to say that they believe she is out of the state because she has broken parole. No wonder he was so devastated. The thing he feared had indeed come true. His mom had left him, and to him, at least, it looks like for good. Maybe it's true that when we finally come up against the thing we fear most, we are somehow less afraid of it than when we merely contemplate it.

CONCLUDING THOUGHTS

Kenny is going to get on with life. At such a young age he is practicing resilience. He is reframing his stories and putting himself in charge of them. The tangible product of the poem itself shows that he has not been allowed to dodge the responsibility of learning how to communicate with someone through print. And the depth of emotion and willingness to share such a personal entry with the class tells me that there were plenty of times that his physical retreat during story time may have been a learned technique of self-defense or a cocooning of sorts for another reason. It suggests that perhaps he never left our presence at all, but buried deeper into the place where story is created and understood.

On the last day of school, I had the children fold a paper in half and on one side write what they remembered about first grade and what they want me to remember about them. Kenny wrote, "I want you to remember about me that I am smart."

I look at the picture he drew to accompany what he had written: a happy-faced little boy working at a computer. This is one of the few pictures he drew of himself with arms. Whole, I thought, he has the whole picture now.

Kenny need not worry about my memory. I will remember him as I first saw him—smart. The power in his request is that he knows it too. I hope the descriptor attaches with a fierce stubbornness to his identity. It's a keeper.

CHAPTER 4

The Firth of Forth: The Power of Memoirs in Narrative Inquiry

Journal Entry (autumn)

The children were in their book nooks, the place in the room each child claims, permanently for the year, as a read-alone spot. The task was to select three books from the classroom library, "read" them, and decide on just one to share something from with the group. The aims are to provide time for self-selection of books, to establish books as a good topic of conversation, and to model good selection procedures. I walk around interviewing as many of the children as possible in the minutes before we have group share. Today, I have a small tape recorder in my pocket.

Two boys, seated some distance from each other, both happen to have chosen copies of the same book. My time with each boy was punctuated by interviews with other children. I began with Eric.

Me: Which book are you going to share with the group?

[Eric holds the book up for me to see]

Me: Oh-h-h! So, tell me about it.

Eric: See well this bear, it's Winnie-the-Pooh, and um-m-m-m he's trying to get the bee's honey because he likes, um, wants their honey. [Flipping pages back to beginning] His pots of honey are empty, see? [Turns more pages] He gots a balloon and it's big . . . but, um I . . . think a balloon can't really do that . . . float a bear in the sky. Just . . . well . . . not in really life but . . . um-m-m . . . if he was a real bear he could climb the tree. But so then um um the bees got him and [turning the pages] he . . . he fell in the mud because the bees stinged the balloon. Yuk! Now he's a mud bear 'stead of yellow.

I then spoke with Tommy.

Me: What book are you going to share when we go to group, Tommy?

[Tommy holds his copy up for me to see]

73

Me: OK! So tell me about it.
Tommy: It about Winnie-the-Pooh. [Silence]
Me: Hum, Winnie-the-Pooh, huh? Tell me more about it.
[Silence; but he's turning pages]
Me: So . . . now, which one is Winnie-the-Pooh?
Tommy: There [pointing] . . . it a bear.
Me: Real or make-believe?
Tommy: [Long pause] . . . I have one.
Me: What?
Tommy: A Winnie-the-Pooh.
Me: Oo-o-h . . . like this one?
Tommy: Yes.
Me: Fun! So what's Winnie-the-Pooh doing in *this* story?
Tommy: [Silence]
Me: The Pooh in *this* book. This one . . . what's he up to?
Tommy: [Silence]
Me: Well . . . tell me why you picked this book.
Tommy: [Long silence]
Me: Hey, practice what you're going to tell at group share about
Winnie-the-Pooh. Just say to me what you'll say to them.
Tommy: [Silence] . . . [Referring again to the pages as he turns
them slowly. Finally, just shrugs his shoulders and looks at me]
Me: Well . . . you'll decide what to say I'm sure.

One isolated event and the reader has formed an opinion, or several, about the boys; the activity; or me, the teacher. What you know with certainty is that I formed an opinion as well. In my case, however, the event is not isolated, as it is here. The event happened in the milieu of the day, bathed by recent past experiences, and marinated in preformed expectations.

Oh you take the high road
and I'll take the low road
and I'll be in Scotland afore ye.
     ("Loch Lomond")

This is a narrative of embeddedness, a word picture of overlapping circles of time and children's lives. It has little to do with Scotland but everything to do with traveling metaphorical high roads and low roads of narrative journey as well as our proclivity for separating people into dichotomous highs and lows. This narrative also has to do with "be[ing] there afore ye," complete with the same surprise of finding that low roads lead to a destination as surely as the high road does.

TIME AND MEMORY

This narrative forces me to consider how many layers of time affect our interactions with people; for "no personal experience story is ever an individual production. It derives from larger group, cultural, ideological, and historical contexts" (Denzin, 1989, p. 73). Think of arguments with spouses and partners that have little to do with the matter at hand and everything to do with years of hassling over differences in perception ("you *never* have understood what I'm saying"), a scenario that in fact has even more to do with the way life was negotiated within the family of origin.

It works that way among school people as well. I think of the year I taught seventh-grade English and discovered that my responses to children were tempered by my own negative sojourn in junior high school. The passage of time had not erased the narratives I perpetuated of events all those years ago. We allow some events to fossilize without the benefit of reflection, and they serve to immobilize any creative interpretation of an experience. When we grow into that awareness, we sometimes make the mistake of dismissing all interpretations of past memories as unreliable. The historian Montalembert once said something to the effect, "To *judge* the past, and really know what one is talking about, it is necessary to have lived the past. To *condemn* the past, one need only feel that one owes nothing to it." We are a part of all we have lived and all that the important people in our lives have lived. We relate to one another in the power each of our pasts has to hold sway over the negotiations. I realize how intricately the pasts of my family affect my teaching and acknowledge that I owe much to that past. A memoir of my father's that appears later in the chapter is one of the embedded circles of time I address as part of Tommy's story.

WORDS AND LABELS

When I was in graduate school, the bulk of my reading focused on the disenfranchised, the powerless, the marginalized children in schools. I spent considerable effort in addressing my own ideology concerning children I have named "other." I was literature savvy and had a post-reflection confidence that I had detoxified my vocabulary about children. If the use of a word is the tool we use to build a concept (Vygotsky, 1986), then, I reasoned, it can also become the tool for dismantling a concept. I assumed that if I dropped a word, certainly attitudes and assumptions left with it.

I did use my new vocabulary to guide some decisions. During the first week of school, for instance, a class list was in my box with instructions to circle the children's names who were "at risk of school failure." I angrily refused to play. I wrote back in effect that I would not label a child in the *first* week of *first* grade as a potential failure! The person needing the data came to me apologetically, stating the need for the data and that we were up against a deadline. I asked if I could see what the other teachers had done. She handed me the other lists. I pointed out to her that nearly all the children circled were African American. Most were male. She didn't seem surprised at all and wondered what I objected to. "So? They are the most at risk. We can't help what is," she said. "But, see, maybe WE cause them to be 'at risk' by seeing them as at risk," I ventured. She left the list with me, and I "misplaced" it. Finally, the third time the list came to me, now during the second week of school, a simple note—including "please"—from the administration was attached to it. I circled the entire list and wrote at the side, "At risk of being labeled."

I wasn't contacted again. Unfortunately, the making of lists is not always so tangible and public. I actually thought that by not circling the children for that list I had not already sorted them to a place inside my thinking. I had, I assumed, safely avoided the trap of naming and dichotomizing children. Although I still defend my boycott, I do so admitting that I learned the power of unvoiced attitudes to do the very thing I fought so hard against.

This narrative centers on an African American boy, Tommy. But it can only be told as it is embedded in the story of his best friend, a European American boy named Eric, and as it connects to the story of Billy, another European American boy from decades ago whom Tommy never knew. The thread connecting this set of narratives is the most circuitous in the collection. It dips back and forth from the high road to the low road and right through the landscape separating one road from the other. I am reminded of Miss Amelia in Augusta Trabough's (1997) *Praise Jerusalem*, who remarked, "Maybe time isn't really a road that goes off somewhere else . . . maybe it's more like hills, with layers of rock and soil going far down, and with the top part of the hill getting its shape from what's underneath" (p. 109). When we hear another person's narrative, we prefer linearity and by our questions often coax the person to add details that help us to organize the narrative in a time frame we can reconstruct. Any narrative of our own that we tell, as Miss Amelia knows, has always pushed itself up from surrounding events and is pulled off the linear to a place of temporal meaning.

There are layers of living far underneath the temporal present of Tommy's first-grade story that have shaped me both personally and professionally. My narration reveals some of the layers of thought and story that gave shape to my growing understanding of Tommy as a student. Tommy became who I named him to be—twice. We are, as Heidegger (1927/1962) reminds us, talking beings, and we live and talk our way into being. Sartre (see Denzen, 1989) believed, as I also understand, that "all we have are words. Our humanness and our selfness lie in the words we speak and attach to ourselves" (p. 78). Teachers must pause to consider the power our very thoughts hold to label a child. We can then be brave enough to recognize the power students have to name us. I became all the multiple definitions of *teacher* inside the heads of those involved in Tommy's story: Tommy, his mother, and my father, and I became them within my own narratives. I am more "teacher" now than when I met Tommy because I am more student as well. When we open our inquiry toward ourselves, it often has the effect of opening our understanding of another. Just as Miss Amelia understands the layers of time involved in an event, Maxine Greene (1995) asserted that those layers of time define us. "I am not a view from nowhere," she writes (p. 94). All those layers of time, acknowledged or not, spoken or silent, caused me to narrate the events as a unique construction, in a way different from how others who lived through them would remember or narrate them. The reader will not even read the same story I'm writing because you bring to your reading layers of time and a view from somewhere I have not been.

Detractors from narrative inquiry could cite that very statement to support the problem of narrative research. It cannot be repeated or verified. I submit that Tommy cannot be repeated or verified or even triangulated; nor can our relationship. The power of this kind of narrative research lies in its complete dependence on "a psychic geography; an intricate construct, whose language dominates the thoughts of a narrator" (Bruner, 1994, p. 31). Tommy and I, indeed our whole classroom family, constructed a narrative that in the physical geography of school has the power to foster success or failure based on the psychic geography we created and shared together.

You will have faith that I have a plan, a project, envisioned as you read the beginning and watch as the stories begin to connect. You will be glad that you did not live the slowly unfolding set of events with me. I recorded them weeks and months apart without the promise of connection, without a plan, and blind to the possibilities the fragments held to create an assemblage pregnant with new "habits of mind" (Greene, 1995).

Naming Tommy

Journal Entry (first week of school)

Tommy is in my class this year. I had hoped he would be. He seems very different from last year, more alive, more responsive, this fall. His best friend, Eric, who moved to our school late in the spring last year, is also in the class. The two of them make a calendar-perfect picture, something that should end up on a diversity poster. They are alike physically only in height and weight. The contrast of Tommy's brown skin next to Eric's fair and freckled skin is only slightly less dramatic than that of their carrot orange and jet black heads together. They tumble about in a wrestling hold on the floor each time we assemble, so much like playful puppies that I fully expect them to nip at each others's ears! Neither of them gives a hoot about reading or writing, but they seem to enjoy hearing stories—when you can get their attention. I think back on my introduction to Tommy last year before Eric moved to our school.

(Kindergarten year [based on several journal entries])

> Something about seeing a 5-year-old fall asleep during the reading of a book makes me angry, not at the child but at the knowledge that he doesn't get enough sleep. Five-year-olds are supposed to have trouble being still, not trouble staying awake at 9 o'clock in the morning. Of course, it is also comical. He falls over in a heap, with his legs still crossed pretzel-style. He just rolls to one side like one of those round-bottomed baby toys. Only he stays down instead of popping back up.

> Another day:

> Tommy looks so confused and dazed when we assemble for story time. I make a special effort to call on him or to touch him as I read to keep him with me. I add in his name as I'm reading along, "So the puppy went up the hill slower and slower, Tommy." He frowns, confused looking, and squints. His whole face gives the impression that he understands the rule "Sit still and listen" but that what he hears is elusive. Any question I direct to him is met with that frown, squint, hold-my-breath-until-she-calls-on-somebody-else look.

> Another day:

> Tommy's interaction with other children, unlike his time with me in group, is on par with that of the other kids—he is

verbal and active. He likes to build; to play in the drama/
housekeeping center; and to use the toy animals, trucks, and
cars. Puzzles are somewhat challenging. He avoids the
painting easel, the writing center, and books. He seems to be
one of those children who could get labeled quickly as having
some deficiency. I know because I fight the building set of
assumptions about him daily.

Another day:

Well . . . I understand that a phone call to Tommy's house
today got the answering machine, with a sultry female voice
that said, "Hello-o-o-o, yes this *is* Peaches. For a good time
call before 2." No wonder! Poor little kid. The questions fly
faster than I can separate them. Is mom there at night? Does
he get any monitoring? Does anyone tell him to go to bed at
night? Are drugs involved? Who else lives there? Can she do
that and keep her child? What does he see? Is there some
pimp involved? No wonder he is so thrown together most
mornings and so sleepy!

My contact with Tommy during kindergarten was limited to a language arts block 2 days a week. Often because of the way we rotated
our groups, I saw the children only once during the week for instruction. I remember that Tommy was well behaved though roly-poly, cute
all the time, sleepy much of the time, and confused over the activities
involving writing and reading. His answers were rarely verbal; he just
shrugged shoulders, furrowed his brow, or twisted his mouth. In those
small groups with limited time, I am sure that I called on children most
often who could give some kind of answer that the whole group could
use for instruction; and I also know that I avoid embarrassing a child
who can't answer. The limited time I had with them had to be positive.
There was little chance to make up for a negative.

Perpetuating Assumptions

As I reflect on getting to know Tommy in depth during first grade,
I reread all the questions I had about him and his mother during kindergarten and at the beginning of the year. Those questions themselves
draw certain parameters around my perception of him and his home.
More solidifying than my questions about him were the answers I
thought I had—long, pious, quickly generated ones. Basically I answered
them myself. It is jolting to remember moving off my position that his

home was a obviously a brothel, full of the wrong kind of people doing the wrong kind of thing, and that his mother didn't give two cents about him as long as I didn't bother her. Jolting because of the discovery that the answering machine voice (of "Peaches") was his teenage sister, who was playing a naughty joke. I don't remember the way we eventually discovered that, but I do remember thinking that I would have responded differently to the same message on many other answering machines. I would have assumed that I had the wrong number, or that it was a joke—maybe even played along. How quickly we confirm assumptions.

When I saw how much time Tommy spent with Eric, I jumped to another conclusion. I assumed that Tommy's "coming alive" had more to do with Eric than with Tommy. So it became my hope as they both entered first grade that Eric would be a role model for Tommy, leading him into school behaviors that would work better for him.

As the first weeks of school passed, I was surprised to discover that Eric was as limited a reader and writer as Tommy was. Eric seemed to know so much about books and so little about decoding. He was artistic and creative but couldn't begin to label his drawings. I was making several observations about this duo. In various journal entries, I noted that Tommy only did his homework on the days when he went to Eric's house after school. Tommy rarely returned things that were sent home, often losing his take-home books for days. I also noted that Eric's difficulties with reading and writing were beginning to look like something more than not paying attention. I made constant comparisons of the two boys even when the entries about each of them were not next to one another. I had not met Tommy's mother, but Eric's mom was a weekly volunteer in my classroom.

It is important for you to read a couple of journal entries from the week of parent conferences. It will help you see what I only saw later, the difference in tone between the two, the unstated perpetuation of a middle-class agenda, the negative assessments I made.

Journal Entry (November: parent conference week [from notes I made after each home visit])
    Eric is the son of missionary parents, who, by the way, don't fit my image of people living a hand-to-mouth existence. They have four young children, who are like little redheaded stair steps. If I'd had their house growing up, I'd have felt like Shirley Temple! It is like a child's dream come true. The entire second floor is the children's living space, and mom, an artist, has connected the bedrooms, playroom, bathroom, and hall by use of a Disney motif. The walls are a combina-

tion of hand-painted murals of a larger-than-life Mickey and friends, muted wallpapers, and surfaces displaying unique wall-painting techniques. The rooms are well organized, full of play and study space. The yard is a playground, complete with trampoline, swings, and playscape and with room to play ball. Positioned at the end of a cul-de-sac, full of small children, the lot allows the kids to have access to the street for bike riding and running remote-control vehicles. The family room, where we met, gives off an aura of peaceful energy that is contagious. We sat at a long table built to accommodate a large family and its guests. From where I sat, I saw huge, handwoven baskets of books, drawing materials, and soft stuffed toys. Eric jumped up to retrieve the dog, who had run into the room behind us. His parents laughed as he took the dog the shortest distance to the door, going *over* the sofa rather than around it. They said, "Eric began the day he was born doing things his own way and on his own time line." They explained that he was born, prematurely, in the backseat of a taxi in Paris, France! When he was 2, his parents were transferred to Brazil for several years. But Eric's respiratory condition, including asthma, was so bad in that climate that he was consistently ill and failed to grow for more than a year. The mission sent them back to the United States. When he entered kindergarten late last year, he was getting better but faced some surgery. After that surgery, in the summer, his health improved greatly. He had never lacked energy, but had to take frequent breaks. It was "nice to be able to relax, now, when he runs all over the place," according to mom.

During the first few weeks of first grade, he seemed to be happy. Anytime he was with Tommy he was happy. He was creative, artistic, and able to predict and infer even the most obscure messages in a story I read aloud. His world traveling allowed him to speak with firsthand experience of many things that other children knew relatively little about.

His older brother and sister are strong, task-focused students who learn quickly and work on projects and homework independently. His mother noticed how tense Eric was becoming when they sat down together to read his take-home book and write a response to it. He always selected a read-to-me book, and I always added one of the emergent-reading selections as well. When his 4-year-old sister began to read them, he became angry and told his mother that he was stupid! The uppermost question I'm left with after the visit was asked by Eric's father: "But where does Eric stack up with the rest of the class in reading?" Their concern is growing—and so is mine.

Now read this one about Tommy from the same week:

I'm going to be mad if one or two kids keep me from being able to turn in 100% of the conferences! I have sent triple notes (all ignored) and have called nightly for 3 nights. I think poor Tommy lives in absolute chaos. At his house, when the kids answer the phone—and it's always the kids—they are so rude. When I ask to speak to mom they ask, "Who dis is?" When I tell them, they scream at the top of their lungs, without covering the mouthpiece, "Ma!" and the call is yelled over and over—"*Ma!*"—and even louder: "MA!! until it overrides the airwaves of the TV (which is going full blast), conversations (and the arguing and crying of smaller children), and the radio or stereo (the loudest of all), until there is a response. Then the child holding the phone yells, "Some White lady. Something like Ms. Hanky . . . something"—as if I can't hear what he's saying. Then I hear Tommy's voice: "Hey, that's my teacher." Then, "She have to call you back."

On one of these calls, I asked to speak to Tommy, and the kid holding the phone, although really exasperated, handed the receiver to him. We talked, or I talked, for a minute. I asked him what he was doing and he answered softly, "Watching TV." I suggested he remind his mother to call me so we could have 100% conferences and he said, "OK." Then I left my number with the older brother, who had hassled Tommy the whole time I was talking to him to get the phone back. Of course, no returned call. I don't know why I'm even surprised! According to Becky (Eric's mom), Tommy's mother is rarely there when Eric's parents deliver Tommy after he plays with Eric.

Finally, I get the message in writing that Becky will come to school instead of my visiting the house. I always feel suspicious when parents don't want me to visit. Now the wait is on to see if she actually shows up.

Later (the week after conferences)

Tommy's mother came today during the school day, not at the time or on the day she had indicated on her note. We all adjusted, covering one another's classes so that we could meet with her. She is so different from what I expected. She has a small, wiry, athletic build, a loud voice, and an engaging smile. She delivers one-liners with adeptness and enjoys it. When she came in, she said, "Hey, didn't I just meet with you! I swear you look just like Hamp's teacher! Know what they say, all y'all look the same. So how Tommy doing?" She took charge of the conference from the start. From the way the rest of the conversation went, I could tell that the only thing she wanted to hear was that he wasn't getting in trouble. She wasn't surprised he couldn't read; none of her kids liked to read, she told me. "But long as he act right he probably pick up soon. He real smart. I bet he and Eric talk all the time? He loves that boy. I never seen nothing to beat how he love Eric. Eric this and Eric that and his mom say Eric love Tommy like that." I assured her that they seemed genuinely good for each other and that they were rambunctious but respectful and usually followed the rules. She was pleased. The thing I'm left with after the conference is the lack of focus on how far behind he was in reading. She just dismissed it, and I guess I hated to harp on it. She was curious to know why we didn't have school teams for sports. It's hard for her to get Tommy to practice. "Seems like he could just stay at this school and be on a team 'stead of me getting him rides to some other school to practice with kids he don't even know." Makes sense really. She wanted to know about parties and field day. She talks sports, parties, field day, friends. I am thinking: reading, writing, math. How far apart we seem.

So even though early in the year I'd written the words "I'm glad I have Tommy again this year; maybe *I'll get another chance*," a retrospective look at the journal uncovers the still largely negative assessment I carried of the way he lived. In effect, much of what I wrote but never stated specifically is that he'd never be one of "us," a monstrous revelation. We prefer to think of ourselves as incapable of housing a shadow side—at least I do. There are two kinds of remembering: fossilized, nonreflected-upon remembering that governs us, and a purposeful revisiting from the middle of the living present to the sometimes monstrous governed actions that thankfully are malleable enough to be reshaped. My writing gives me a tangible entry into fossils of some of the more negative reasoning that molds my actions. Narrative inquiry's strength lies in the writing that can be revisited. Revisiting the writing with a new question each time or checking to see how it meshes with a new narrative cannot be overattended to. The recursive look into the written accounts become both the genesis and the revelation. Had I not seen my attitudes revealed in the writings, I never would have believed they existed. As you read you may want to ask me, "But isn't it a pious, maudlin kind of self-battery? Is anything served in such a pathetic and public purge?"

We send scientific expeditions to Loch Ness because if the dark and monstrous side of fairy tales can be proved to exist, who can be sure that the blessed side doesn't exist, too? I suspect that the whole obsession of our time with the monstrous in general . . . is at its heart only the shadow side of our longing for the beautific. (Beuchner, 1992, p. 113)

So I write on even when the monsters appear, hoping and longing for the beatific that must exist in order for me to claim the name *teacher*.

HELPFUL LITERATURE

This year, I went to two conferences. I met and talked with two of my favorite writers on education, Lisa Delpit and Lucy Calkins. I was already grappling with shaping materials of the craft to meet specific needs but feeling afraid that I would misjudge these needs. Calkins opened her conference with "I do not support teachers who are afraid to teach." She lectured on ways to construct bridges for children who have not had the experiences that children in the mainstream take for granted. There was nothing soft in her delivery or in her demand that teachers expect *all* children to read and write fluently and, further, that we not makes excuses when they don't and that we not allow them to make choices in our classrooms that detract from that goal. How does "afraid to teach" look? Is there any of that in me?

Delpit's opening was no less haunting: "A school can be an excellent place for some children and totally unsuitable for others." I have a heterogeneous group of children who can easily be divided into "school works for" and "school doesn't work for." How do I make it work for all of them? I talked to Delpit briefly and told her my dilemma. She recognized it and had dealt with it in her own teaching. She encouraged me to stay open, keep listening, and not run from what I heard. She autographed my copy of *Other People's Children* and introduced me to Michelle Foster, whose book, *Black Teachers on Teaching*, I'd just bought. I began rereading Delpit, in light of her speech, at the same time I was reading Foster. The tandem reading of those books raised my awareness once again of the "modern prejudice" (Delpit, 1995, p. 115) that was infiltrating our schools. Foster (1997) complained that some of the worst miseducation of African American children is at the hands of "liberal White teachers who pampered and coddled them but demanded little" (p. xlvi). Is that how afraid to teach looks? Over and over again, the teachers interviewed by Foster urged today's educators to make instruction relevant and undergirded that with the plea that we not lower expectations for children of color.

Journal Entry (spring)
Foster and some of the teachers she writes about make me ask if I demand the same of Tommy as I do from privileged White students. Well, he and Eric are moving right along together. In some ways I can answer yes, but the question still niggles at me. They are at about the same ability and production level. They are reading in the same group and going at about the same pace, a snail's pace for sure, but a pace together nonetheless.

ERICANDTOMMYANDTOMMYANDERIC

Or were they? Reading the followinig set of entries embarrasses me a little. How did I not see what is so plain to me now?

Journal Entry (late November)
Today I was so excited! I watched one of those magical moments of connection with my own teacher eyes. Tommy tracked the words in a sentence in order to identify a word. We were reading a familiar chart rhyme and I was asking different children to isolate words with *ing* in them. I asked for *sing*. I saw Tommy squint and point to each word from a distance, mouthing the first sentence until he got to the word *sing*. His hand flew up. He came to the chart and pointed the word out, even underlined the *ing*—leaving off the *s*! Eric was busy tying his shoes the whole time. So, I asked him to find the next *ing* word and, as usual, saw that he struggled to find a way to isolate a word. I asked Tommy to help him. "Pretend you're the teacher, Tommy, and show Eric how you did that."
Tommy repeated his pattern from earlier on in another sentence. His ability to recite that chant proved invaluable today. Eric tried to see what he was doing but failed to. His parents continue to worry about him, and I wonder if I'm being fair to tell them that he will catch up, that he is just young. I'm beginning to wonder myself.

As I revisit that November entry, it seems fraught with an emphasis on my worry about Eric in the midst of my joy over Tommy. And it clearly indicates that Tommy was moving ahead of Eric. Yet in my mind both of them were still walking along beside reading and not stepping into it.

Journal Entry (December)
Tommy had fun at reading today. He has enjoyed reading Bill Martin's (1967/1993) *Brown Bear, Brown Bear* now that he attends

to the words as well as the illustrations. I asked if the kids wanted to write something together, using the brown bear, brown bear pattern, inserting characters from the *Nutcracker* ballet. He bit! He was calling out the sentences fast as lightning. Eric, Chris, and Jamel thought of the things they wanted to "see" and Tommy put them into the pattern. He ran to get the book. After each member of the group had chosen a character to illustrate, they began working. I called children to read to me individually. I noticed how much fun Tommy and Eric were having. Once Tommy said, "Look I'll be the teacher again, OK?" He showed Eric how the answer was not on the same page as the question. Eric is such an artist he can draw anything, so they made a great team. Tommy's drawings all look the same. Anything alive is represented by a circle with attached loops for legs—no arms, no body; four loops for animals, two for people. He struggles to form letters and doesn't even write his name consistently the same way. Eric can copy anything and draws detailed, though childlike, representations of objects.

Once again I recorded Tommy helping Eric, but I ended with their teamwork. I saw them together and responded to them together. Even when I did note them individually, the multitude of foci in a given day masked the strength of their individual efforts, especially Tommy's. Here are two wonderful little boys whose worst acting-out is no more than kid wiggles. They are polite, considerate, friendly, and cooperative. They weren't at the top of the academic ladder, maybe, but they both seemed bright enough. I chaffed at the pressure to assess them under one spotlight called reading when I enjoyed them in so many other ways. They were so refreshing and I knew I'd take them just the way they were any day of the week! But always it was "they," until mid-December, when I was forced to think of them so separately.

Eric

Journal Entry (late fall)
    Eric has been tensely measuring my responses to him lately. For me there is a degree of sadness as I watch that tiny set of hands hold some piece of print that makes him so nervous. He wants to read and knows that he can't. I think often of the rude trick his premature birth played on him. A few weeks' difference on a certificate places him in one grade instead of another. It would have been so good had his family waited until after summer to put him in school and just put him in kindergarten this year. He is so small and is dealing with

culture shock on top of having to regain his health. He's had enough on his plate without a developmentally inappropriate school day being added on.

I hate to hear that he is giving himself such negative messages at home. While he can't read yet, he is incredibly bright. His parents and grandparents are all caught up in the question of why Eric can't read. I don't think I've ever had a long-distance phone call from a grandparent before. Eric's grandmother had taught reading once upon a time, she said. I could tell she was checking me out. I think I "passed," but we both agreed that it just doesn't make sense that Eric is not yet reading. "He's had every advantage," she reminded me. And that's where I'm confused as well.

Just before winter vacation Eric's mom, Becky, was helping me in the classroom. We were rehashing our usual subject together. I ventured toward some of my new thoughts about Eric. "You know there really is nothing wrong with Eric that time won't fix. Too bad we can't just stick him back in an oven and let him cook a little longer." We laughed at the metaphor and talked on the surface about it.

That night his dad called. He wanted to hear my side of the conversation, which Becky reported to him. I took a deep breath and offered what I thought would sound like a wild card. "How about if he spent the rest of this year in kindergarten and then came to me next year?" We discussed it realistically from several perspectives. We agreed that it seemed like a good thing, if Eric didn't reject the notion. How I wished for the more fluid construct of a multi-age grouping. But of course that's not what we had.

The levels of personnel for a decision like that had to be addressed: the principal, the kindergarten teacher, the counselor. Would it even be a possibility numberswise? Everything checked out except in regard to the counselor, who had a real problem with retention. "This isn't really retention, though," I told her. "It's more like . . . starting over." She wasn't convinced. I admitted that none of us could really be convinced, but we had an unhappy child who was likely to become even more tense and less able to produce. As always the parents were the main decision makers in the mix and they would take their cues from Eric.

His mom asked him how he would like to be in his old classroom again and then go back to my room in the fall. "COOL! I'll be the smartest kid in there!" he answered. Then he asked, "Can Tommy come too?"

He was willing to go without Tommy as long as Tommy came to play in the afternoons. His dad wanted everything taken care of before winter break so that after the break he would just go straight to his "new" class. We met several times with all parties involved.

We made the move just as his dad wanted us to. Every time I saw Eric, he was happy. He had that old jaunty spirit again. His parents, and the reading-teacher grandma, felt we had made the right decision.

In the end even the counselor had to agree that though the move was unprecedented at our school, it appeared to have been a successful choice.

Tommy

Just before we went back to school from winter break, I got a phone call from Tommy's mother:

Journal Entry (winter break)

Tommy's mother just called. She had talked to Eric's mom when the boys played today and was concerned that Tommy might be sent back to kindergarten. I assured her that the decision about Eric was made after much thought and with all parties, including Eric, agreeing.

"How is Tommy doing in school?"

"I'll be honest," I said to her. "If Tommy got marks for good behavior he would skip the next grade. But if he doesn't learn to read it will be a disaster to send him to second grade."

"What do we have to do to get to make his pass?"

"It's January. Almost half the year has passed and he is very much behind."

"I work till late, so I don't help him with homework. His sister can, though. Just send us some extra work."

"Well, he doesn't need extra as much as he needs to do what I assign every day. But here's what I'm going to do. I'm going to continue sending home books for him to read and some flash cards and matching games. But he can't do them without someone checking to see if he is getting them right. He needs to be read to and someone needs to hear him read every night. He will need 30 minutes every day from someone at home, including Saturday and Sunday."

We went on to talk about Reading Recovery. He would be the next child in after someone came out, if she would be willing to sign for him to participate. She seemed positive about that. I told her we would have to work together, become a good team in order to get Tommy "up with the class."

In the background I could hear the family. The noise of the TV, the stereo, people talking, and children tussling was so distracting. She said that she would get her daughter to work with him.

She asked me to do one more thing.

"You tell Tommy that if he don't learn to read he won't make his pass. Show him that he's behind and what books he have to learn to read before school gets out. It will mean more coming from you. You the teacher. He'll believe you."

Hard Questions

I had to write about Tommy's story in the context of his relationship to Eric to help me answer that haunting set of questions: Do I expect more of the privileged White child than I do of a child like Tommy? Did I hold lower expectations for poor children of color? Am I afraid to teach? In *Composing a Life*, Mary Bateson (1990) used the analogy of jazz in constructing the stories of the women she wrote about. It fits my view of Eric and Tommy as "at once individual and communal, repetitive and innovative. Each [boy] sometimes providing background support and sometimes flying free" (p. 3). Now that the boys had been separated I had to learn the melody Tommy made as he flew free. All narrative accounts, even those of subjects flying free, have multiple layers. "There are always stories embedded within stories . . . multiple levels . . . and these double back, laminate, and build on one another to provide the context of the larger story that is to be told" (Denzin, 1989, pp. 72–73). This series of embedded contexts speaks to both the interplay of our teaching lives in multiple connections to students and to the necessary dip we take into the past—our own and those of others— in order to makes sense of where we are today and where we need to go next.

Journal Entry (winter)

I am bothered by Tommy's mother's call. There are things that weren't said. Maybe we didn't know how to say them or were afraid to. We both understand that Tommy and Eric, so much alike, always viewed together, were treated differently. When the privileged White boy couldn't read, none of us could make sense of it. When the nonmainstream African American male couldn't read, no one was surprised. My indictment of his "failure" was aimed squarely at his home, the mom, the lack of parental participation, the lack of value placed on reading in that home.

How is it that my visit to Eric's home, with the dog running through the house, and Eric jumping over the sofa, and the neighborhood children's voices coming through the window, and the three other kids moving around as we talked didn't register as chaos? There are the same number of people in Tommy's house as in Eric's. Every time I talked to Eric's mom she had to apologize and solve a fight going on right around her, but I never wrote about it. The same kind of noise can be viewed either as rude and close to violent or as emitted by lots of people in a small space who want attention. My attitude was listening harder than my ears were.

I realize that Eric's inability to read was treated as an illness that needed aggressive treatment—a Mayo Clinic, a team of specialists, and if that doesn't work we'll go to the experimental.

Tommy's lack of skill in reading was treated more as an allergy: awful to deal with, but something some kids just have. I was inactive, not ambivalent, but just sure that the solution to his nonreader status lay beyond my control. There are common teacher gripes about children that I abhor, argue against, am sickened by. There are statements such as "He started behind." "If we could teach parents how to raise their kids before we get them maybe there would be some hope." "I know what to do; I just need better clients." I fight those words but accept too easily the confirmation I see everywhere that education is not the promise for poor children of color that it is for "us." It is monstrous that I moved all kinds of boundaries in my thinking when Eric couldn't read and added extra support to the fences of acceptance that Tommy couldn't read.

A MEMOIR TEACHES ACROSS TIME

My early research dealt with the power of memoir in research (Hankins, 1996, 1998). My inquiry centered largely on dissecting my ideological frame of reference. It was enlightening and painful. So I was shocked to discover that even when I was armed against myself, certain prejudices still proved to be motivating factors in decisions I made.

Although I was unaware of how my attitude defined Tommy's position, I was cognizant of the power that memoirs and family stories held to shine a bright light on such an unawareness. I have learned to trust those "one moment in two times" feelings (Hankins, 1996, p. 27). Luckily, as Tommy followed the low road, he had company: my father, who as a boy was called Billy.

Journal Entry (written after the event and shared in writing with my
father for accuracy)

He sat at our dining-room table with an itinerary in his hand, a
way for us to track where he and Mom would be on the trip to Scotland. Our family stays in constant touch. It's almost a curse to be so
focused on keeping everyone's schedule in your head. It's born, I
think, from our roots in a mill village, where life beyond the village
must have looked far away and inaccessible; and most specifically from
Papa Hale, who wanted his children with him at all times, certainly at
dark and during storms, and most especially as he lay dying, when my
father was just 7 years old. Daddy was somewhere in the middle of
9 children, big enough to understand the importance of staying close
because Papa wanted him to but too small to be of much help. In the
very end they weren't all there. Someone ran to a nearby neighbor,
hunting for a phone; another ran to get the oldest son. And my father,
7 years old, watched in horror from just outside the door, as the panic
of adults tried to coax his papa back into this life. That moment lived
alone must have ensured a feeling that the world could tilt suddenly,
spilling everything dear. For the following years, school felt like his
place of exile from home. He needed to be home. School was a place
where he had to stay on guard, a place where he could not concentrate because it would take his attention away from protecting Mama.
For the most part, he was unsuccessful in elementary school. For one
thing, he was too sleepy to learn much. He was busy waking his
mama up all night long to make sure she hadn't died. The strong urge
to keep track of everyone, keep them all there, was such a big responsibility for one so young, though it never occurred to him that it was
his own job construction.

It is surprising that he has traveled so far from the village now. It is
not surprising, however, that we still report in, check up, and roll call
frequently.

He double checked the notes he'd made for us, paused, and said,
"Sometimes I can't really take in all that has happened to me. How far
I am from where I ever thought I'd be. Why . . . I couldn't have even
thought it possible to do all I do now back in the village. I really had no
idea anybody did stuff like this . . . except in a movie." His grin revealed a combination of thrill and embarrassment. "I am just so
excited I can't stand it. The only thing I'm worried about is the limou-
sine taking us to the right terminal. Once that's behind me I'll be fine!"
Our family magnifies small things into giant worries when life is
proving to be too good to be true.

"I'll tell you one thing I'm going to do in Scotland. I'm doing it to settle a score, as proof to myself of just how far this ol' lint head has come. Just to thumb my nose in the air and say, 'See there, you scumbuckets!'"

I looked puzzled.

"I'm going to a place called the Firth of Forth. I'm going to stand and throw a rock into it or touch it and think how *I'm* the only one of us, even the boss's kids, that's done that.

"You have to understand, they all thought I didn't know anything. They thought I was dumb, an 'ignoramus.' All I had to do was get called on in school to make them laugh. I didn't even have to answer for people to start giggling."

He laughed. There was no hint of bitterness in his delivery as he said, "I really was dumb, back then I was. I mean I guess . . . I really didn't know anything much at all. I couldn't read hardly at all . . . sure couldn't spell. Arithmetic was better but I really couldn't do that either!

"But in the fourth grade, every day after lunch, Miss Walton asked someone to go to the map and show us some spot she'd not talked about before, a place we had never heard of even. I loved that part of school. She could make those faraway places sound so grand. George [my father's older brother] had gotten a map from somewhere and I began to look at it at night to see if I could find the place we talked about at school. I could always find it. It was kinda like a puzzle. We didn't have books or magazines at home, nothing to read, really. But George did have that map thumbtacked to the wall. It was the only thing that resembled any part of school at home.

"The first day she called on me I heard them start giggling and muttering right away. I pointed boldly to a place called the Firth of Forth. As I read it they laughed out loud. 'Cause see it sounded like I'd made a mistake in reading, as usual. Old Jimmy Truett, one of the boss's little kids, said, "You know Billy cain't read! He cain't read a lick!" I was turning red, but I knew, or hoped, I was right. Miss Walton came close to the map and looked. She put her arm around my shoulder and smiled real big. She said, 'Billy has shown us the Firth of Forth, in Scotland. I've never noticed it on a map. How wonderful that you've shown us something new. I can't wait to read about it. Who knows what a firth is?' Nobody did. And she just went on and on acting like I said smart stuff all the time. She didn't act the least bit surprised that I got it right.

"They all looked at me in shock and quit laughing. How could I, dumb ol' cain't-read Billy, scared of everything, get this right! I knew I was dumb . . . no, really, back then I was. I mean truly, I . . . didn't . . .

get . . . it. Nothing connected or made sense at school. It interfered with my main goal. I just wanted to stay alive and keep the vigil to make sure Mama stayed alive too.

"We all loved that teacher, she was nice, not mean like so many of them were then. If she liked my answer then everybody liked my answer. When that teacher smiled at me and thanked *me* for teaching *her* something I felt something in school I'd never felt before. A teacher believed in me. She took my response, the one they all expected to be stupid, the laughable one, and suddenly turned it to pure gold. A place was eked out inside me that I can go back to and almost touch it was so real.

"I learned to spell and locate continents, countries, capitals, rivers, oceans, and mountain ranges, especially the funny-sounding ones like Constantinople or Madagascar.

"I still 'couldn't read a lick' and missed all my spelling words every Friday, except for the bonus word that was always a country someone had shown us on the map that week. I was the only one who got them right week after week.

"One day, when I was in middaydream, she asked me gently, 'Where you been, Billy?' when I was not paying attention. I shrugged my shoulders. 'Home with Mama, I guess.' That same day she asked me why I could spell Madagascar but none of my easier spelling words. I remember her smile when I answered, 'Ah, I wadn't never too good at spellin', but I can do geography . . . Madagascar is geography.'

"I know it sounds comical, a punch line worth $50 in *Reader's Digest*, but life was compartmentalized like that for me. She told me that Madagascar *was* spelling and reading and that I could do it other places as well. She believed in me and I believed her, I guess.

"In her smile and approval, a geography student had been born, in her words a new curiosity was awakened, and in her hand on my shoulder I was led into teaching and well . . . she never knew it . . .

"But one day next week I'm going to do what—I am sure, because I've checked—none of those smart kids ever did. I'm going to go to Scotland, listen to that so-far-from-the-mill-village-brogue, taste some haggis, and touch the walls of its castles. But no king's castle will have the impact of coming right up to the lapping waters of the Firth of Forth. It will remind this lint head of what I was doomed to be until that teacher treated me like I was one of the smart ones. There was a whole lot of difference in her smile and their laughing. When the water meets my eyes I hope I remember her smile more than their laughter; I want it to be a good feeling.

He stood up and handed me the itinerary, complete with every possible phone connection we could use to find each other at a moment's notice—not that there was any impending need, you understand. As he left he said, "While I'm in Scotland you'll be teaching. Remember to smile."

He walked out the door and up the walk to his car. I watched my dad. As he got in the car and waved to us, I was thinking of Billy but I was seeing Tommy.

It is important that the reader know that Billy, now Bill, my father, earned his Ph.D. in education from Florida State University. I was 10 years old by that time. He retired from teaching at the University of Georgia several years ago and continues his own consulting firm. He is a commanding and well-known speaker in the field of human motivation and communications. It is important for teachers who read his story to realize that we never know which of our students are scholars waiting to happen. We never know how one event may figure into the course that a person's life may follow.

Reframing Through Memoir

Lisa Delpit (1995) says that "we do not see with our eyes or hear through our ears, but through our beliefs" (p. 46). My beliefs about Tommy are central to the point of this narrative. The night I read the itinerary of Scotland I began to deal with my part in the many strikes against Tommy as he tried to navigate the system.

I remembered that evening how Tommy looked the day I talked to him, at his mother's request, about his reading. He looked at me deeply, without taking his eyes off of me. Before I started talking, I had felt a little bit as though I was about to deliver news that his dog had died. As he listened, I became braver. He *wanted* to know what was required and was trying to cut through my message to the specifics. So, I actually got some books that are considered primers and some that are considered at first-grade level off the shelf. I asked him if he thought he could read the words in those books yet. "No." He shook his head. "Well, when June comes, Tommy, you really have to be able to read books like these to be able to do the work the second-grade teacher will give you next year." (I could not say to him, "You will not go to second grade." I wanted to hug him. I wanted to say, "*You* matter more than a reading level.")

As if to force my hand to confirm what he thought he had understood from home he asked, "My mama said what book I got to read to make my pass?" I sucked in my breath and said, "Not one particular book but books like these, books this difficult. Here, take this one home and show it to your mama." I knew that more was involved, but we'd take it one day at a time.

The time Tommy and I had the conversation about "making his pass" coalesced with the night I heard the Firth of Forth narrative, and a miracle began to take shape. The sequence of the miracle is hard to completely identify, but what is important is the outcome.

The year was more than half invested now. We were somewhere toward the end of winter. I immersed myself in Delpit and Foster, went back to Heath and Cazden, Smitherman, anyone who would remind me of specific ways to reopen my mind to the multiple voices around me.

Randel, in Chapter 1, had already preached and I had orally rehearsed that event story many times. I don't think I had recognized the power of his voice completely. I think that I saw his as a unique voice, a gifted voice that I could have overlooked had he been able to be silenced. I was building an appreciation for the connections his narrative style had to my own. His story style felt familiar to me in its inflection and its constant hypothetical questioning. Rereading the literature gave me renewed respect for the connections I saw between his voice and Tommy's. I began to reflect on the way I listened to a wider variety of African American voices. I began to stop myself in mid-response to check the genuineness of the invitation to academic conversation that I had delivered to Tommy. I worked to become aware of what Bakhtin (1981) called the "heteroglossia" of the everyday. It's one thing to hear the heteroglossia and another thing altogether to gain a fluency of communication within it.

The events recorded next represent my efforts to hear Tommy differently and to respond with some degree of relevance to him.

MEMOIR-LITERATURE-REFLECTION-CONNECTION

Journal Entry (spring)

Last night I was reading Smitherman (1981) on African American writing styles and it reminded me of Sara Michaels's sharing-time stories. The thesis I carry from them is that difference is not deficiency. Smitherman gave four specific guidelines to follow:

1. Capitalize on the strengths of the cultural discourse.
2. Encourage field-dependency (where the writer writes with a total involvement with and a non-distancing from the subject at hand).

3. Design strategies that incorporate the black imaginative storytelling style into writing.
4. De-emphasize concerns about Black English Vernacular gram-
   mar, to keep from suppressing the rich, expressive African
   American discourse (p. 95).

Reading this kind of literature for a graduate class discussion entails
a less impassioned agenda than that of reading them with the face of
Tommy popping out from between the lines. But I was still surprised at
how soon I was able to draw on Smitherman's suggestions.

The very next morning I entered the room, still distracted by the
phone call I'd had to take in the office. My aide was with the class,
hearing them read from their journals to the group.

I walked in as Tommy finished reading, and she said to him, "That
doesn't make sense, Tommy! I mean, what is this story about?" (First
off, her tone is enough to send me into orbit and I fight against embarrassing us both by saying something equally as rude to her!) She
picked up the journal and read aloud what I'd not heard him read as
I entered the room.

> I love Winnie the pooh
> My Mom love Winnie the pooh
> My Mom gon wup me
> I love Winnie the pooh

His little face had that dashed-to-the-floor look of embarrassment
as he took the journal she handed him. He looked at it, tapping the
writing with his finger as if that would somehow produce the answer
for her.

I intervened, thinking about my father's charge, "Remember to
smile."

"Wait . . . Tommy. I think I know what this is about. I bet your
mom was teasing you, saying that you couldn't like Winnie-the-Pooh
because she did!"

His eyes lit up as he nodded his head.

"Did she tell you that she was going to get Winnie-the-Pooh?"

His smile took on a hint of surprise at my "getting it" and his ears
seemed to perk up a little.

"I bet she said" (I was acting now, inflecting my voice), "'You
cannot have my Winnie-the-Pooh, he's *my* Winnie-the-Pooh!' and you
said, 'He's mine!'"

He was with me now, saying the words almost in unison with me.
He added a soft-spoken but well-done reenactment:

"I love Pooh."

"Uh-uh! I love Winnie-the-Pooh!"

"I'm gonna hide him."

"Gimmie that Winnie-the-Pooh!

"No mine . . . mine . . . mine! He like *me* best!"

"I'm gonna whup yo-o-o-u! Boy! Don't you take my Winnie-the-Pooh!"

He acted out the whole scene, taking her part and his part, stepping into each part by blocking with his elbow and spinning to hide the invisible bear. Some of the kids laughed with him as they recognized that familiar joke between a child and playful adult.

The writing that he had painstakingly put together (copying the name from the front of a book, *love* and *Mom* from the word wall, and *gon* and *wup* with help from children at the table with him) had been read with equally painstaking attention to calling a word for a word written. It's not surprising to hear so little of the giddiness of the family scene in the text or in his delivery. That's the way with most early writers. The aide's response to the "rereading" of the journal was "I don't know how you got *that* from what he wrote!"

I didn't have time to answer. I was on a roll, paying allegiance to my father and homage to Tommy-the-writer and listening to Lisa Delpit, who seemed to be standing at my ear saying, "Don't run from what you hear." I was able to put my fingers right on Vera B. Williams's (1990) *"More, More, More," Said the Baby*. We had done an author/illustrator study with her books earlier in the year. I told the children that Tommy's writing reminded me of that book about parents and kids, even reading her limited text as a comparison with Tommy's. After Tommy went back to his seat, we had time for several more children to share. As they read and children responded, I noticed Tommy writing instead of listening, a "no-no" in our classroom. I moved over to whisper to Tommy that he put his eyes on the speaker to show respect. One survey of his work, and I didn't have the heart to stop him. He was meticulously drawing a colorful, patterned, Williams-like border of X O X O around his entire Winnie-the-Pooh entry. Love and kisses Vera B. Williams style, a self-made connection between his work and hers. Who knows, maybe his oral responses to literature will follow.

How did I get that meaning from his story? I listened to the memories of his mother's teasing banter and the squeals of a chase when I called his house. I also listened to a game I had played recently with my grandson in which I claimed that his shoe was mine and tried to put it on my foot. He was laughing, and when I acted angry that he took "my shoes," he laughed even harder. And I remembered my grandfather, who never went to church, making the excuse to me "How can I go when you are wearing my Sunday dress!" "But it's *my* dress, you are a man!" I giggled. "Mine," he insisted. We whispered that mine-mine-mine joke all morning long. When I guessed the meaning of Tommy's writing, the rest of the story was his to recite, and he did so, revealing the "field-dependency" of his writing (Smitherman, 1994, p. 94).

What I saw in his reenactment was evidence of what Delpit called a verbal adroitness, which is so highly valued in most African American communities. Heath (1996) reported that children much like Tommy tell story-poems from the age of 2; they embellish them with gestures and shifts in voice and repetition. "They only gradually learn to work their way into any on-going discourse with their stories, and when they do, they are not asked questions about them nor are they asked to re-peat them" (p. 187).

I think back now on the first Winnie-the-Pooh encounter, the book Tommy chose early in the year and the "ongoing discourse" I tried to have with him. He may have tried to begin a story when he said, "I have one." I had asked him if the bear was real or make-believe and was lis-tening to my questions instead of his answers. Maybe he meant, "Of course he's real, I have one, don't I?" He didn't respond to "Why did you choose the book?" But he obviously chose the book because he had a Winnie-the-Pooh. He wanted to tell me about his own Pooh. Our dis-tance produced a silence that he filled with thought and I filled with words, words absent of communication.

It is good to recognize that I have made progress. I can acknowl-edge the transformative power of rereading all those passages I had highlighted earlier in Cazden, Delpit, Foster, Heath, Michaels, and Smitherman. They not only made a different kind of sense in the con-text of knowing Tommy; they were in fact shaping the specific craft of communicating in the heteroglossia of my class. I see evidence that my actions were guided by new "habits of mind" (Greene, 1995).

Instead of being thrown when I entered a spot of silence between myself and a child, I could actually recall verbatim Delpit's (1995) writ-ing that questioning styles outside a child's cultural narrative would "cause a child to lapse into silence or to contribute very little informa-tion" (p. 56). In that same argument she also challenged me and all teachers to structure the classroom so that all children can acquire the verbal patterns they lack while further developing the ones they are most proficient in. The tension lay in learning to recognize those very sophisticated expressions, and celebrate and employ them, while model-ing entries into ways of questioning that schools most often use.

Journal Entry (March)

Time to get the old projects off the walls of the room to make space for some new ones; anyway, the children are all eager to take them home! I decided that spring pictures and poems and writing would be just the ticket to get us through these surprisingly cold March days!

I began the project with a brainstorming session. I was hoping to compile a list that would provide words for writing and ideas for illustrations of stories and poems.

"Let's make a chart/list of things that remind us of spring," I said to the children.

Tommy, who tunes into these discussions more energetically now, raised his hand.

I called on him right away and he said with confidence, "Winter!" (Oops! Why did I call on him *first*!)

"No!" some of the children told him. They were waving their hands and making, "O-o! O-o! O-o!" noises.

"Wait," I told them. (I was thinking how Daddy had said, "The teacher took my laughable response and turned it to gold. They laughed but she smiled.")

"Tommy, I know why you said that. When I said spring you knew it was a season like winter, spring, summer, fall! Right?"

He nodded more in trust than as affirmation of my guess. I proceeded. "So . . . when I said spring . . . you thought . . . " I spread my arms wide to catch the answer and he said, "Winter?"

"Winter," I repeated. In school talk repeating means "right."

He nodded, but knew there was more.

I tried to model the process. "Now, Tommy, if I said tell me something about winter, I might expect you to say snow, mittens, hot chocolate, because those things go with cold winter weather. Now think, when spring finally comes what will we expect to see?"

He tried to think, his eyes darting at the kids who were impatiently making bids for a turn.

"Put your hands down. It's Tommy's turn. He can't think when you do that," I reproached the group, who became silent.

He relaxed and answered, "Flowers?"

"Yes, we think of flowers in the spring." And I wrote *flowers* as the first word on the chart.

His hand went up several more times as we compiled the list. I noticed as we read the chart that he was right in step with us. He is just on the edge of reading alone. He is working hard to figure out what it is that I expect of him. I'm trying to learn from him as well.

The confusion between our efforts cannot be attributed to nonchalance or lack of concern on either of our parts.

I don't know what actual impact those events had on Tommy, but his smiles and his exponential growth in class discussions confirm that they were positive for our relationship with each other and for his with the class.

MATCHING FAMILY EXPECTATIONS

At about the time of this incident, an interesting and informative phone call taught me even more about Tommy and his family. I was called to the office and requested to bring Tommy also, to hear a message. It was a long message with multiple steps for him to follow. The secretary was concerned that he might forget so many things and when she read the directions I was concerned also.

Mom had called and said she would not be home when he got home and that he was riding the bus alone that day because his brother was sick and she was taking him to the doctor. Did he still have his key and if not there would be a key hidden under the rock by the back door. Don't forget to bring the key back inside. He was to go home and get his basketball uniform on, his top was drying on the line outside. He needed to get dressed, call his coach, whose telephone number was beside the phone, and tell him he was home. The coach would pick him up for the game and she would get him after the game. The dog can stay on the back porch. He had a sandwich in the refrigerator and 50¢ on the table to get a drink at the game.

This child is 6 years old! I was blown away. So many things to remember. The secretary gave me the list and I took it with me. It was 10 o'clock. Would he remember all that by 3 o'clock when he got off the bus? As the day progressed I made several stabs at taking control. I could find an older child on the bus; no that might alert too many people that he was alone. I know, I'd just follow the bus home and make sure he remembered. No, his mother might think I was trespassing or something. Around lunchtime I asked Tommy if he remembered all the things in the note and he reeled them all off fast as lightning. I was impressed, and I did let go of some of the anxiety I had carried around about it! Just before he climbed on his bus I called him over and he began the litany with some exasperation in his voice before I ever told him why I called him over. I referred to the note as he recited what he was to do; I was glad his memory was better than mine.

Clearly, he was a man in charge and more interested in getting to that game ready to win than anything else. He was confident and focused on his mission.

His mother saw him as capable of managing himself. There was no reason I couldn't/shouldn't demand the same. No more feeling sorry for him if he forgot his book, lost his book bag, or didn't record the books in his reading log. I thought back to his mother telling me, "Show him what he has to do to make his pass. Nobody in this family ever failed their grade and he is a smart kid. *You* tell him, *you are the teacher.*" They held him responsible for his own learning. I was reminded of a dialogue a teacher had had with the parent of a Black child who was using his journal not for writing but for drawing. The teacher asked the mother what she would do to encourage him to write first then add the drawing later. If he was at home how would she handle it? She said to him, "In Black families we would just say, write first draw later" (Delpit, 1995, p. 180). He took her suggestion, told the child exactly what to do, and suddenly full-page written entries appeared in the journal. Tommy was capable and independent at home. It was time I stopped coddling him and gave him the same message at school that he got at home. I needed to stop feeling that I didn't have the right to demand quality from him.

One day he goofed off and turned in an incomplete assignment. I handed it back to him and reminded him that it was part of a group book and that he needed to finish it for homework so we could bind it the next day. He looked a little shocked. Then he came to me and said he couldn't do it at home because he didn't have any crayons. I'd given the children crayons for Christmas, he sometimes added drawings at home to his journal, and, besides, they rented videos by the truckload in that house and crayons cost about the same as a video. I told him nicely that he needed to tell his mom if he couldn't find his crayons and she would help him figure out what to do. I added, "Don't wait till bedtime, Tommy, you'll need to work this afternoon." The next morning he brought in a colorful, well-done assignment. I asked him what he had done about the crayons. He looked as though he didn't know what I was referring to at first then answered, "I looked for them in my toy box and there they were!"

HIGH GOALS REWARDED

I promised you a miracle some pages back. The events I've narrated since then all figure into a sudden dawn of realization that connected Tommy to reading. It was almost as sudden as that memorable scene in which Helen Keller finally understands the point of the finger games, when the running water pulled the past right into the palm of her hand.

Journal Entry (spring)
     Today as we were doing a together-whisper-read (when a small group reads along in unison to get the sense of the story without getting too bogged down in the decoding), Tommy's voice was a word or two ahead of the group the whole time. I noticed and he noticed, both of us showing some surprise. He looked at me as he finished as if to ask me if I'd seen it too. I asked him if he had read this book before. "No." He shook his head. A half smile turned into a big one that covered his whole face.
     "What a great job you did!" I held him by the shoulders and looked into his face, almost whispering, "Tommy, you can read!" I hugged him and twirled him around and around before standing him back on the floor. "Look at me! YOU . . . . CAN . . . . READ!!!"
     He was grinning as though he had won the lottery or something equally as desirable but truly unanticipated. He was breathing hard as he said, "I know."
     Today, I watched a new birth of sorts. This babe moved from incubation into a new way to breathe. Now, his world has exponentially exploded with possibilities that had been locked away from him before. What a reason to celebrate!

     I remember Tommy asking to take the book home that night. He came back the next day and read the whole thing to the class. He was blossom and flower all at once!
     When he began Reading Recovery a few days later, I had to convince the teacher to keep him because he tested so high, at level 9. (It was still below the expected performance of the average first grader in March.) I bribed her, begged her, then convinced her to keep him. She kept him as an extra, seeing him right after he got off the bus each morning. I wanted him to be able to use multiple sets of skills to foster his reading independence. His family valued one's taking charge of one's own learning. I wanted him to be at maximum efficiency as soon as possible.
     He made rapid progress. Our parallel block schedule afforded us the opportunity of having only half our class at a time for directed reading lessons. At the beginning of the year I split my class into two performance groups based on alphabetic knowledge, facility with writing, and knowledge of sight words used in kindergarten. Tommy was in the group

that needed more teacher support. When the year began he was struggling along with Eric to pay attention, to make sense of the print, and to contribute in a meaningful way. After the "miracle," and during the one-on-one tutoring, his ability seemed to mushroom. Now, close to the end of the year, he claimed leadership of that group, which by now did have a share of grade-level readers. The groups had never been static in my mind, and I often shifted kids for a while from one group to the other and back again for a multitude of reasons. So when I moved Tommy to the other group, there was no fanfare, no announcement made. The reality was, however, that he was bored with the books that the others were slowly working to decode, so he would just blurt out the words or take over. One day during centers (the whole class is together for centers), he went to a reading spot where there was a child who was a very strong reader. Tommy was telling this child the words that the child stumbled over; among them were *disappointed* and *argument*, not exactly from a first-grade sight-word list. I was so proud of him—but no prouder than he was of himself.

In the second half of the school year, our class held three different reading incentives. The chief goal was to read 1,000 books in a combined effort from January to the end of school. The incentives all required me to make a fool of myself in one way or another, from wearing my pajamas to school, to standing on the roof in a clown suit blowing bubbles while the children ate ice cream. Tommy was a nonparticipant in the first 250 books that we logged in during January and February. He lost his list, or mom didn't sign it—there were all manner of excuses. In the spring, he was the first to turn in a list for the last set of books that would bring us to 1,000. The final incentive required each child to read 25 books at her or his reading level. Tommy's list was completely recorded in his own handwriting, though his mother did sign it. As one of the first to finish, he was paired with a child who was not reading or not recording at home. The child read to him or he read to the child, and I signed off. This meant that they had to read during recess, but they were willing to do it. (Anything to see me act like a clown!)

One morning in May, I listened as several boys came into the room, greeting each other while they unpacked and readied themselves for the day.

Journal Entry (late spring)

Mark Twain said once that there is no difference in a man who can't read good books and a man who won't. I note the attitude of some of the middle-class and socialite parents about the reading I demand be done by their children nightly. The sometimes stated response is, we just don't have time. They labor under the false assumption that their children are so far ahead that little is required to keep that spot. Their children know what is required, however, and talk about it.

Hayward: "Dang, I couldn't read last night. I had tae kwon do and then all kinds of chores to do with my mom.

Tommy: I read!

Spencer: I didn't read either. Mom wouldn't let me after my game.

Tommy: How many did you read, Christopher?

Christopher: I read one but my mom forgot to write it down.

Spencer: Liar!

Christopher: Uh-uh, I did too read!

Tommy: Look how much is on my list! 1-2-3—then the other night so . . .

Christopher: [Helps count] 4-5-6-. Hey I read that book!

Tommy: It's funny.

Christopher: That lion went "Na-na-naaa!"

Spencer: And he was pestering everybody.

Tommy: No the lion was getting somebody to read to him so at the end though he could read to *them* . . . but they all fell asleep!

Hayward: I'm going to take that book tonight, OK?

Tommy: OK, here. [He hands the book to Hayward]

Evidence of all I wanted for Tommy academically when I first met him is contained in that one conversation. He can read, and he likes to read. Most important of all, he talks about the story with such facility that another child wanted to read it too. The kids in that conversation knew who had the academic goods that morning: Tommy.

"If teaching can be thought of as an address to others' consciousness, it may be a summons on the part of one incomplete person to other incomplete persons to reach for wholeness" (Greene, 1995, p. 26). I am a teacher, but an incomplete one each year until my consciousness meshes with others. The miracle of Tommy is not a supernatural kind at all; it is the miracle of human connection despite the odds that we had created against it happening. The miracle speaks to finding the beautiful side of the fairy tale to balance the fear of monsters we hold so easily.

INTERPRETATIONS AND MEMOIR

I try to remember when it was in the spinning coalescing of this story that I told my father about a bit of the power that his memoir had held for the education of one child this year. I remember above all that he winced at my admission of the negative view I had once held of Tommy's family, especially when I used the word *chaotic*. "You know," he said, "when I was his age I was active and rambunctious but there were also three *little* sisters and one infant niece living in that four-room house as well. I can't imagine that there was ever anything but chaotic bedlam. I mean, really try to imagine four preschoolers, toddlers really; a wide-open 6-year-old boy; and four older kids in one small four-room house." He just shook his head.

It was an old song, really, one that I have heard from both my parents of large mill families. I had just not played it in this context. For me that song was always an amusing flip side to the song of their success. The song of getting out, rising above, while still appreciating their roots.

Now it will serve as a powerful reminder, along with Tommy's song, that surroundings, family, home life, choices, and culture do not define our intellect nor encode our ability to learn. Tommy's intelligence and his performance did not match at first, but we must recognize that it was his performance that changed, not his ability or his intellect.

According to *Webster's*, a firth is "a narrow inlet of the sea"; "a shallow place where a crossing can be made." So frequently during the year I heard the voice of Lucy talking about "crossing bridges" and of Lisa saying, "Listen, and don't be afraid of what you hear." How could I have guessed that writing down that silly song that ran through my head accompanying Daddy's memoir would help me find the firths between Tommy's world and mine? I listened again and again to the memory of Daddy's voice, and remembered how proud he was to be at the firths of Scotland *afore* any of those "smarter" school boys from half a century ago. I heard it every time the children giggled when Tommy spoke and especially when an adult put him down. The story itself became a firth, the place that made the passage shallow enough to enable me to understand how to use the things I had learned from all the literature I'd read.

Really listening to all the parties involved allowed me to find a geography of the mind that contained the crossing places. It was the crossing itself that became a transforming act for both of us. Freire (1985) talks about a process of "conscientization," which involves "a constant clarification of that which remains hidden within us while we move about in the world, though we are not necessarily regarding the world as the object of our critical reflection" (p. 107). Tommy and I sought clarification not only of what was hidden within our individual selves

but also of what was hidden within each other and also between ourselves. Neither of us uncovered it all—how would that be possible? We
uncovered just enough to give us more faith in questions than in answers, more joy in the journey than in the destination, and a greater
assurance that the psychic geography we created and moved in together
will exist, in many ways, forever.

CHAPTER 5

Singing Songs of Silence from Below Time: A Triple Narrative

Open my eyes that I may see
glimpses of truth thou hast for me.
Place in my hand the wonderful key
that shall unclasp and set me free
Silently now . . . I wait . . .
—Clara H. Scott,
"Open My Eyes That I May See"

To enter a psychic geography with Tommy was to participate in a positive movement between time periods and events and even generations. Connecting his story to my father's creates a cohesive narrative. The bridges are logical and progressive. The span of generations, the mesh of cultures, the driving metaphor—all flow, and it seems to work. It was not very difficult to see in retrospect how ordering those scattered events became a working precept for moving my relationship deeper with Tommy. It is not always the case that connections between events are so evident. In fact, most often the narratives kept in journals, at least in mine, are much more erratic. The set of narratives that you will read in this chapter are about three little girls who from time to time became selectively mute, withdrawn, and disconnected from the present. It is also in large measure about the power of a written phrase to open a place in one's understanding. In this case the phrase "once-below-a-time" (Beuchner, 1982) opened that understanding place for me.

TIME, PAIN, AND SILENCE

Because their stories run parallel to one another instead of being woven into one, these narratives reveal something of a struggle. They lack the steady flow and connecting threads that are a feature of the other narratives in the previous chapters. I found myself wondering after multiple rewrites if it was possible to tell three stories at once. They do work together, however, as confirmation of what happened in *my* head about what I was observing.

If reading about three similar children at once can become confusing, imagine *teaching* them at the same time—and in a classroom of 21 other students. The process of writing about them in parallel sections, as disorganized as it may seem, actually brought some order to my own confusion. Teaching them had a life-altering impact on me. I had never been exposed to any child who was selectively mute or who withdrew excessively deeply into him- or herself. Now, here were three children in the same year with those striking behaviors. My first response to their behaviors was to define them: one as manipulation, another as a sign of developmental disability, another as evidence of physical illness or improperly administered medication. As my association with them grew, I understood those behaviors to be evidence of suppressed pain.

I began to recognize another face in their frightening withdrawal. It was difficult to reexamine the time I watched my own daughter disengage from the present, withdraw to a place where I feared she would stay forever, inside and locked away. Fifteen years ago, divorce hit our family with all the surprise and force of an earthquake. My children were traumatized as a result of the abrupt parental desertion that they experienced. Each displayed grief in a different way. Late one night, my 12-year-old daughter seemed to grasp the reality of our condition and her lack of control over it. At first, she became hysterical; and then mute, withdrawn, lethargic. The panic I felt as I watched her change into someone I didn't recognize still haunts me all these years later. I called my mother, who came immediately. We realized that we were no match for what we were seeing and sought professional help. Although that one episode did not repeat itself, it was a precursor of the slow unraveling that would consume my daughter for years. As the children and I reeled from the change in our family and our circumstances I went through dramatic alterations in both appearance and demeanor. Not only had their father left, but in a very real way their mother had too. At one of the lowest points I experienced, my mother kept the four children and arranged for me to visit with some old friends in another state.

As I left on that long trip, one that was sure to be a lonely drive, she gave me a set of audiotapes to listen to in the car. "Just listen to the sound of this man's voice, even if you don't think you can concentrate on what he is saying. Time is what you need," she said. "You need to walk in a different city, hear different sounds, think different thoughts, and see time moving forward again. Listen to someone else's life. Sometimes we need a break from our own."

The three tapes were labeled "once-below-a-time," "once-upon-a-time," and "from-beyond-time." Imagining them to be a set of short stories, I inserted the first tape into the deck, to break the silence of the trip. Although the trip took only 5 hours, that morning I journeyed a lifetime inside that car. The tapes were from Frederick Beuchner's (1982) memoir *The Sacred Journey*, and they produced a tearful epiphany that gave me renewed strength and faith in life itself. On that day I realized that I would, someday, come out on the other side of my pain.

In my life, though nothing like his, there was a surprising resonance with his story. I am female and grew up in an entirely different region of the country from where Beuchner was raised and in a family that in comparison to his, was not at all similarly constructed. Even our generations were different, as were the experiences afforded us by our families and by the circumstances of our lifestyle.

The power of the names he gave to life's stages, once-below-a-time, once-upon-a-time, and from-beyond-time, yoked our lives together. The juxtaposition of his life narrative with multiple other narratives—including my own—created a jigsaw puzzle. Oddly shaped jigsaw pieces somehow fitting together to make a bigger picture seems a fitting metaphor for oddly shaped lives being placed into other contexts. It makes sense that "the narrative of anyone's life is part of an interlocking set of narratives" (MacIntyre, 1981, p. 203). Recognizing and piecing together what we understand of our own narratives and then connecting them, with some understanding, to the lives of others is somewhat like finding small pieces of a jigsaw puzzle that fit together, however gradually, to create a more complete picture.

Once Below a Time

Beuchner (1982) uses *once-below-a-time* to define that part of life when everything is "by and large *now* time and apparently endless. When every day is lived for its content more than for its duration, by its quality rather than its quantity—happy times and sad times, the time the rabbit bit your finger, the time you first tasted bananas and cream . . ." (p. 9).

Once Upon a Time

Once-upon-a-time is event tied. For many of us there come events that can forever separate life into before and after: before we moved, before the baby came, before Daddy went away. Once-upon-a-time

starts at whatever moment it is at which the unthinking and timeless
innocence of childhood ends, which may be either a dramatic moment or
a moment or series of moments so subtle and undramatic that we scarcely
recognize them. But one way or another the journey through time starts
for all of us. I think that journey is primarily a journey in search. We search
for a self to be. We search for other selves to love and we search for work
to do. (Beuchner, 1982, p. 58)

Beuchner says that on the day his father committed suicide, the door
forever closed on his once-below-a-time and situated him squarely, at
10 years old, into once-upon-a-time. Forever after, he spoke of his life
in terms of before his father died or after his father died. The family
never really spoke of his father's death. So he buried the sense of loss
deeper and deeper as he grew, until even as an adult when anyone asked
him how his father died, he would reply, as he had taught himself to
believe, "Heart trouble." For many of us, as it was with him, we can't
or don't speak to that pivotal event as a part of the story of our lives.
The silence of what we don't say can be deafening.

From Beyond Time

In the last metaphor, *from*-beyond-*time*, Beuchner (1982) addresses
the epiphanies of his life that connected him to the Creator. "I choose
to believe," he says, "that from beyond time, a saving mystery breaks
into our time at odd and unforeseeable moments" (p. 96). The memoirs
that he wrote come from his early to middle adulthood. Connecting to
the whole of humanity and looking at life as greater than his own helped
him to heal from the suppressed anger and anguish of his childhood and
adolescence. From-beyond-time is not referenced in the story of the girls.
Assuredly, I write from having reached that stage myself. I fully em-
brace his notion that the events of our lives, though seemingly random,
do have a shape and direction of their own. "They lead us somewhere"
(p. 95).

My fascination with the dramatic events that began in Frederick
Beuchner's (1982) once-upon-a-time gave me a wondering place as I
wrote about the girls. Who they are does not have to be who they become. I wrote into my "imagination to become able to break with what
[was] supposedly fixed and finished . . . to become able to look at things
as if they could be otherwise" (Greene, 1995, p. 19). The narratives as a
collection give evidence of my attempts to visualize the girls, my search
to get to know more about their early lives. Learning about their early
lives was a way for me to begin to think about the girls' response to the

pain they experienced and about the varied ways they began to construct their stories, to narrate bits of their own lives, sometimes with success but more often with confusion.

A MAP OF THIS CHAPTER

There are three overarching foci in this chapter: alarming behavior, metaphors of time, and the necessity of memories to anchor life narratives. As I wrote, I asked the same questions over and over: Why do they choose silence? Why and how do they withdraw so deeply? What makes one throw tantrums, another inflict pain on herself, and another give away everything she receives? Where did time go for them when they withdrew from us? Were they blocking out the pain of the past or of the present? What do they remember and how accurate are those memories?

As I read the literature on different concepts of time, I was more and more drawn to the idea that telling one's own narratives depends on an understanding of one's place in time. Polkinghorne cites the point that "appropriating the past and anticipating the future require different narrative strategies. When the strategies are mixed the resulting self-narrative is confused, inconsistent and even chaotic" (Crites in Polkinghorne, 1988, p. 106). I believe that when a person is not able to use those narrative strategies successfully, whether to appropriate or to anticipate, that person's story may remain in an inaccessible place buried in silence. It was such silence that caught my attention.

I have placed the narratives in groups, each group containing one narrative about each girl. The girls always come in the same order: Santana, Nickole, Clarrissa.

Section I, "Narrating the Beginning," documents my earliest encounters with the girls and my bewilderment over their behaviors.

Section II, "Narrating the Common Thread," encompasses narratives I composed as I began to hear about the girls' infancy. In addition, in this section I begin to address questions of time, especially of how chronological time and a psychic geography of time can become confused.

Section III, "Narrating the Girls as Students," contains examples of the kind of narratives I write about children's responses to the curriculum. They reveal the girls' relationship to the class and to me through literature, writing, oral response, and conversations.

Section IV, "Narrating the Storms," speaks to the angst of that year. How do I balance needs and keep priorities in order? When must the academic override the emotional, and when must an emotional need take precedence over an academic one? And, as I asked in chapter 1, How do I hold reading up as the beacon of life to children who struggle with issues big enough to swallow us all alive?

In section IV, I address the crushing realities of both the girls' continued struggle and my inability to right the multitude of wrongs that immobilized them.

This set of narratives, unlike the others, is not a flow of writing that brought closure to a set of events. Rather these narratives speak to the reality that some things, though defined and understood, are by nature open ended.

When curriculum, projects, workshops, programs, and agencies fail us, we are shoved toward our imaginations, philosophies, and faith. If anything, these narratives are a record of my own movement between failure and imagination.

I. NARRATING THE BEGINNING

Santana

Journal Entry (first day of school: first grade)

That little girl with the big vacant eyes is in my room. I remember her from last year. She could never find her breakfast card. I drew a large star on her card, but it was the same color as the writing so it didn't help. Later, I affixed a large clown sticker to it. I expected her to smile at me, to show some sense of delight in being able to retrieve the card herself. But always she stared at everything and nothing at the same time and walked as if she was moving in water. Later, she found her card without struggling and on occasion made eye contact or touched me if the card wasn't immediately visible to her. When she patted my arm for help she didn't use words, just a touch, barely a touch, with the pressure of a butterfly.

On this brand-new, first-day-of-school morning, her grandmother delivered her to the door, outfitted in new blue-striped overalls and with her hair in two tiny ponytails, way on top of her head and adorned with red plastic bows. She had that same dazed, expressionless face. I remembered her as soon as I saw her and began wondering if I'd missed a special education folder in the before-school stack of paperwork. She stood slightly behind her grandmother as I met them. Other parents and children were coming to the door; I needed to be in so many places at once! The children were gathering in clusters on the floor around hula hoops that delineated work spaces. Each hoop encircled objects defining a different task: puzzles, blocks, books, and so on, providing children a chance to talk to one another and explore some of the objects as everyone arrived. As Granny filled out forms, I led Santana by the hand across the room toward a hula hoop. Her little hand clung with surprising strength to mine, in a way unlike how she touched me last year. Midway across the room, I was forcefully jerked backward to a complete stop. I was sure I'd run her into a table. My neck hurt so badly I wondered if I had whiplash. I turned to apologize, only to discover that Santana was her own obstacle; there was no other. She had stopped dead in her tracks in the middle of the floor, pulling back on my hand. She was staring at the children she was about to join. There was no doubt that she saw them, no doubt about the strength she used to stop me. Her grandmother saw my surprise and came quickly across the room. She pried open Santana's hand, moving her toward the group, saying, "She'll be all right. . . . she'll be all right." Was she afraid I'd not want Santana to stay?

"She do like that but when she get used to you she be fine. It take her a while to get used to somebody. She always scary like."

To Santana she said gently, but with some urgency, holding the child's face in her hands, "San! San, Granny got to go now but I be back. You go find you a little friend to play with." Then moving quickly as if to distract her, she added "O-h-h-h, looky here, San, here some friends now. Here, you play with them." She pushed her into place. Santana sat down, but she didn't touch the toys or talk to the children. She pulled her knees up to her chest tightly and rocked, her feet planted flat on the floor. Granny hurried away. Santana's eyes didn't follow her. I wondered what in the world would happen next. As the day moved on, however, what I thought would be problematic must have been lost in the other trappings of the business of the first day of first grade. I can't remember any behaviors standing out significantly other than the silence, but most children are shy the first day of school.

Nickole

Journal Entry (first day of school: first grade)
    She is one of the prettiest children I've ever seen, this Nickole. Maybe she was nervous today. I know I was. I couldn't get a handle on her at all. She went from one emotional display to another, which I

found alternately humorous and exasperating. Thank goodness she is pretty to behold, because I beheld her plenty. I noticed something in Nickole's countenance that stopped me. It was haunting, as if there were moments when her big smile gave off no light. Her attention-getting behavior broke through my determination to maintain a very positive, nurturing, you-can-do-it tone even in the face of mess-ups (deliberate or otherwise) on the first days of school. It seems that her best defense against me is withdrawal. When I talked to her privately about her behavior, she giggled hysterically, shaking her head back and forth, which caused her beaded extensions (attached false braids) to whip forcefully and repeatedly across her face. It had to hurt. When I took her face between my hands to stop her self-battery and get to her eyes, she veiled them over and wouldn't look at me. At lunch, I asked her kindergarten teacher, frankly, if Nickole was "all right." I was told that she'd pull that "goofy act" but that she was smart as a fox and not to let her get by with anything. She did state, as an afterthought, something about a new foster home and that maybe she was "going through some changes."

The last ounce of my patience ran out when Nickole began to cram the front of her shirt down her throat, gagging herself, because she was not first to share her writing after lunch. I went up very close to her ear and whispered—no hint of Mr. Nice Guy—"If you throw up, I'll leave you in here all by yourself while Mr. Fred cleans it up. The rest of us will go out to play, and *then* I will send . . . you . . . home!" She slowly let go of her shirt, and at the same time she shut down her eyes. Her vision just seemed to leave; her body grew limp and her mouth slack as she slowly pushed the shirt out of her mouth. I sensed that her haunting, vacant eyes were exactly the opposite of what they appeared to be. That appearance of loss of control was a lie. She was completely in control of the withdrawal and I was not invited where she went.

Clarrissa

Journal Entry (September: kindergarten)

The first person I saw this morning as I struggled to balance all the bags I bring in and out of school each day was a bus driver. He was standing beside the bus helping the little ones off. A kindergartner I see each morning when I am on breakfast duty stepped down. She is one of the children I noticed first out of the hundred-plus who pick up a breakfast ticket from me each morning. She has a wide, curious, unforgettable smile. I greeted her as the bus driver helped her down, but today she made no eye contact. Her usual greeting, never spoken, is a big smile and a big hug with a long pause that lasts until I speak. I joked, "Hey sleepyhead, don't I get a hug today?" She looked toward me without really connecting. Ever so slowly, she turned to face me, unsmiling. I felt a wave of sick panic at the hollowness of her eyes, eyes that looked without seeing. Was she sick, injured, on medication, sleepwalking? Her cousin got off the bus a few kids behind her. Her response to questioning showed no concern: "She not sick she just do like that sometimes. I don't know why." She couldn't say how often but indicated that it was certainly nothing out of the ordinary for Clarrissa to pull into herself.

Clarrissa went zombielike into the building. The bus driver stopped me to ask if I was her teacher. "One of several," I affirmed, not going into the limited time I actually spend with her. (That year I was an augmented literacy instructor, going into two of the kindergarten rooms each morning.) He said, "Something's not right in that house." He looked off into the distance and shook his head. "You can see it in that child's eyes. I don't know what it is but something's not good there. If ever she doesn't get on the bus I worry till next day."

During breakfast duty, I stayed fairly close to her table, trying to make contact and encouraging her to eat. After she left her untouched breakfast, I walked her to the kindergarten wing. She was still staring vacantly ahead as I held her hand, which didn't hold mine back. Her teacher's concern matched mine, though Clarrissa did reach out to cling to her "real" teacher. I had to hurry off to other duties, but I stewed about what I had seen and checked on Clarrissa all day long.

This day, she slept until early afternoon in the clinic. The school was unable to reach any family member; the Department of Family and Children Services "noted the observation" but did not visit. When she boarded the bus to go home, her earlier hollow expression was replaced with a weary one—less frightening, but no less haunting in its very pointed connections to the eyes of her teacher and to mine. Her teacher and I stood together as the bus pulled away. Clarrissa looked back at us; she gave no smile, but her fingers touched the window as she locked eyes first with one and then the other of us. Now it's after midnight and I can't stop thinking about her, wondering, worrying.

We hear the adage "Eyes are the windows to the soul" and smilingly nod our agreement, perhaps thinking of someone whose eyes always reveal exactly what he or she is thinking; or we may sadly re-

member when the light of connection left the eyes of a loved one en-
trapped by dementia.

I have spent my adult life relating to children, and except in the
case of the few autistic, blind, or severely developmentally disabled
students I have encountered along the way, I have not peered into
cloudier windows to any soul than those eyes of the three little girls
I've just introduced to you.

I was so busy during the first part of the school year doing what
was necessary to move a group of 24 small persons in tandem from one
place to another that I was not attuned to the connection I had recorded
about the girls vacant, hollow eyes. Clarrissa's entry was picked up from
the journal I had kept the year before. I had taught in her kindergarten
class as an augmented teacher. (With the exception of Nickole, I had
contact with each of the children described in this book during their
kindergarten year.) It took that backward look into entries in the previous year's journal to link the common aspects of the girls' response
to stress. As the weeks unfolded, I was increasingly impressed with what
those retreats inward did to my ability to bring the girls into our community and into the teaching arena. I also was becoming aware that
understanding parts of each of them separately filled in a picture of them
as a group. I wondered why they withdrew, why this withdrawal showed
up in their eyes, and why it was more pronounced sometimes than
others. Why was it so unpredictable, why did some stressors produce it
and others not? As we went into fall the episodes dropped off dramatically, so dramatically in fact that I was surprised by the intensity of my
first journal entries on each of the girls, especially when I later read them
as a collection.

I believe—otherwise I would not teach—that persons are never
completely defined. Despite the definitions I have penned on the children here, I still see them as "persons in process, in pursuit of themselves and, it is to be hoped, of possibilities for themselves" (Greene,
1995, p. 41). And yet the silence signals something. If Bruner's asser-
tion is true that "language not only transmits, it creates or constitutes
knowledge or 'reality,'" then I fear that the silence signals detachment
or breaks from reality (1986, p. 131).

Discovering the facts of each girl's early life was much like learning information through eavesdropping: in the latter, sometimes the
clearest words mislead because the context has been muffled. It is especially difficult to eavesdrop on silence.

As the year marched on, I began to contemplate more often the kind
of time we use to hold memories or to make plans for the future. I also
began to wonder about the time that elapsed for the girls when they

retreated behind their eyes. Was it a safe place, a scary place, a past place, or a kind of limbo? Was the time behind their eyes different from the time the rest of us were experiencing?

II. NARRATING THE COMMON THREAD

Santana

Journal Entry (second day of school)
This morning "Gran" came back to school at about 9 o'clock and stood around talking to me. Thank goodness we were taking a little walk outside. She clearly meant to stay. She had come to make sure I knew that "San's mom" could have no contact with her. Gran wore a bright orange tam and her blouse was flamboyant, colorful and flowing. She looked different from how she had appeared yesterday, dramatically so. She told me she was 49 years old, but reported this age as though it were 70. "I'm too old to be taking these children but somebody got to." Fast and furious, she related the story of her own daughter: "I can't understand how anybody could do the things she did to these babies . . . her own babies. It's that devil drug! Full of evil, full of evil!"

I was given more information than I could possibly absorb at once. What Santana and her sister have been through! No wonder Santana withdraws in stressful moments. Would I trust life if I were in her shoes?

San and Gran rhymed, not only in their names, but also in the balance each gave the other as opposites. Gran talked nonstop, revealing every thought. San remained selectively mute. Gran sought attention and San retreated from notice. Gran expressed emotion openly, unashamedly, while San tentatively, silently tested each emotional response she offered.

As Gran revealed San's story on that second day of school, I longed for a tape recorder. If I'd only known then that I'd hear a repeat performance each time we met, I could have relaxed a bit. I've memorized the telling, even the order of delivery. With each subsequent telling I absorbed other small pieces of her puzzle.

Gran told how Santana had been left alone, unfed and unclothed, and was then brought to her one day by the authorities. She felt too old to care for her but didn't want to have her sent into the foster care system. Santana's mother had been out of the picture for some time, but over the past several months an attempt was once again being made to reunite the child with her mother. Gran's biggest concern now was with what she perceived as interference from Department of Family and Children's Services (DFACS). She was also angry with her daughter, who had physically assaulted her and had tried to take San one night several years earlier. Over and over she would say to me, "They say they trying to teach her how to do and all like that. What they think I did her whole life? What they think they gonna teach her? Drugs doin' the teaching I tell you! Drugs! All I know is this baby see her mama coming and she hide!"

Gran always made me uncomfortable with the way she refused to posture our relationship as equal partners. She addressed me in a discourse style that I had not witnessed, except in films, since I was a child in the 1950s. "Ms. Hankins, *you* need to call them and tell them how she make them scary eyes when she know she have to go see her mom. They believe what White folks tells them. Here's the number now. Just call them.

Telling her that I held less clout than she did made no difference. Eventually, I did call them, not because I was White, but because she wore me down one day and I promised. I was, after all, concerned over the child's fear, her muteness, and as Gran called them, her "scary eyes." The worker I talked to had a different agenda from mine, of course, because she worked with Santana's mother as well. Her job is to reunite families. The agency seeks ways to pull someone out of drug addiction and back into responsibility and to provide avenues to help that struggle along. I can't imagine having that set of issues before me, only to have a schoolteacher call with a complaint. She reminded me that there were two sides to the story and I knew only one of them. I offered back that there were in fact three. Santana had a side that she was unable to present. Once again history repeats itself in the plight experienced by so many children—irrespective of race, economics, age, or gender—who are both elevated and castigated by being made the object of contest in a family custody battle.

Nickole

As you may remember, I'd known from the first day of school that Nickole was in foster care. Her dramatic outbursts compelled me to meet with her foster mother early in the fall. Her foster mother took charge of the meeting, telling me in great detail about the 11 months in which Nickole had lived with them and a little bit about her past.

Nickole had been molested, emotionally abused, and physically neglected by her birth mother, who apparently was mentally unstable as well as physically ill. Nickole had been in foster homes since she was about 3½, but nobody would keep her, because of her behavior. Nickole's foster mother wanted my "expert opinion on child management"; I wanted her expert opinion on "Nickole's management." After the meeting we agreed we needed more than the two of us could put together.

I have juxtaposed the next two journal entries about Nickole because they go together in a way that I was completely unaware of for months. It will help you to experience the necessity of revisiting the writing in narrative methodology with new eyes every time. It also sheds light on narrative inquiry's penchant for "casting a portrayal" (Piantanida & Garman, 1999) of a participant from the scattered particulars collected over time. These two entries, containing scattered particulars and recorded at separate times, are examples of the power of revisiting and of reflecting through words that have been recorded earlier.

Journal Entry (October)
Nickole and the book bag are driving me crazy. She won't put it down. She keeps it wrapped around her legs, her face down in it, apparently sniffing it. I was sure there was candy in it for a while. When I took it from her, she was more than sad—she became hysterical! It was more trouble to make her believe I'd give it back after the story than it was to endure the distraction of her rattle-rattle, sling-sling with the thing.

The book bag is ratty and smelly and the straps are coming off. There are holes in the corner of it so any pencil she transports can easily slide out. The zipper is stuck half closed, meaning that she is going to rip past it any day now.

The problem is actually bigger than the ugly, distracting book bag. The problem is that her foster mother keeps asking me to look for the new book bag. I keep telling her the new book bag is here. I cannot get Nickole to take it home. It is a wonderful book bag, one of those pink-and-purple created-just-for-a-little-girl bags with sparkles and unicorns flying over a rainbow on the front. I have found it in the bathroom, in the lost and found, left on the hooks in our classroom. Yesterday, I flew out the door with it and told her to take it home and leave it there until she was ready to carry it. After the buses left, a safety-patrol officer found it behind the bushes!

Today, I got another message in my box, to please send the new bag home with Nickole's neighbor. As Nickole was leaving, I noticed that she bulged peculiarly. She had stuffed the old book bag under her dress and into her panties to keep it from falling out. The new bag was in the trash can underneath some paper.

She can choose the oddest things to stress over. She chooses an annoying, irrational-seeming behavior and carries it to the extreme. I gave the neighbor child the new book bag, and guess what? I'm *done* with the old book bag struggle. She can have it for lunch if she wants to. As long as she doesn't hurt anyone with it, she can wake the dead cramming her feet and face and arms inside it! I'm going to ignore it. A week at this is too long. I'm going to ignore it. No, really I am. Promise! (But it *is* the loudest book bag in the world . . . OK, OK. Forget it.)

I included that entry with all my frustration and sarcasm left intact. Writing through frustrations provides some distance from the event and helps me see it more objectively. Writing how I felt was honest and the journal provided a far better place for that tirade than the teachers' workroom. It is, however, painful to read it now, knowing what I discovered later.

Journal Entry (October: Halloween party day)

Why am I still surprised and angered by the inappropriate ways that some parents address time in the classroom? I had to fight anger when Jodie, Nickole's foster mother, came to the door and began to ask questions about Nickole at the absolute worst time of the day for there to be an interruption.

As I opened the door and tried to listen to her, I was thinking, "Can't she see that I am not free to leave the children alone?" The 5-minute transition after lunch can make us or break us. Today, Halloween day, the children are halfway settled, and then—a knock that has all the potential of wreaking havoc. She didn't want to come in, so I was only half listening to her. Distractedly attending to the disorder rising in the room behind me, I noticed the huge tray of party treats (unsolicited) she has brought for the party. "What will we do with all this extra food?" I wondered in my half-listening mode.

"I just wanted to see how Nickole is doing," she began.

"We *do* need to talk," I told her aloud but was thinking that for the past few weeks Nickole has been going backward. I wondered if I dared plow on with my list of complaints (tantrums; hitting; tearing up work; the book bag stuff; and, most alarming, wetting her pants). At the same time, I was intermittently flipping the light switch in the room, with my arm around the doorframe, as a message to the kids— "I'm able to monitor you from outside this door!" I was smiling, kind, but quickly trying to answer, monitor, and deliver the message that we needed (desperately, I was thinking) to sit down at *another* time. Balancing on one hand the tray she had handed me, so I could keep flipping the lights, I began to list possible meeting times.

She interrupted. "Did Nickole tell you her mother passed?"

I stopped midsentence. "*No!!* When?"

"Oh . . ." She looked toward the ceiling, calculating the date. "I say beginning of October!"

"But . . ." (That's when all the new problems started.)

"Oh." My hand went to my mouth. Tears heated the corners of my eyes as I stuttered out, "I feel awful! I mean, if I'd known I could have . . . maybe . . . I was no support for her. What she must have been going through. I don't even remember her missing school."

As I talked with Jodie, I was wondering if Nickole had tried to tell me and I hadn't listened. Good God, was she *afraid* to tell me? Did she think of me as being that distant?

"Well, she didn't hardly know her mother anymore anyway," Jodie said, "But she went to the funeral and over to the house. I thought she ought to go."

"I just wish I'd known."

"I thought surely she would tell you . . . but then she didn't act like it bothered her. She hasn't really said anything about it at home either."

The number of thoughts I carried multiplied beyond the already unmanageable number as I added in memories of events with Nickole over the past few weeks *and* the tough day we'd already had today.

As Jodie left, telling me to let her know if Nickole cut up in class, I felt embarrassed at the things I'd thought as I'd opened the door to her earlier—don't interrupt my agenda, my need for control. I had come a finger snap away from missing invaluable information this time.

The tray of goodies represented this parent's cold assessment of the school's invitation for parents to visit: parents who come bearing gifts are more welcome, more valued.

Life can just smack me in the face sometimes, especially when I get too legalistic, too rule conscious. I keep making the same mistakes! I catch myself acting as though I think myself above "those parents." I keep asking, "Why don't *they* get it," and all along I'm the one who doesn't get it. So they knock on the door with life-and-death news and

I wonder why they don't see that what we are about here at school is too important for an unannounced interruption.

My anger was gone when I walked back into the room. It was replaced by guilt-laden promises that *next* time . . . next time.

I remember trying to get through the following 50 minutes of reading instruction that preceded sending the children off to music. When the others were delivered, I asked Nickole to help me get the party ready so we'd have a chance to talk for a few minutes. I sat down with her and told her that I didn't know her mother had died and how sorry I was about it. She looked at me like I was crazy. Her response was to stare at me until I became uncomfortable with the silence and began asking her questions. "Who was at the funeral? Did you go in a church?" Finally, she made one comment: "What's a fume-er-al?" After I told her, she offered a nonchalant "Oh." That was it.

When I talked further with Jodie that evening, I learned that Nickole had gone to see her biological mother that fall for the first time in months and had got to spend the day with her. She came home talking about when she would go back "home" to live. The next morning, family members found Nickole's mother dead: the next time Nickole saw her mother after her visit was in a casket. Her foster mother said that Nickole had expressed little emotion over what had happened and had said nothing about the funeral to them at all. "But that's Nickole for you," she offered.

Over the following few days, Nickole's mother's house was stripped of everything. According to an old acquaintance, Nickole's mother had owned some beautiful things. No one thought to save anything for Nickole; not even her old toys were left. It was only months later, when she was receiving therapy, that Nickole would reveal that she had "stolen" (although in fact it was hers) the old book bag when she went to see her mother. As it turned out, the bag was all she had to remember her mother by, the only thing she could touch that was inside her mother's house. I'm sure it carried the smell of the house and of her mother. It was, in essence, a piece of time, a fragment of an unverbalized event.

We walk in a time-bounded classroom, but the spirits of the past walk with us. We are a bunch of I's that of necessity become "we" (Buber, 1957). Becoming "we" takes in a host of others whom we never see or meet but who, like Nickole's mother for Nickole, unwittingly shape our responses to others. I am continually impressed by the overlapping circles of time that converge in any moment. I am also admittedly embarrassed by my ability to become fixed inside my own circle as though it overlaps with no others. That "ratty old book bag" finally pushed me outside my own circle to acknowledge its silent message. It became a kind of icon to me. The thing I once despised became something I protected, something of great meaning. I became ever more aware of where it was and found myself hoping that I would never have to know when it was lost.

Clarrissa

Journal Entry (December: kindergarten)

Today I read aloud the book called *When I Was Young in the Mountains*, by Cynthia Rylant (1982). I asked the children if they could remember when they were "very little," before they went to kindergarten. I did the same exercise with small groups of children from two classrooms. Out of close to 50 children, Clarrissa was the only one able to remember a time, other than right now, absent of photographic data.

"I remember that there is a house that I have some Christmas toys in. I don't know where it is but there is a doll in a little pink stroller. I have a tea set too with flowers on it. And I remember that me and my brother and my mama were there. [There is a long pause] And . . . . we was happy." She adds this last sentence looking off into the distance. She was so pensive, I didn't respond. Then she looked back at me and said, "One dark, dark nighttime they took me to another auntie house, not Debra's. It is up in Atlanta. This auntie is so nice! She put me way high up on a cabinet and made me a jelly sandwich. She let me eat the whole sandwich . . . all to myself."

"Who took you there, Clarrissa?"

"Some lady I don't know . . . and my brother went too. But not my mama. I don't know where that nice auntie is. I guess she up in Atlanta."

"Do you ever see her now?"

She was busy thinking, not hearing the question.

"I keep telling people I need to go get my Christmas toys. Maybe one day I'll go back to *that* home. I do have a brother, my own brother, he might be there too."

For several years, I have asked the same question and read the same book to children. Out of at least 100 kindergarten children, Clarrissa is the only one who seemed to recount an actual self-sustaining memory. Most of the time, children tell something someone else has told them, or they replay a photograph or home video. Standard fare for "I remember" is "I got stitches at the hospital." After that *everyone* has had stitches, and amazingly the same set of events had happened to them as happened to the original teller. So I was stunned as I watched Clarrissa's face and heard the change in her inflection. She seemed to tap a place she visits often in her thoughts. How I wonder about this small child. She seems to attend to every feeling around her, responding with genuine caring for any child who is hurting. The response is held largely in her face, as if words escape her. Today, however, it was her turn to remember. I am still able to remember catching myself holding my breath as I listened to her. When I took her back to her classroom, I asked the aide about her mother and was told that she had not lived with her mother for several years. It was then that I realized she and her "cousin" lived more as sisters.

Clarrissa couldn't say how old she was when she ate the sandwich. She couldn't remember the sequence of events, or even if the memories were connected to the same evening. Clarrissa remembered a feeling—"we was happy"—and toys, objects that belonged to her somewhere. She remembered things that were hers and hers alone and that had brought delight on that awful-blessed day when she was rescued from the neglect and abuse that she lived in.

Much later, she would add to the story, "That's the day I stopped living with Betty [her biological mother]." I learned from her cousin, Miranda, that Clarrissa had come to live with them when Clarrissa was 2 years old. "Betty act too bad on crack, she forgot to feed her children. My mama is Betty sister so now the welfare say that she got to be Clarrissa mama too," Miranda reported.

I commented to Miranda that I bet she was a good big sister. I said, "You will be a big help to her as she is learning to read. Will you help her with her homework, Miranda?"

"*No-o-o!* She's weird and too light. I hate her!" I was shocked at the quick, unashamed way she stated her feelings about Clarrissa.

"Oh, everybody thinks they hate their little sisters," I said. "I bet you have fun!"

"Well, I wish Betty would come get her. I can't stand her skinny-bone self, my mama can't either! She too much trouble. We got enough to worry about. Betty need to straighten out."

Those did not sound like the words of an 8-year-old to me but repeated bits of conversations she had heard at home—conversations that I am sure Clarrissa heard as well.

Clarrissa told me in different contexts over 2 years that she better be good or they would send her away. "They said they'll let my real mother have me even if the police did say *no!*" Was it with hope or fear that she contemplated going away or back to her mother?

I do believe that the account of the night when she stopped living with Betty, with all its errors, gives her hope that she belongs somewhere, but it is laced with a fear that she cannot express. I would hear a refrain over and over again from her: "Somewhere there's my Christmas toys. I didn't take the top off the tea set yet."

As heart wrenching as her story is to hear, the ability to construct memories from her past gave Clarrissa an emotional edge over Santana and Nickole. It gives her a past to spring from in building a self-narrative. Our personal story, that self-creating narrative, is a recollected story "in which the more complete the story that is formed, the more integrated the self [the personality] will be" (Polkinghorne, 1988, p. 106). Persons who practice the level of withdrawal that the three girls practice seem to give evidence of a nonintegrated self. Psychologists know that people conceive of themselves in terms of stories. Clarrissa was building the story from what she claimed of the past. Although Nickole and Santana have a past, they had forgotten or suppressed it. And why wouldn't they?

In common they had all experienced the unthinkable at the hands of their mothers. It is hard for one to absorb such a reality when one cannot even imagine it as a possibility. There is a surreal quality in the knowledge of the neglect and abuse they experienced as infants. Reacting to it is akin to walking out of a scary movie: you convince yourself that it is not real . . . you don't have to think about it.

The most traumatic events for each of the girls took place before they acquired language. Language is necessary for creating reality. However, before we have language, we do begin to order experiences and create awareness of life's operation around us (Britton, 1993; Bruner, 1995). We all observe infants who seem to know the heartbeat of their mothers from the first day outside the womb, and we watch as they respond with pleasure to repeated sloshing sounds. Feelings come early and babies begin to respond consistently to the stimuli.

"A reflective grasp of our life stories and of our ongoing quests . . . depends on our ability to remember things past" (Greene, 1995, p. 20). Aside from the memories, however, being able to narrate, to tell about, to connect, past events depends on language as well as the ability to impose sequence and unity on the memory of that past.

Though I cited it earlier, I continue to find the following quote helpful in understanding my students. "Appropriating the past and anticipating the future require different narrative strategies. When the strategies are mixed the resulting self-narrative is confused, inconsistent and even chaotic" (Crites cited in Polkinghorne, 1988, p. 106). I wondered what happened to children who seemed determined not to see the present at times. I began to think that my girls shut out the present at the same time they worked to repress the past. If appropriating the past was not only difficult but very painful and the future was filled with insecurity, it is no wonder that at times silence or tears or rocking seemed the best means with which to deal with stress. So, where were they in their ordering of time?

A Common Ordering of Time

You may recall how Randel, from chapter 2, "The Preacher," brought three levels of time together in one stunning morning. That event's uniqueness springs, in part, from the unexpected ability of a 6-year-old to operate for so long within an abstract interpretation of time that usually develops in middle childhood (Friedman, 1990). While 6-year-old children can correctly order cards on which are depicted daily routines or put in proper sequence events within familiar stories, those activities are "unlikely bases for developing representations of longer patterns" (Friedman, 1990, p. 97). The abstractness of moving from the present into the distant past, even one's own, in terms of counting time in segments, remains undeveloped until about "nine years old when historical time increases in importance" (p. 97).

Whereas Randel seems precocious in his ability to abstract time and cross over temporalities in a narrative, the girls, each rooted in events that occurred before she could talk, were impeded in their ability to perform these tasks. Perhaps they were impeded because they had repressed the events that caused them the greatest pain. More likely, they were unable to talk about the past because the abuse had happened to them long before they had words to think about it. That doesn't negate the memory of feeling, emotion, or lack of trust. The girls' difficulty can be viewed in part by considering them in the frame of two metaphors of time: time standing still and time marching on. In a sense, time stood still in one area as time marched on in all other parts of their lives. Time stood still in the unarticulated memory of abuse and hostile neglect. Time marched on as they grew into language along with going through other developmental changes and as they experienced moving to new homes and into new classrooms, participating in family as an add-on.

Beuchner (1982) experienced his father's suicide, the end of his once-below-a-time, at the age of 10. Even though the words were available to him to allow him to speak honestly about the tragedy, he chose words to couch that once-upon-a-time event in a more acceptable vocabulary. It masked the pain for a young boy to think of his father as a victim of untimely death rather than as a man who had intentionally ended his life, leaving the boy forever. Still, Beuchner says of repressed memories, "we never really forget anything. All our pasts lie fathoms deep in us somewhere waiting for some stray smell or scrap of sound to bring them to the surface again" (p. 48).

For Nickole, Clarrissa, and Santana, too young chronologically and developmentally to divide time into before and after, the jolting thrust of that once-upon-a-time life-altering event came too early. Although they were not then able to form language about the events, their pain is carried just the same. They have once-upon-a-time events trapped below-time in ever repeating episodes without words, waiting for "some stray smell or scrap of sound" or sense of pain "to bring them to the surface."

My girls experienced events too tragic to blend with childhood's once-below-a-time, and those events splintered into fragments of time: disconnected, emotional memories to be either skirted or perseverated upon. They were too soon jolted from living as if there is no reason to measure time in increments, when one snowfall is all snowfalls and any summer evening of firefly catching merges with all firefly evenings.

Clarrissa's Christmas toys are caught below time. Nickole's book bag was rescued from below time. Santana withdraws to a place she thought safe once-below-a-time. Now for each of them there are some once-upon-a-time events that remain silent because they cannot be remembered in words. When every night was a duration of pain, every day a duration of hunger and neglect, when a cry for comfort was met with a slap, it is difficult to know if the once-below-a-time was constant pain and the once-upon-a-time event was felt as a rescue; or if the once-below-a-time was the bond of a mother who lived out her love for her child before the first abusive event opened the door on once-upon-a-time. It may have been different for each of them. What finally made sense to me was that they were robbed of childhood's right to an incubating once-below-a-time.

Extending Once-Below-a-Time

If it is possible to provide small dips in and out of once-below-a-time, I believe it is through the process of creating something with paints, clay, collage, or building materials. I watch children daily as they are composing or creating and envy the pure joy they take in simply using the materials. No deadlines, no building permits to secure, no pressure to sell gets in the way of that moment in time and space.

I believe that self-expression should be encouraged and celebrated as the expected way of coming into the teacher-learner relationship.

Perhaps children cannot always narrate their experiences effectively, but they can practice the process. They can practice what it feels like to paint, to sing, to draw and sculpt and build. I never feel that I am being frivolous if I purchase good paints, good crayons, and reams of paper for my classroom out of my own money. Artistic expression through music, painting, drama, storytelling, and writing produces offerings from that intuitive way of knowing we are born with (Gallas, 1994; Eusden & Westerhoff, 1998). Those experiences provide possibilities of connections to ourselves, others, and the environment. It was literature, writing, and drawing that provided a place where the girls could practice the process of claiming a personal narrative.

III. NARRATING THE GIRLS AS STUDENTS

Santana

Journal Entry (December)
     Writing and drawing seem to be a bridge for Santana from behind her eyes to the outside and vice versa. She becomes completely absorbed in drawing, even more silent and fixated. But her drawings, at least one of them, became her avenue into the community. We were reading and writing about animals. One of the center choices involved researching a favorite animal and drawing it by using good observation skills—"just like a scientist," as I told them. We had a big blank bulletin board labeled "Animals Everywhere" just waiting for the drawings. The pictures went up in the quick-draw fashion of most 6-year-olds . . . ready to move to another center. Santana, however, continued to work. She worked all through the 30-minute center time for 2 days in a row, never taking an opportunity to move to another one. It was on the second day that other children who chose the writing center began to notice the deer drinking water from a stream that was emerging from Santana's careful drawing. She had copied, not traced, a deer from the front of a book. It was a beautifully rendered drawing with an ability that far surpassed mine! Dylan saw it first.
     "Ms. Hankins! Come and look what Santana did!"
     "O-o-o-o, we-e-e-e!" others whispered as they also came to see.
     "Santana is a real artist, huh, Ms. Hankins?"
     "How did she do that?" asked one. She then turned to the source. "How did you do that, Santana?"
     Santana beamed, embarrassed, and shrugged her shoulders. I said (ever the instructor, always making a point), "Well . . . she must have

looked at that deer for a long, long time. She *took her time* observing and she *took her time* drawing, just like a scientist does. She used her eyes and her hands at the same time."

At about that moment, one of the children with better observation skills than mine said, "Look, it says Santa!"

"Where?" asked the children.

"There, wight there! S-A-N-T-A!" Dylan, our resident keeper of the imaginative spirit was ecstatic, beside himself, as he pointed to the place where Santana had written her name.

I realized, then, just what he saw. I'd been trying to help Santana remember the right order of the letters in her name . . . but all those *a*s and *n*s just confused her. So we started with the part she always got right, SAN, and were adding a letter at a time. We were up to S-A-N-T-A.

"Oo-o-h, well, that's part of Santana's name," I began to explain objectively, but then caught Dylan's face, his need for the story, and allowed my imagination to play too. "But . . . it sure explains why her eyes twinkle and why she's so sweet! I never noticed it before but sure enough *Santa* is a part of *Santana*!"

"Hey!" And the storyteller inflection invaded Dylan's words. "Maybe that's why she knows so much how 'weindeews' weally look!!"

Dylan was so excited I thought he'd explode.

I looked at Santana. She was grinning all over! I hugged her and asked her if she thought that's why she was so sweet. With a big grin, she said in a low husky voice, "Might be I made out of brown sugar." That's the most she's said to me on her own.

As I revisited the power of that scene, I knew that Dylan's story had released Santana's imagination and allowed her to risk remembering someone, maybe Gran, who had made her feel good too. She was reaching across time to another event where she felt as special, as loved, as she did right then. Maybe that's the reason the story caught on.

Journal Entry (continued)

Santana being one of Santa's helpers became one of our shared class stories. She seemed to enjoy the attention as much as Dylan enjoyed the telling. As Christmas approached it was common for me to hear, "That reindeer's not as good as Santana's." Or "Maybe you can weally see Woudolph one day, huh Santana." One day I heard her pretend to Dylan, who sat next to her, that she *could* see Rudolph. That was the day I discovered she had a voice that I'd never heard before or at least that I'd never acknowledged as hers. The children were creating a drama/game over in the large-block area during center time. The game apparently involved yelling, "Hey, hey, pack up the sleigh. I think Rudolph's on the way!" Then they'd "pack up" and act as though they were flying. Great game, but too loud. The giggling was totally unnerving, eardrum piercing, and irritating. I warned the group several times before I finally made them clean up silently and go to another center. They all protested, "See there Santana! Told you!"

I couldn't quite believe what I was hearing. They were accusing my silent little San of being the noise maker that got them thrown out of the center! I told them they were all responsible and not to blame one person. I thought they were just blaming the weaker one, the one who wouldn't defend herself. She shed great big crocodile tears as they cleaned up. She went to the writing center and worked alone. Later in the day as we were packing up to go home, I heard that same irritating eardrum-piercing laughter and witnessed her playing a rough game of tug-of-war with her neighbor as they got the same jacket off the coat hook. It really *was* her. The next time I saw Gran, she asked me, "Have you noticed lately how San talk soft and play loud?" I'll say!

What I see, now that I look at the connection between Santana's loud, carefree playing and the "weindeer" story, is the manifestation of a child coming into her identity. She is one of the children Maxine Greene (1995) referred to whose "identity is contingent on the existence of humane school communities. Individual identity takes form in the context of relationship and dialogue" (p. 30). The drawing had given San a way out of her silence and a way to play with others. I know that for Santana, Clarrissa, and Nickole, imagination will be central to moving across time and will need to be acquired and practiced. When Dylan took time to look at and appreciate Santana's artwork, he also begged me, the teacher, to respond imaginatively and to tell a story, to leap beyond the ordinary. The group's responses to her writing encouraged her to risk interaction through pretending with others.

Nickole

Journal Entry (December)
I wondered if they were ready for Patricia Polacco so early in the year. Polacco's gift of story is sometimes lost on children so young. But this class is different. They seem to run deeper in their memory banks. The children responded very well to an oral retelling of her version of the tree of the dancing goats, so I decided to try *Uncle Vova's Tree* (Polacco, 1989).

The children took up their usual stances for listening—some at the back of our large-group rug and some at the front, some positioned to be unnoticed so they could wander to places in their minds other than the story I presented. Nickole moved quickly to grab a spot beside my leg. She likes to play with my shoes, rub my legs or skirt. If she is foiled in claiming her spot, she moves to the back and refuses to participate. Today she found her spot and seemed satisfied. As I began to read, she played with the hem of my pants, tucking them into my socks. I tried to read, but was soon distracted and had to grab her hand and hold it as I read. She relaxed but moved so close that she was able to watch her own breath move the pages of the book . . . and did so!

She seems to need to be inside my personal space and claims more and more right to be there.

As I read the story, its beautiful illustrations lured her more front and center as she tried to get a better perspective. She became, as I did, mesmerized by this story of children visiting the uncle and aunts with the full-of-hard-consonant names and the blended traditions of December.

As I looked across the faces, I imagined what it would be like if those comic book thought balloons suddenly appeared, so I'd know what each child was thinking. I envisioned their thoughts in floating orbs of handblown glass with all the potential of a Humpty-Dumpty collision above their heads or a crash onto the floor. Suddenly the whispered phrase I read from Aunt Svetlana, "We remember," seemed tangibly fragile as it floated out to meet the children's own floating glass-orbed thoughts.

Maybe it was Nickole's move away from me physically, her face uncharacteristically focused on the book—but I sensed a change in her.

After I whispered the words "we remember," Nickole said softly, "*My* mama died." I looked at her and she jumped up and began that head-turning routine, saying, "Oh, oh" with that impish been-caught grin returning to her face. Maybe she thought my look had been a reprimand for interrupting. I touched her, prompting, "No, no it's OK, Nickole, what did you say?" And she repeated her words more strongly, seriously now, without the grin, without the head turning. "My mama died."

"Yes, I know, Nickole. I was so sorry and sad to learn that."

Randel, ever the sensitive one, lowered his head into his arms, saying, "O-o-oh Lord! Please, God . . . this is too sad!"

Ian looked disturbed. Anna wanted a better view of Nickole's face, which had now returned to its usual grin. I read the rest of the book not listening to myself or to the story until the last page, which told about the miracle.

Nickole, into the book again, asked, "Did he come back alive to decorate the tree!?"

"No. They were thinking about Uncle Vova so strongly that they felt him there . . . almost. When you remember someone, they are never all the way gone, right?"

Randel wiped his tears and said, "It's just like my granddaddy. I can't see him till I go to Jesus in heaven."

"Uncle Vova in heaven?" Nickole asked.

"Yes," several children responded.

"My mama in heaven too."

Randel put his arm around her and said, "Nickole is my cousin."

I don't know if that's true or not, but it somehow seemed appropriate and in character for Randel to offer to be her family when she had experienced a loss.

I continue to be overwhelmed by the power of story to break through barriers we've erected in our memories. Nickole had never said the words "My mama died" until today.

It may have been that she was unable to talk about death because she didn't understand it or perhaps subconsciously she knew it sealed forever the possibility of going home. Or maybe she became mute about the incident because she had other silent places in which to shelve the pain and it felt normal to put that pain there as well. Any suggestion I have is pure conjecture, but I do believe that Polacco's art opened a door that had a transformative power for Nickole. Greene (1995) suggests that "the world that the arts illumine is a shared world" (p. 150), and in that shared world, Polacco offered Nickole a place in which to see herself, a place in which to "remember," and she took it.

Clarrissa

Journal Entry [several entries from late November to January]

Clarrissa loves to write. She writes strings of words to accompany her standard illustration of happy girls under umbrellas of rainbows and flowers. They always have big bows and pink shoes. The happier her drawings get, the more unkempt her own appearance seems to become. She is growing taller or thinner or both. Her hair is wild most days, her shoes sometimes don't fit, and she never wears socks. It's getting colder and she seems to wear less. Maybe the only clean clothes are the summer ones. The other day I suggested looking under her bed for something she had lost. She replied, "We don't have any beds. They had so much bugs in them that my uncle had to burn them!" She reported that they sleep on the floor and cover up with their coats. A call to her caseworker at DFACS gave me a reality check. He gave a sympathtic but tired response: "There are children all over the world who don't have a bed. Life doesn't guarantee you a bed." My report was not sufficient leverage for a contact. I understand where he was coming from. I think the horror of it is that Clarrissa doesn't expect a bed. She barely expects kindness. She seems above all to crave a sense of belonging. Her writing seems to be a place in which she creates a sense of well-being and belonging. She draws herself into the smiling girls with the pink shoes, holding hands under a cloudless sky. The writing center is her favorite spot in the room and she makes use of all the materials there to create her scenes. It is also the place where she feels free to interact with class members even though these activities are more akin to parallel play than true interaction.

The face of poverty is a visible mark against belonging in schools. Sometimes Clarrissa might as well be a leper. I am overwhelmed by the thought that life doesn't guarantee belonging to school just because you show up any more than it guarantees a bed for the weary. She doesn't interact with many of the children and I have even noticed that some forget her name. Her quietness; calmness; and love of drawing, painting, cutting, and pasting keeps her busy all day long even to the exclusion of listening at times. She enjoys books but she is not reading yet. She's not able to consistently name all the lowercase letters of the alphabet but has control of a few sight words. I feel an urgency to get her reading. Reading—not I, not life—will guarantee at least a shot at success in school.

I am confronted daily with balancing the choices I make for children such as Clarrissa: those who need time to use books the way very young children use them, but who also desperately need to practice skills for unlocking the process of reading. Each choice can be argued as *the* moral and ethical one, given what I know about the crippling effect of illiteracy on even a second grader. I am always forced to interject my own look into the future into her contentment with today. She hates being interrupted when she is drawing or cutting and pasting, which she seems continually to be engaged in, but complies as best as she can with whatever reading task I ask her to do. She tries diligently but is able to decode only the simplest of words. I try not to be impatient in my longing to see progress or with learning to understand the progress I do see.

Clarrissa has an interesting way of using her writing, those rarely varied illustrations and strings of letters. She writes industriously and comes to the circle ready to share. She just never refers to what she has written when she reads to us. She holds the journal but looks at me or the class, telling us about whatever important issue is on her mind. The public forum does not deter her at all; instead it seems to invite the most intimate of stories, such as the one that was created just after Thanksgiving break:

Journal Entry (continued)

"Last night I was a hero, Ms. Hankins!" Clarrissa greeted me the way all the children do first thing in the morning—telling the most important things all at once while some teacher or parent is standing at the door with vital adult information as well. I responded as I do every day, hurriedly. "Go write it in your journal and we will have journal share in a minute. You can tell me anything you want to in your journal and you won't forget."

At journal share she held her drawing of people and rainbows and told her story without consulting the paper. "We was sleeping in the car but all of a sudden it start to roll down the street. So I jumped over the seat and grabbed that stick thing and it quit rolling! And everybody said, 'You saved our life, you saved our life!'"

"Who was in the car sleeping?" I asked her.

"Me and Miranda and Antwon. He a baby, 2 years old."

"Why were you all asleep in the car alone?"

"It was time to go to sleep!"

"Were you on a trip? Where was the car parked?"

"No, it was in the front of the house. They having too many grown folk in the house. Minnie friends over there." (Minnie is Clarrissa's aunt and caregiver and the sister of Clarrissa's biological mother.)

"Well, you certainly were a hero," I responded.

Before the week was out she had been placed with Alice, her first cousin and the grown daughter of Minnie. I thought that my report to DFACS had finally made a difference; in fact, Alice reported her own mother for neglect and has got temporary custody of Clarrissa and Miranda.

Journal Entry (continued: the next week)

Clarrissa came in today looking rested, clean, and well-groomed. Her hair is styled in cornrows with beads and she looks proud of herself. Things may get better now. She wrote three names on her picture today. Alice, Antwon, and Antoinette (the cousin and her two small children). This time she referred to her paper as she pointed to the illustration before she looked at the class. "When Alice get her check we going out to eat and get new shoes. I can't wait!"

I am so excited. What a great Christmas present for Clarrissa. It appears that she feels at home with Alice and that she belongs there. She has needed a break in life for a long time.

Over winter break I sent home enough crayons, paper, scissors, and glue for all four children to use every day if they wanted to. I also sent a sack of books. I guess I felt guilty for thinking that teaching her to read was more important than her need to create something on those days when I may not have understood what she had lived through the night before. The days she had come to school so unkempt may have followed other nights when she had slept in the car or on the cold floor.

Journal Entry (continued)

Clarrissa is able to go to Reading Recovery now. She was so thrilled to get an extra teacher and the sparkly pink plastic folder the teacher had given her to hold her take-home books. She bounds to the door when Mrs. Razor comes, to report that she is moving quickly. There is a reading metamorphosis happening and she seems to be blossoming in all areas. All of a sudden she is writing more than just random words and lists of names across the paper. She still likes to draw her happy little girls on the picture but she occasionally draws other things in addition to her practiced repertoire. More and more her text and illustration support each other.

This morning, however, she came in angry and reported during her journal share, "Nobody will let me read to them. They just keep saying, 'Get out my face with that book.'" It makes me so angry that I have to be careful in my response, and that is not easy for me at 8:30 in the morning. I did stop and wonder if Clarrissa had not asked to read until it was time to go to bed or if she had asked at another inappropriate time. I suggested she think about a better time to ask for help.

Journal Entry (next day)

"Ms. Hankins, I didn't get to read again! Last night Alice got to drinking. We had to stay upstairs and not come down. I told her I had to read and get my list checked and she said if I didn't shut up she would throw my books in the Dumpster."

My faith in Alice is taking a turn for the worse. I had such hopes, but things are just not right there either. Something is brewing with Betty (the biological mother) too.

Her journal share today included a drawing of a house, the moon and stars, and a tree—no people, no rainbows. She wrote, "I see the moon." But she held that paper to her chest and spoke in a voice that made her sound at first as though she were reciting a very carefully read passage: "Betty got cut last night by those mens she got in the car with. She got 40 stitches in her face. When she get out the hospital she have to stay with us. And I have to go to Atlanta and I will miss you." She was looking me straight in the eye now. "Because I will never get to come back to this school and you won't see me no more."

She dropped her head and began to cry.

I put my arms around her and told her that that probably would not happen. How could I promise her that it wouldn't? I wondered what they had told her.

At lunch I called her caseworker, who assured me that a knife fight would keep the mother from regaining custody and taking Clarrissa to Atlanta. She came to the school that day to talk to the girls and assure Clarrissa that she was not going to Atlanta to live.

These entries speak to the transformative power of both the process and products of writing and drawing and responding to literature. They are powerful reminders to me of the work of Karen Gallas (1994), who asserted that priority must be given to reading literature and to providing writing time even for the youngest learners and that we must cast a wide net over the definition of *narrative*. Gallas, an insightful classroom teacher who also writes, has observed the agency that drawing and painting gives to children's narratives.

School time, our now time, has much to do with future time. The future is always lurking behind the questions the public dwells on, such as, How are your test scores? People rarely ask about real children in real school. So while I was wrapped up in the stories of my children, I still had the stated agenda of a first-grade classroom to worry about.

This priority of producing readers is a complicated issue, to which with multiple interlocking factors contribute. "The more you read the better you read" seems a simple enough motto, but infiltrating a value system, or fighting second-shift work schedules or caregiver illiteracy are competing realities. Combine those factors with the hard reality of poverty and set the whole scene adjacent to groups of students who *do* read more, who *have* in-home tutorial help, who *are born* into the expectation that one must read—then the dichotomies of success appear etched in stone.

Time during the school day has much to do with the art (and business) of reading and writing. It is, however, attached to a firm expectation that reading and writing are practiced outside school time. How tempting it is to speculate that the problem of lagging progress lies outside school completely. I would absolve myself of much of the responsibility if I chose to think that way. There must be something I can do, something I haven't thought of yet. I know that books and the ability to read can enable the girls, and indeed all of us, to "imagine what is not yet" (Greene, 1995, p. 24). Building memories through the experiences offered during the day may provide the connections needed to envision what is yet to be. The shared narratives of our time together will help me to build a bridge from my memories to theirs and from our present to the future. "Memory is more than a looking back to a time that is no longer; it is a looking out into another kind of time altogether where everything that ever was continues not just to be, but to grow and change with the life that is in it still" (Beuchner, 1982, p. 21).

IV. NARRATING THE STORMS

Beuchner's naming of time as once-below-a-time, once-upon-a-time, and from-beyond-time helped me to understand the girls' behaviors as representative of an inability to reach across places in time (McInerney, 1991). It may also illuminate for you how the complicated set of factors involved in the mind's ability to protect itself can interfere with learning. School is not a stress-free environment. Learning, moving ahead, rarely takes place without some level of discomfort.

I pushed, prodded, coaxed, bribed, danced, acted, and sang to make reading an attractive and palatable place for contemplating what we can do now, what we can remember and what we can become. Reading requires an amalgamation of skills, not the least of which is communicating a sense of story. This requires a modicum of success at telling one's own story. The problem may have become evident to you by now: The girls had experienced the unusual, the tragic, before they had words to form thoughts. That part of their personal narrative belongs to the "silent language that embodies thinking" (Gallas, 1994, p. xiv). What could I do to increase the opportunities for the girls to "uncover the threads of silence that speech is mixed with" (Merleau-Ponty, 1964, pp. 43–46) so they could express more of their personal narrative?

We all tell our stories to give meaning to who we are, to where we belong, and to where we anticipate going. "The reasons for which we tell stories are rooted in the same temporal structure that connects our rush towards the future, our attention to the present and our capacity to emphasize and to recollect the past" (Ricour, 1981, p. 34). Without memory, there is no anticipation. With an overrehearsed memory of pain, the anticipation would be of more pain. If pain was all they anticipated of the future, it would make sense that Santana would continue to drill on a way to be safe, Clarrissa would remember only the jelly sandwich and not the reason she was offered one in the first place, and Nickole would choose to remember nothing.

This section deals with the girls' continued responses to the seared-in place of loss, separation, and fear. It also charts some of my struggle to make sense of their pain and its manifesto, ever present in our community. The narratives are representative of the overwhelming number of things that a teacher monitors at any given time. I had 24 children to contemplate in any one moment with all the rough-and-tumble activity, dialogue, conflict, and playfulness that accompanies any school day. I observed and listened to single events with distracted eyes. The child of focus in the narrative was rarely acting as a central figure or a star standing out in relief against a backdrop of insignificant events. The miracle is that any story shoves to the surface at all. In this section I continue to probe the question, What am *I* supposed to do? In addition, evidence is provided here of the two planes of inquiry—the academic and the personal—that I weave together on a daily basis and of how, of necessity, one takes precedence over the other as I attempt to answer that question morally and ethically.

Santana

Journal Entry (spring)

As the months have unfolded, Santana has become more verbal and for longer periods of time, and on occasion she even hugs me. She does this stiffly, tentatively, never like a child who is accustomed to hugs. She does it impulsively, always heading into my stomach with her head, to maintain some distance, and brings one arm to my waist quickly, releasing the instant I hug back. Still, it is a physical connection. Just as her gran predicted, I have learned to take less notice of her silences. Although her usual stance when we come to the rug is to contort into that flatfooted rocking fetal position, she can be drawn into the lesson, if we read a book or sing songs she likes. I have accepted her quietness, her need to move into books, and I do admire her artistic talent. I am witnessing a child developing a love of books and moving into reading them. She seems for the most part happy at school and is making progress.

The only time she ever expresses anger toward me is when I force her to stop writing, drawing, cutting, and pasting. I follow Dewey's precept that teachers couch education in art to keep teaching from being brutal (1916). So much of my interference seems brutal, I think, to Santana . . . her eyes show pain at returning to us from her "drawing" world. She usually puts her head down just after she glares at me. The drawings seem to take her to the lovely thing she is contemplating. Her drawings seldom surface from her own imagination. Most often they are renditions of a picture she has copied. However, when the art teacher or I give instructions for a project, she understands them and produces beautiful works that stand apart from those of the other students. I have searched for ways to let her have more time to draw. But she never seems to have her fill. Where does she go when she draws? Is it close to the place behind her eyes?

Journal Entry (March)

This was a day I will never forget. I cannot believe I didn't see it coming in some way. At another level, I cannot fathom it happening at all. How do I begin to identify the factors involved?

Santana has been in Reading Recovery all year. It is a one-on-one teaching situation built on what the child already knows. It has been a struggle because San is so reticent to speak. But oddly enough, when she realized that the words she needed to say were all on the page, she began the process of learning to read in earnest. With her Reading Recovery teacher she reads in a whisper, barely audible. Fortunately, she feels more comfortable in our classroom, and I know the child can read. She has good strategies and uses them.

The Reading Recovery teacher began to use some of Santana's morning journal drawings as material to write from. Since Santana had already spent time contemplating the drawings, she had something to say about them that could actually be used to coax her into writing. The writing time began to makes sense for her then, and she began to see the connections between reading and thinking and writing about her own thoughts.

As her confidence grew, so did her interaction with others. One day recently, she surprised me by telling a child to "put your finger on the word, boy, then get your mouth ready to say it." She was ready for him to get on with it so she could have a turn. She quickly looked up at me, a little surprised at herself, and our eyes shared a silent giggle.

I am reminding myself of the good and positive work she has done against the events of today.

I am stuck on today, but still I know things had changed before now. Last week, she folded in Reading Recovery. A new, harder book sent her under the table, knees to chest, rocking, tears running down her cheek.

All week she has crawled under the table when confronted with any stressor. Consultations with the school counseling intern and the grandmother were of no help, except for my becoming informed that Family and Child Services had reinstated visitations with the mother. Gran told me that Santana had cried and didn't want to go but that Gran had to make her, to keep from "breaking the rules." When they went, Santana refused to "visit." They made her stay in there for a while, but she sat mute, withdrawn, uncommunicative. What the family caseworker saw as either the grandmother's fault or recalcitrant manipulation on Santana's part, other professionals who were involved defined as a disassociation syndrome linked to posttraumatic stress disorder. So who is right? Is there an element of truth in each definition?

We have the mother back on the scene and at the same time Santana is feeling school pressure that I am unaware of. The Reading Recovery teacher has been pressured by her lead teacher to exit Santana from the program. The hierarchy of the Reading Recovery program has little confidence in the onsite teacher. It sends the leader in to test children who are ready to exit, as a sort of validation, operating a checks-and-balances system. I met with the leader this morning to confirm what the Reading Recovery teacher had warned her about. I told her that Santana was reading very well for me but that she may not perform for a stranger, especially right now.

She seemed to take offense at my contact and assured me that things like having to read with a stranger didn't interfere with the ability to read. I reiterated that Santana was afraid of change, distrusted testing, feared many women in authority, and might become mute, especially today.

At testing time, the woman came to get Santana. She was warm and talked to Santana nicely; nevertheless, San looked back at me as if I was sending her into a den of lions. They were back quickly and Santana was tearful. The report was that she took one stab at reading, was told to speak up, and crawled under the table.

The tester said, "Well, she obviously cannot read fluently at that level or this wouldn't have given her such problems. Readers read without thinking about it *if* they can read." I let her know that I didn't really care whether Santana exited the program or not. I didn't care what the leader found out or thought she found out. I did care about making a reading experience so negative for a child already under stress. I'm embarrassed as I remember my heated response to her. The way she looked at me told me how "off center" I must have appeared.

Was it the test, the mother, or a combination that caused Santana to frown and rock all day, slap a child in line, shove her feet into a hole in the playground and dig, dig, dig into the red clay with a vengeance?

All I know is that I will never forget the multiple factors of the day. It was the day of the test, after my rudeness, after lunch even. Santana's reading group members were at tables and I was instructing as I walked around and between them, offering support and guidance. She remained silent, slow moving, distracted. She was proving to me that she was not listening. The task, involving cutting and pasting, was hard for her to ignore. I gave instructions at the same time as I worked to regain Brandon's attention, turn Charles's paper right side up, coax Nickole to stop pulling her extension braid out of her head—the usual four things at once. Amid the efforts to continue teaching through the distractions, I sensed, more than saw, her slow and deliberate move.

Although I saw it before it happened, I was unable to stop it. Those seconds felt like they took place in a dream in which one's feet just won't move. Santana had a pair of blue-handled scissors open. Her tongue was out, and she slowly, sickeningly, slit the side of it and watched the blood drip onto the page in front of her. The table full of children became completely and totally silent.

The whole of that moment was surreal. Her move was not simply impulsive, as have been those of other children whom I've been unable to stop from cutting their hair, faster than lightning. I'll never know what Santana was thinking. I can't even really reconstruct what I thought in those milliseconds, which stretched into unmarked time. But I think that I will always interpret the act as a warning of, a pre-cursor to, a final silence. "I will not talk . . . I'll cut my tongue off to keep from it . . . you . . . old . . . so-and-so."

From below-time there is a silence that keeps her safe. Screams may have brought pain . . . but silence brings a safe hidden harbor.

My shoulders were bothered by a sudden pinched nerve for weeks as a physical reminder of Santana's power. I remember the moment, but I cannot reconstruct the aftermath, even today. I cannot for the life of me remember what I did, or said, or how we resolved that event. I remember the sadness I felt, the reminder of the shock was with me for days, the feeling of helplessness and the certain knowledge that I was over my head in deep, deep turbulent waters. Her tongue healed with ironic quickness against the pain she tried to cover with the self-inflicted injury.

Nickole

Journal Entry (March)

I am writing this against the background of Nickole's tantrum. Rising and falling high-pitched cries and low-pitched moans and long hollow whines. Really I am. I wondered if it would help to localize me in her fits of temper to tape record one and play it at home. This style of tantrums is a new behavior but she is already close to perfecting them. Maybe I'm growing tired of being unsuccessful in my attempts to stop the tantrums. I know I am tired of dealing with them. It is both painful and frustrating to watch; and it is not without its terrifying aspect. As I watch her slender, attractive, 7-year-old body revert to the stance of a 2-year-old in the middle of a meltdown, I can't help but wonder where the crying takes her. What does it protect her from or immerse her into? What screen does it serve as in her psyche? The tantrums come when I am least able to deal with them, at reading time. I am caught in the role of teacher, director, facilitator of academe. My paid occupation is to move an entire group of first graders to the tune of a reading curriculum, from "cannot" to "can," from "won't" to "will."

This kind of tantrum began in the spring, when a class from the University of Georgia became writing buddies with us. As the girls stepped into the classroom, I saw Nickole's eyes choosing one of the students, named Angela, for her own. She recognized her as a volunteer worker at a Boys and Girls Club.

It was a great match, too good, actually. Nickole could not let Angela leave the first day. I assumed everything would be OK when I explained that she would come back the next week. The next week Nickole refused to accomplish anything unless Angela promised her to come every day. And each ensuing week brought another emotional display of control. I was unaware of the problem for several weeks because the UGA student felt that she should be able to handle it on her own.

Then, Nickole's crying was a tearless whine. Now she has gone several levels beyond that. Lately, the tantrums have been so disruptive that she has had to be removed from the class. We end up having her reading lesson during the time she should be going to specials (art, music, physical education, and so on), which of course allows her to have me all to herself. I finally understood the reward I was giving her.

She is less and less productive now in the classroom, attaching everything to a reward. I lose patience with the quickness of the storm. But I ache for her as well. She needs more than I can give her, but she also needs what I *can* give. I have to help her understand that when she interferes with the learning of others, she is not being a responsible member of the group. When she throws a tantrum instead of doing her work, she is not respecting herself. I have to diffuse the impact of her tantrums over me, over the class, and ultimately over herself.

Nickole's tantrum is still going in the background. It is clearly an impossible task to manage that reading group with the tantrum going on. But the most unbelievable truth I feel right now is that there was no place to take her at that moment. The office was "full." Reading time was robbed from nine other children. Suddenly I am not as impressed with that scene as I am with the memory of the statement she made that started the tantrum today, "I wish I was dead."

We were on the way back from lunch, which should be such a simple thing. Anyone who has ever taught knows the potential for disaster that any transition holds, but from lunch it's even greater. So there I was watching the kids at the tray window, the kids leaving the table, the kids lining up in the hall all at once. I was hearing children talk right underneath the big sign that says "Quiet Zone." I was also watching the clock for the quickly fleeting minutes we had before half the class was picked up for extension lab. Then I moved the whole wiggly group toward the bathrooms to continue the potential for chaos.

Nickole's face carried all the jealousy and anger she could muster over Megan choosing Emily to have lunch with her on the patio with her mom. Her arms were crossed and she muttered, "I wish I was dead."

"Oh, Nickole, it's not time for you to die. I would miss you!" I tried not to overreact, giving her a quick hug and a smile.

"If I was in heaven I could see Jesus and I could talk to my mama."

Christopher told her seriously, "Well God is the only one can decide when you die. If you kill yourself you go to hell!"

"Ah-o-o-o, Christopher said the *h* word!" several children reported.

"Who left a red lunch box on the table?" the lunchroom aide broke in, and several children ran to get it for Anna, who was in the bathroom. I was admonishing them over the dangers of running in the hall and tussling over an object someone was holding. The conversation continued.

"If you not good you won't see no Jesus even if you do die," Kenny retorted. "And you . . . ain't . . . acting . . . good!"

"Are we supposed to talk in the halls?" I asked the children as the principal walked by. I wanted her to know that *I* knew we were supposed to be quiet, whether the children did or not.

"I'm looking for some first graders who know how to be silent in the halls." I began to scan the line, which was quickly becoming silent with children who hoped to be so identified. Such a goofy game, but it always gets results.

That whole startling conversation took place in the few minutes we traveled from the cafeteria in the din of dinnerware, scraping chairs, loud echos of children's voices bouncing off the numerous hard surfaces of a cafeteria. I heard it with my ears but not with my heart, which I was so busy managing, but Nickole's storm warning had been issued.

Such large thoughts for 6-year-olds and so ignored, so unheeded by their teacher until this writing.

I'm reviewing all I know about Nickole, including the day she whispered, "My mama died." Is it possible that Nickole wasn't so much feeling neglected by Megan as she was feeling without a mother?

I keep coming to these understandings so late . . . so very late. And the tantrum still plays in the background as I write.

Maxine Greene (1995) recalls Martin Buber (1957), speaking about teaching and the importance of "keeping the pain awake" (p. 116). She suggests that the pain he had in mind must be lived through by teacher as well as student, even as the life stories of both must be kept alive. I believe that Nickole cries to keep the pain awake. Knowing her mother was painful, but forgetting her may be even worse. Nickole's cries force me to live through pain. I can make them my frustration or I can live her pain with her. Her cries serve to remind me that her pain is indeed awake as it awakens my memories of other children and of memoirs I've read. How familiar, how Maya Angelou–like some of the weeping silences of voice become now.

Journal Entry (continued: the next day)

Aha! Today Nickole showed me that she had not forgotten how to read. She read with us as a group and she read a story individually and she worked effectively with two children at the word work station. Reading was wonderful today! Oh it didn't start out that way. But after last night's immersion into her tantrum and the the time I afforded myself to reflect on her, I was in a better position to respond effectively.

As we moved to the group, she asked if we could sing a song we had sung just before lunch, and I said, "Later." It was the trigger she would respond to today. If it hadn't been that it would have been something else. When she began the low moan I have come to call stage 1, instead of removing her from us, I pulled her into my lap where I sat on the floor. Instead of ignoring her or isolating her, I wrapped my arms tightly around her. I whispered directly into her ear, "If you stop crying I'll give you a piece of candy and if you do the reading lesson with us I'll give you two." Immediately she stopped. Outright.

So chastise me for setting her up with candy. Somebody else can handle that problem! I learned that the tantrum is not out of her control.

We had reading and she ate candy. She read well and didn't break her stride. No tantrum—we had a deal—she didn't write, but that was not in the deal. I didn't push her; one step at a time, one step at a time.

I have become convinced that Nickole will be able to keep the pain awake at times other than reading group. It was not likely to be put to sleep because of a piece of candy. If *Uncle Vova's Tree* had the power to help her sort out the pain, another story could help her to find more of her own narrative. The candy just offered the possibility that she'd be quiet enough when that story came along for her to hear it.

Does it matter in the course of education as a whole that I interpreted this event as representative of Nickole's attempt to spin the pain awake? No. Does it matter if a psychologist picks this up someday and questions my assessment? No. What matters is that I, the teacher, found a way to view her tantrums as temporary interruptions rather than defining who she was. It matters that hearing Nickole's cries in the light of the computer helped me lay them down, dismantle them, take them apart, and diffuse their impact on me. I could move beyond them and believe that one day she would too. Spending the time necessary to write about the multiple layers of this event and reflecting on the interrelatedness in creating Nickole's story has given me a tangible way to shape and reshape the materials of my craft: the craft of listening, the craft of building community, the craft of reshaping my attitude and of redirecting a child's behavior toward an academically oriented place.

Clarrissa

Journal Entry (a cold day in early spring)

If words could add tangibly to one's warmth I'd have no need for a coat on our brisk morning walks across the playground. Based on the sheer numbers of words that Clarrissa speaks, in 15 minutes' time I would be sweating rather than clenching my teeth against the brisk, unusually cold March wind.

Clarrissa is so different inside the classroom. She's so quiet, easily missed in the course of the day. She appears to be busy, on task, self-motivated. Even when she comes to something she doesn't understand, she just writes anyway. She never says, "I don't understand." She never raises her hand for help and seldom volunteers an answer. Sometimes when I call on her, she jumps as if scared out of a reverie, even though she'd been looking right at me. As soon as we leave the building, she becomes a magpie. Her talk continues over the din of the others and she seldom leaves my side.

She finds my hand as the others trot, spin, run ahead, and double back. Today her hand found mine and she was silent for a time. She usually jumps right in talking. I thought that like mine, her lips were too numb to produce much talk yet. Her opening statement hangs in the balance of my memory like the cold air cloud that came out of her mouth; "You know what I need, Ms. Hankins? I need a mommy. I need one who cares about me."

I was glad I was too numb to speak. I squeezed her hand and kept walking, glad to be interrupted by the comments of other children. She wasn't distracted.

"Betty was at the house. She is going to take me away.

Alice wouldn't sign my papers, said if Betty gonna be the mama she have to sign the papers. Betty say I have to change my name if she sign the papers. She don't like my name no more. I was scared. They made me go to Betty's house 'cause they say she got to take me back. She come bringing me back after two nights. She don't let me stay asleep 'cause she think I be sleeping wild.

"Ms. Hankins, do you know about crack? Its' a secret that you cannot talk about. I'm scared of it too."

I have learned as the year progressed that Clarrissa will keep talking no matter what, so I just said nothing and sure enough she went on. In typical childlike fashion, she switched to another topic altogether and asked, "How can the moon be up at the same time as the sun?" Finally a safe place to respond. I pointed it out to the others.

"O-o-o-w-e-e-e!!" The children began talking at once about the moon in the blue sky, and the talk of a mother was dropped.

I am reminded of yesterday's outside time. In the middle of her running family commentary she asked me, "Ms. Hankins, if I dial 911 will you answer?"

"No, Clarrissa, the police answer. It's just for emergencies like a fire or something, remember?"

"Oh, well I can't call *them* then. If a policeman comes he will take me to a bad place. What's the welfare look like? The police came *one* time but they hide me upstairs. *Next* time the police came again and they woke me up and said, 'Are you all right?' It was in the dark, dark night!

"What is a foster home? If you bad you'll have to go there, right? Not Antonette and Miranda and Bubba. . . they belong to Alice . . . only me. They all hate me. Seems like I didn't do anything to make them not like me. They just don't. They said I am a white skinny-bones girl." (Clarrissa does have light skin, but she's not white.)

My assurance of how beautiful she is seemed to fall on deaf ears.

Today's conversation reminded me of multiple statements she has made under the open skies of the playground. So odd that Clarrissa would choose such a public venue for those discussions. I hear the biggest questions and issues she wrestles with in the middle of watching out for the antics and safety of 24 other children. Her sentences are spoken to a distracted listener and I realize now they were voiced with little expectation of help. I certainly reinforced that expectation.

What does she mean, If I call 911 will *you* answer? Me! Me? Why does she think I will answer the 911 number?

"*If I*, she begins (while so much is going on).

"Owen! Watch out for the mud!" I yell.

go to a

"Ms. Hankins, we found a snake coat!" A group cried out.
"What?"
"See?"

foster home,

"It *looks* like a snake skin but . . . Owen! I know you saw that mud! . . . But I think it's a piece of broken strap or"

you won't see . . . me . . . no . . . more."

Silence . . . The children run off to scare someone with the "snake coat." Owen moves away from the mud. Clarrissa stays beside me, holding on tightly.

I answer her while still scanning the playground and modulating to an optimistic decibel level: "Children who go to foster homes often go to a home where they are very much wanted. Often they stay in their same schools. That's what would happen to you too. But mainly, Clarrissa, I'm just glad you're here today." (Tight hug to the shoulder.) "I'll still be your friend wherever you go."

Good God, where did I get that stuff I just said! Was it OK? Was it wrong? Is it enough? Too much? It sounded like someone else talking. What exactly do I feel? I am not sure, but it feels like fear.

What did she mean—the police came in the dark, dark night? She was hugging me tighter still, talking a mile a minute, not interested in playing with the others.

"O-wen!" I called sharply. The cold mud splashed onto his jeans as the rock he "mistakenly" threw crashed though the thin ice on top of the puddle.

"OK!! Line up! Time to go."

I have schedules to keep. A pace to follow. A lesson plan to carry out. Clarrissa is the door holder. She runs to her spot to open the door, to follow the plan. She will go on silently.

The next hectic minutes began. Get clothes for Owen. Set out the paint. Get the paper for the reading group. Change the chart. Don't be late for lunch. Hurry, hurry. Pay attention. Keep up . . .

And the rest of the day took care of the thoughts about Clarrissa, until now. Her words stick in my memory, accompanied by the other thoughts I attended to at the time, along with the remembered smell of the cold, the sounds still so clear I could be replaying a video; even the flush of anger warming my face comes to mind. It makes me understand what Frederick Beuchner (1982) said about writing your life: that indeed any moment or all moments are important ones.

I believe it's the telling that makes them so.

HOPEFUL INTERPRETATIONS

The first time I heard the song quoted from at the beginning of this chapter, I was in an auditorium filled with 500 young girls. I wish I could hear that mass of treble voices again singing, *"Open my eyes that I may see/glimpses of truth thou hast for me/Place in my hand the wonder-*

ful key/that shall unclasp and set me free." I hummed that song frequently as I observed or wrote about the girls. I always changed the pronoun from *my* to *their*. I always wrote hoping for *their* eyes to be opened, wishing *they* could view truths that would set them free. When I wrote and rewrote their narratives, I realized that I might be better served singing that song with the original pronoun. The narratives constructed in this form revealed my part in their story as well. I realize in retrospect that I was the one who needed to ask for open eyes, open heart, open mind, and the ability to use even a glimpse of truth as a key to hope. I suppose that more than anything, I wanted to believe I could set the girls free from the place they retreated to behind their eyes. The truth I learned, finally, and the truth I couldn't face all along was that I could not. I could free myself of the pain I carried for them by telling the story my way. They would have to learn to free themselves, and it would be a lifetime of work. Teaching is not a search-and-rescue mission. There are no heroes in the sense of deliverance or liberation, only when it comes to survival. Writing about children and musing over situations do not produce solutions; nor do they point with certainty to what needs deliverance or changing.

Narratives offer not solutions, but interpretations that we can live with, interpretations that sustain the children and me. The last thing this book should become (were it possible for it to do so) is a compendium of definitive knowledge about this set of children. I recall Einstein's statement that imagination is more important than knowledge. I had a limited knowledge base of the girls and even less knowledge of posttraumatic stress disorder and child psychology. It took all the imagination I could muster, upon my acknowledging their struggle, to look within it and move beyond it. I am not a psychologist; nor am I well read in the field. However, just as I searched the literature on autism when I taught a child with autism, and the literature on the effect of crack cocaine inutero when I taught children labeled crack babies, I knew that I would need to search readings in psychology to find the behaviors I saw in my girls. In addition to examining the readings, I sought advice and support from colleagues in the field of psychology. I never attempted to practice therapy; I never labeled the girls. I only mused and wrote, and wondered and wrote, and read outside my field nightly with a dictionary at my side, spending more time in the dictionary than the text, and wrote some more.

The journal documents where my imagination took me. My knowledge base about the girls and about their conditions grew from the scattered and imaginative search to understand them and to construct cohesive stories from disordered fragments of information I collected from and about the girls. Cronon (1992) believes that all narrators work by "creating plots from disordered experience to give reality a unity that neither nature nor the past possess so clearly" (p. 1349). I suppose it was the search for unity amid the disorder that drove my construction.

The capacity of even one of those girls to hold her pain is a remarkable testimony to the resilience of the human spirit. My knowing one of them would have been remarkable enough; knowing all three at once had an unprecedented impact on my teaching.

I have obtained a new appreciation of how all students perceive school. School is supposed to be a place of new beginnings, new accomplishments, a place that "depends on breaking free, a leap, and then a question . . . why" (Greene, 1995, p. 6). It takes faith both in yourself and in your teacher to take risks, to be willing to break free, to leap, and certainly to question.

Bishop Desmond Tutu said once that "faith is hearing tomorrow's music but . . . hope is dancing to it today." The ethical choice of the teacher, then, is to supply the music for those who cannot hear it for themselves. In answer partially to the question, What am *I* supposed to do? I respond that I must choose most often the avenue that delivers hope to a student. Offering hope is not at all the same thing as getting one's own way. It doesn't mean taking the easiest path or offering the most immediate comfort level. It means rather that I learn to acknowledge a student's strength when they have to move out of the more comfortable place or have to take a risk. It means giving them assurance that they are capable of making the difficult choice, a choice promoting peace over self-gratification. Part of the answer to, What am I supposed to do? is to do all I can do to prepare myself to see, appreciate, and listen to every form of a child's narrative rendering of life, especially the silent ones, as though they were music.

I think of the girls coming to the place we call school full of all the same energy and curiosity other children bring to school. Out of their lived experience, however, they carry their fragile anticipation within an unspoken question: Do I belong here? Unfortunately, for each of them, their differences were so apparent that I am afraid an affirmative answer might be as fragile as their anticipation. Faint as it was, however, they all seemed to hear "tomorrow's music" in the daily affirmations of school, through a walk hand in hand, a story, a drawing, a stack of books, a hug, a smiley face on a paper, drawing girls with pink shoes under a rainbow, being the line leader, choosing the song we'd sing or the story we'd chant, and learning to read words someone else had thought up and penned on a page just for children.

The shape of future questions for my teaching lies in what I have learned from the silent songs of the girls. How many children come into school needing not only a new start but also a way to bring closure to their beginning? How many children come to school within that fragile question, Do I belong here? The girls are three such children whom I grew to understand, but I think that in many ways, hopefully less dramatic, many children step into school needing someone to offer them hope. Teaching the girls was not always easy and was always framed by their particular difficulties. Yet the sweep of our time together gave me a sense of accomplishment, pride, and encouragement. Living their questions within my own questions renewed my commitment to activities and curriculum that fosters community in our classroom: class meetings, character education, journal sharing, group sing-alongs, shared literature, group dancing, and plays we do together. I am more committed than ever to providing daily contact with materials that allow self-expression through drawing, painting, building, and constructing.

Once-below-a-time is that "intuitive way of knowing which is at home in the world of timelessness and eternity. It is nurtured by dance, drama, music, literature and the visual arts" (Eusden & Westerhoff, 1998). Children so immersed in the moment that they can't recall with certainly the events of today contrasted with the rest of the week have the gift of dwelling firmly in a sense of now. If it is possible at all for the girls to delve into once-below-a-time in a positive way, I imagine that it can happen during experiences that celebrate the gifts of music and visual art and story and dance.

Richard Niebuhr wrote, "Our habits become our habitations. To make our vision clear means to unwrap the habits of our imaginations that enfold our minds and hearts and keep the light out" (quoted in Eusden & Westerhoff, 1998, p. 1). The girls, each in her own way, deal with habits of imagination that keep today's light at bay. Beuchner, through the art of writing, received the power to explore his own once unarticulated pain. Writing gave a place for a connection to the hidden and a way of altering the habits of his imagination, allowing in a light of understanding. The art took him back to the world of intuition from the more logical linear intellectual world, from argument to story. The intuitive realm of knowing is characterized by surrender, mystery, imagination, experience, surprise, and passion. It is at home with anti-structure, ambiguity, chaos, and risk. It is a way of knowing that leads to consciousness and revelation. All of us in the beginning are intuitive by design; more *being* than *doing*.

So . . . once-below-a-time there were three little girls, yes, but there were also the rest of us. And once-below-a-time we felt the world as being one with it, dissolved into something larger and more complete than just ourselves and those we knew. Dwelling once-below-a-time more often, by whatever artistic mystery we use to get there, will enable the unwrapping of our imaginations. And with clearing vision we *all* will walk together in the hope that is our human birthright.

CHAPTER 6

At the End of the Storm

Now when the storms of fate o'ercast
Darkly my Present and my Past,
Let my Future radiant shine
With sweet hopes of thee and thine.
                        —Edgar Allan Poe,
                        Hymn (emphasis added)

As we close the book on the year of El Niño, you carry in your thoughts the incomplete narratives of seven children and a teacher, as incompletely written as our lives are open ended. You carry their problems now while still mulling over your unanswered questions. You find yourself in dialogue with my interpretations and wonder if you had all the particulars, all the journal entries I did not include, whether or not we would agree on interpretations. You leave the last narrative knowing that, after all, there are tens of thousands more children who could be so uniquely written about. Still, I suspect, you find that you can't just shrug and say, "So what?" For to do so would in some way diminish your own way of living. It would discount in some way the faces of children you know personally who may have emerged as you read about the children I have written about. Perhaps it wasn't your students you saw in the narratives but your family, colleagues, and relatives. I am certain of one thing, and that is that at some level you have met yourself in these pages. It may have been through the children or through the teacher. Or it may well have been that you met yourself in the silences, in the spaces you were not. And perhaps those silent spaces are the cloudy areas that you carry every day. I urge you not to ignore those spaces but to tackle them. The cloudy areas are most assuredly pregnant with agents of change that will be born only as they are given a narrative. Venture into the middle of those issues; reflect, write, discover.

WRITING THROUGH THE STORM

Too often today, educators find themselves on the political plat-form of the ill informed and self-righteously motivated. Too often the research backing their assertions seems to be outside my own experi-ence. If you, like me, have found more of yourself in what is left *out* of the dialogue on schools, I urge you to come into a more exacting narra-tive discourse on your teaching.

I think teachers are able to feel hopeful, because we are witness to the progress children make every day. It gives hope to watch children such as those I have described here make strides in literacy, math, and community building. It gives hope to know that the children who were not filled with storms coexisted peacefully with those who were, and made equally impressive progress. Although I pulled the narratives of the storm together for all the reasons previously stated, it would be a mistake to leave the rest of the children completely unaddressed.

An academic profile would show several children who were per-forming well above expected grade level, a strong mix of children who were moving with ease in the prescribed curriculum for first grade, several more who struggled to keep up but moved in and out of the expected target performance, and several who were still performing way below what is expected. I selected reading material at instructional levels from emergent through grade 3 to meet the needs of the class. I had several who wrote with a depth and volume I seldom experience in children so young. When it came time for a schoolwide vote on a book to be nominated for the Georgia Children's Book Award, a media spe-cialist remarked to me, "Of all the classes in the school, yours were the only children who voted for books because of what they meant to them. They were serious about the vote and they could talk about *why* they were voting for the selections they were. I tell you, Hankins, they are a puzzle! To be so wild—they are very astute as well."

If we look at the children from the perspective of this media specialist's first description, "wild," it reminds me of what colleagues who have read this manuscript have said to me: "You didn't even write about the 'bad' ones!" While it is true that Nickole and Kenny were part of the reason we were dubbed the "class from hell," their behavior was only one small ingredient of the fracas. The ones who got the attention of the rest of the faculty were fighters, disrespectful of people and of property, children who were not able to operate without being the cen-ter of attention, no matter how negative the attention seemed to be. Perhaps one of the reasons the children in this book required so much written attention had to do with my needing to separate their behaviors out from those of some of the ones who took center stage all the time. Yet the effect of the poor behavior was tempered by children who were able to ignore it and continue working, children who did not hold the startling behaviors of the girls against them, children who were happiest when they were involved in creating something artistic.

When the inevitable was asked—How did they do on the Iowa Test of Basic Skills?—I was able to say that the class average was above the national norm. If someone decided that something could be learned from that score, I suppose one could say that we passed. You know from what you have read about just six of the children that one would be hard pressed to say much of substance about them from the test.

I am now teaching younger siblings of some of the children from that year and enjoying reconnecting with families, recalling events, and even getting rolled eyes when I mistakenly call a child by his or her older sibling's name.

I have taken great delight in seeing awards at science fairs, for citizenship, in oratorical contests, and for reading hours being given to a number of children from the year of El Niño. Most of the students from the class are successful in school and keep coming by to visit or wave shyly if I see them in the community.

Narrating the Stories of "Other" Children

Categorizing the children into "children selected" and "children not selected" for this book runs the risk of "othering" children. The focus on a group that I have variously labeled as stormy children, children of poverty, or children who struggled with identity, among other things, does require a level of categorizing, but it was not my intention to set them apart from myself. The fact that I happen to be middle class and White and have written about poor children of color opens me to the charge of posturing as yet another narrator of a story in which "White hero" triumphs over "Black chaos." The bothersome indictment does have weight, and I am not quite sure how to address it, except to admit that even our roles as adult-child position us at some level to create dichotomies. I hope to make it abundantly clear that I do not see the stories of these children to be representative of all children of color, or of all children of poverty. I set myself apart long enough to admit that politicians who look much like me and live much as I do make decisions that perpetuate cycles of poverty of which most often our children are the victims.

Although I myself am not a hero, perhaps there is a need for heroes to emerge—middle-class heroes who are willing to take action spurred by their hearts and faith instead of perpetuating power and position. As long as we continue to treat children of poverty as though they have made a decision to be poor, not enough stories will be told. To skirt the fact that Blackness still enters into the equation of otherness would be less than honest. To pretend that I don't have a role in making the children other would be a travesty. I—teacher, White voter, middle-class female—too often see "them" without thinking "us."

I hope that tapping into my family's memoirs has made me less able to separate the class into *them* and *us*. The irony is that the more deeply I get to know people who live differently from how I have lived, the more I am able to connect their lives and mine together. The beauty of a classroom is that it affords a better arena to become more "we" than do most daily work environments. I have the intimate, often earthy, experience, unduplicated in other professions, of prolonged contact with children outside my culture. If only for that reason, I must narrate the classroom as I live it, even if it reveals a certain held-over sense of "saving the world" that was so wrapped up in my call to teach.

Writing these narratives, as personally interpreted as they are, has helped me to fashion more continuous face-to-face relationships with children who are less like me than are other children. "It seems clear that the more continuous and authentic personal encounters can be, the less likely will it be that categorizing and distancing take place. . . . [Children in classrooms] are less likely to be made 'other'" (Greene, 1995, p. 155). I am convinced that our ability to cross over to other cultures, to hear voices other than those most like ours, will be cultivated only as well as how we attend to the narrative construction of our classrooms. We will attend to a narrative construction of a class only to the degree that we acknowledge and give voice to the narratives of each of our children. And we will be able to hear the multiple voices of our children only as well as how we listen to and give voice to our own lives.

So, if there is an "aha" in the rendering of these concluding thoughts, it comes in the confirmation of my speculation long ago that autobiography and memoir in research should be more than accidental or serendipitous. Especially in places as founded on relationships as schools are, we must be acutely aware of the shape that our narrative selves gives to our dealings with others and to recognize how the lived experiences of those we teach shape their ability to deal with us.

Balancing Past and Present

As I worked to bring closure to this book, the school bell had rung on yet another year, 2 years after the end of the year in which I had taught the children in this book. As they were entering third grade, I was teaching my new first graders all day and trying to write and revise in the evening and on weekends. The school year began awkwardly and progressed in such a negative trajectory that I lost hope. I felt that much of what I knew about good teaching had flown out the window. The children seemed elusive and distant. I didn't seem to know them any better in November than I had in September. I felt that if I could just bring closure to the book, or be brave enough to lay it down, I could at least get some rest. In the muddled thinking borne of little sleep, I found myself contemplating quitting both teaching and writing, which for me was akin to denying my spirit.

I took several weeks away from school, at the suggestion of my family, with the stated agenda being only to rest, step back, and regroup. As I began to feel rested, I set out writing again. At first I was just journaling feelings. Then I decided to write in earnest again. In the journaling, I had begun several themes of events from this year and in the mix of journaling and following some writing plan for the day, I did what I had missed all year. I wrote about the children I am currently teaching.

I had not written about this year's children since school started, not reflectively, recursively. I had recorded onto tape, had even jotted and sketched, but my reflecting time was spent on the children of the storm. Not writing had rendered me helpless in the unexpected mix of the children I am teaching this year. Writing about them renewed my hope in what our community can become and gave me faith once again in what I know about teaching and about children.

It seems contradictory that writing so deeply about this year became the catalyst I needed to bring closure to the year of El Niño, but it does in fact support what I understand about narrative theory. Writing about this year's children captured the "reality of the way that moment by moment the future becomes the present" (Britton, 1993, p. 12). I teach with more assurance that now is always the most significant moment, the highest moment, but that any now is weighty with past, present, and future.

There had to be worked out, finally, the way that the narratives, which were so "presently" written once, yet contextualized in a question of the children's futures, are being revised from a distance from which I know already a bit of what the future dealt them. Every rewriting, every rereading, is a glance back at a more distant past. Now *their* stories, these very narratives, have become craft-shaping memoirs that influence and guide my teaching today and that will always.

ON THE OTHER SIDE OF THE STORM

One of the joys of belonging to my family was the gradual immersion into a working knowledge of most Broadway musicals. We played them, loudly, on an old hi-fi while we cleaned house. "It will make you work with dispatch," my father told us. We sang them, memorized all the words, and with luck got to see the plays. Even during the lean years of graduate school, my parents sacrificed—once pawning a gold coin—to afford us the opportunity of attending the theater. My repertoire of coping mantras often as not come from show tunes (and hymns). Not that I choose one intentionally; they seep into my strength-gathering, unnoticed at first. Gradually, I realize that a song has begun nestling into my head. I may find myself humming it at the same place on the road to school, for instance. A song from *Carousel*, "You'll Never Walk Alone" (Rodgers & Hammerstein, 1945), carried me to and from school on many days during the year of El Niño. Perhaps the real tornados we struggled against that spring caused the song to creep in. Examining what triggered it, what set me humming it in the first place, provided me with the storm metaphor that connects these narratives. I guess the song reminded me that I weather storms best by clinging to the knowledge that eventually, they *do* end.

Now that the year is preserved on the pages of this book, however, I have to wonder about the last line of one of the verses. At the end of the storm there may be "a golden sky and the sweet, silver song of a lark," but the lark may sometimes sing while peering down on a scene of destruction that is made more visible by the light of that golden sky. I thought the emotional storms we experienced on a daily basis had ended when the buses pulled out on the last day of school. Writing about the storms for the better part of 2 years kept them raging, because writing gave me a chance to view the storms' power in a better light. In some ways the aftermath (the writing) was more painful than the storms (the days in the classroom.)

Even as I wrote, I brought at least some measure of closure, painful or not, to each stormy event. My own sense of closure, though, does not negate my understanding that the children's reality differed from my own. The closure I bring to the narratives does not wipe out the fact that for some of the children, the storms still come, repeatedly.

I would like to have you visit the children one more time, from beyond that year. I felt the need to write one more narrative of each child, with the aim of bringing this book full circle. As recursively as the narratives were constructed, it makes sense to move in reverse order, beginning with the girls and going backward child by child to the place where we began: where "by narrative, we love, hate, learn, gossip, construct, criticize, revise, plan, count, believe, despair, anticipate, remember and hope" (Hardy, 1978).

Clarrissa

Clarrissa's aunt/foster mom died shortly after the school year ended. I paid a visit to the house the day after the funeral and was hit full face with the reality of her existence. I took food into the tiny kitchen, which was surprisingly bare. The cousin (now mom) told me, "All the food is at Grandmama's house but looks like I got all the children to feed!" And there they stood, all five ... wait, four—where was Clarrissa? My peripheral vision picked up some movement. There she was, standing in the narrow space between the refrigerator and the wall. She had on an oversized T-shirt with a huge hole right in front. She made no eye contact, just stood there, barefoot. Her hair, out of its braids and uncombed, made a standing 6-inch mane around her head. She looked wild next to her two cousins, who were dressed and had their hair braided, complete with beads and bows. When I hugged her, she didn't hug back; when I spoke to her, she made no reply from her Kool-Aid-stained mouth; no light of recognition came from her blank eyes. It had been more than a year since I had seen this depth of withdrawal.

"How long has she been like this?" I asked.

"Oh she get that way sometime, CLARRISSA!" her cousin-now-mama yelled, clearly impatient with her. "Talk to your teacher, girl!" She looked toward me but said nothing. I talked briefly while I held her hand, which began to squeeze mine more tightly as I made moves to leave.

As soon as I got home, I called back to her house, arranging to bring Clarrissa home with me for a few days. To stay for "a few days," she arrived wearing a dress that was two sizes too big for her and brought along the same dirty shirt she'd been wearing earlier, for sleeping in, and an extra pair of panties. When she got into the car, she was silent and remained so until we had cleared the neighborhood. Then she said, "They said they *glad* I'm going. Alice got too many kids now."

The few days turned into several weeks. During that time, she went to day camp, to Bible school, and to a chorus workshop. We took her to see Cathy Rigby as Peter Pan, to the movies, to the mall, to church, to the pool, to every fast food restaurant that offers a toy with the meal. But it was the grocery store that impressed her, more than all the other destinations put together. She couldn't believe all that food; the deli, the frozen section, the meats—and the *free samples*! She also couldn't believe how close this store was to where she lived. It was less than

2 miles straight down the road from her neighborhood. She had never seen anything in that area, however, because the school bus turned in the opposite direction, and besides her apartment complex and her grandmother's street, a block over, she knew only the school bus route. In the few weeks she spent with us, she opened my eyes to the real, physical bondage of poverty.

A concert culminated the weeklong chorus workshop she had attended. We went, of course, and had invited her family as well. They declined. From the backseat of the car after the concert, she asked me, "When did I get good?"

"What do you mean, 'get good'?" I wanted to know.

"Like, how your mama gave me a little flag at that parade [the Fourth of July]. And your daddy gaved me a quarter every time he see me . . . and how you always be fixing me up to go places and how Mandy call me over to play . . . and how Mr. Hankins always be reading to me . . . Looks like I'm turning into good."

"You've always been good, Clarrissa."

She didn't agree. "Uh-uh. Like when I got to be on the stage and you looked at me and I was so happy I couldn't stop smiling. It feels like I'm having a dream with my eyes open."

The lark sang for me at that moment, but only against the backdrop of a boiling horizon. I was taking her home. It was time. After several attempts to take her home were thwarted by the cousin ("Can you keep her just till Wednesday?" or "I got some business to take care of, can she stay till tomorrow?"), the cousin finally called me. I had a feeling that relatives were listening, because this time she demanded that I bring Clarrissa home, as if all along I had been trying to prevent her from going home, instead of the reverse being true. About 15 minutes later, the cousin called again and suggested that Clarrissa stay until after the concert on Friday night, because she couldn't get to me to pick Clarrissa up. Clarrissa clearly missed her little cousins, and by the time that evening rolled around she was looking forward to going home. I told her that Alice must really be missing her. I had a feeling she believed me. I hoped so.

It was several weeks later that I read an old journal entry recording a question I'd asked a group of children, including Clarrissa.

"What does it mean to be a reader? What does a reader look like?" I asked them. The first response was given almost in unison: "They be good."

A little surprised, I just answered by repeating, "Good?"

"Yeah, like Meg, Sean, Anna, Abby, you know, they be good." They had named White, middle-class children who were strong, fluent readers.

Urging them to talk about "goodness," I discovered that it was not a quality that those children applied to themselves, but I had believed that their interpretation applied only to the context of reading. It is haunting to remember it now, in the context of Clarrissa's statements about goodness. Clarrissa taught me what *good* more likely meant to them. It described what Janie Larkin in the *Blue Willow* (Gates, 1940/ 1968) meant when she referred to nonmigrant children as "smooth" children. These settled children exercised a degree of agency that was not available to children who moved constantly and who were more acquainted with hunger than with its absence. Janie, like Clarissa, saw school performance as a component of goodness. We would be dishonest to dismiss Clarrissa's intuition as completely erroneous.

The face of resilience does not restore her innocence, but it does signal the hopefulness that undergirds her life and remains a source of inspiration for me. How I wish she could see her gifts from my perspective . . . then she would know what good really means.

Santana

"It's too cold, too rainy, and too late," I grumbled to myself as I drove to the all-night grocery story for some absolutely necessary toiletries that my daughter had neglected to add to the shopping list earlier but desperately needed now. "No one but a parent would do this," I pouted to myself. I walked straight to the aisle I needed, shivering and still holding my damp coat tight at my neck. What a surprise to meet up with Gran, San, and her little sister as I passed the valentine aisle.

They were buying a box of valentine cards for each of the girls to take to school, and in less than 8 hours that's where we would be. Gran acted as though it was the most natural thing in the world to have two small children in a store at midnight on a school night. I knew, however, that her purchase was in its own way as essential as the one I was making. Santana was leaning on the cart that held her little sister, her eyes drooping, her thumb in her mouth.

Gran had been with the child of her employer until the child's parents came home from an event they had attended out of town. For years she had worked as a housekeeper and child-care giver for this family. I knew that often Santana went to their house with her. Tonight, as probably happened on many other nights, the children had fallen asleep there, then had got up and gone to the store on their way home. I remembered from the year before that Gran had shown up an hour before a party with a box of valentine cards for Santana, unopened. I remembered sending three children along with Santana to form an assembly line for signing them, stuffing them into envelopes, and addressing and finally placing them in the red and pink heart-shaped valentine mail-boxes around the room. I thought it was a shame that she was not able to have the time to do them in a more leisurely way. I am sure she would have loved to sort, address, and apply the stickers to them. I feel a little guilty now about my thinking last year that Gran just didn't get it. I think I seriously underestimated her, as well as the power her job held over the way Santana viewed the world.

The following day, when I asked Santana's teacher if Santana seemed more tired than usual, she said she didn't think so. She had not noticed anything out of the ordinary (except that Santana had been addressing valentine cards all morning.)

I realized then that she spent many evenings like that one. The plight of poverty for this little girl forced her to walk into school many days half asleep, and then move from school to the home of a wealthy little boy who had "stuff" she couldn't touch. She could, however, cut and paste all she wanted, using the many old magazines and catalogs his mother gave to her. I only now get the picture of sleep depriva-tion, only now sense the full impact of Gran's incessant remarks to me about how she's "taking care of her White folk so they'll take care of me. If that's the way it be, then I be doing what I can to get what I can for my grandchildrens." It makes more sense now that she still speaks to me out of a 1950's maid's voice. She has found a work rela-tionship that feeds it.

It adds a new dimension to the way Santana avoids the toys and the blocks and games, how suspicious she is of children who look like another boy her age whom she observes daily living a life so different from her own.

When will Santana see herself as one of the rest of us? Will she ever? When will she move into classrooms as if she belongs equally in every corner, not just in the art corner?

Gran's style does not match my own in many respects, but she does have a memory somewhere of what is absolutely essential. Although she may actualize it from the back door, she knows that a child with-out valentines to hand out to everyone might as well stay home that day. I remember her saying to me last year when she came into the room, "You make sure every child gets one, every one of 'em. I told San you give all these children a card and one to yourself, too. All the children deserves to get valentines."

I looked at the boxes of valentines she was putting in the cart and wonder if she had not been able to purchase them until tonight, when she got paid. I watched Santana drooping on the handle of the cart and remembered how Gran had told me on more than one occasion, "I didn't think I would ever be raising my grandchildren. I'm old and tired but I got smarter when I got older and this time I'm going to do it right. You got to keep your eyes open . . . be smart. You got to let these children today know you gonna be on top of things, be at the school, keep them with you all the time they not at school. You got to protect their little feelings." She didn't add it, of course, but I can almost finish the phrase myself with "and make sure they all get valentines."

Santana's third-grade teacher came to me early on. She was witnessing a gradual increase in the withdrawal behaviors that I had seen, that blank face of noncompliance. Apparently, Santana's mother had returned in the spring of Santana's second-grade year. As more contact was made over the summer, Santana began to withdraw again, according to Gran, who dropped by my room during fall conferences that third-grade year. However, the mother's return to drugs caused child protective services to terminate parental rights. Full custody was given to Gran. I cannot say with certainty that the mother was the only issue with Santana, but the events I was able to observe indicate a strong connection between contact with her mother and the periods of withdrawal. I worried about Santana, wondering what she had been through, wondering what that final separation might do, wondering if I had a complete picture, and wondering how Gran could cope financially.

A few weeks ago, Santana's teacher stopped me as we made our way to bus duty. Her hands on her hips, she said, with a twinkle in her lament, "Well, Hankins, I've been meaning to tell you to stop worrying! Santana definitely found her voice. I don't think she has spent a silent moment in my presence in 3 weeks!"

"Really!?" My relief had to show.

She read my pleased inquiry and added humorously, "If she didn't have a smile that melts my heart, I'd be ready to put a sock in her mouth!" Just about that time, Santana rounded the corner. She stopped to give me her signature hug: tentative, one armed, quick, with head down, on the run. I held on to her arm as she stood between me and her teacher. "Are you having a great year or what?" I asked her. She grinned. I pointed my thumb to her young, pretty, energetic new teacher and asked, "So, tell me about this mean old teacher you got?" Santana always "got" my humor. Her answer was to throw *both* arms tightly around the new teacher's waist and giggle! As she moved on toward the bus, her teacher said, "You know, there's just something special about that little girl . . . and does she ever love to read."

"Does she still draw?"

"When she isn't cutting and pasting, which is most of the time. She manages to find glue, and scissors even, to put things on her math papers! She is the original cut-and-paste queen."

Who knows? Maybe she will enlarge on that talent someday, using it to feed her creativity. Something as simple as school glue mixed with the complicated need of staying out of the way in the "White folk's house" may be the unexpected melding of chaotic necessity that inspires an artist.

We watched her lope to the bus in her distinctive way. What a long way she has come from being that little girl so determined to stay silent, angry with anyone who would invade her need to withdraw, always suspicious of the way her thoughts sounded once spoken. I stood absorbing the happy thought that she's a reader, a hugger, *and* a talker. I realized that it truly is the ordinary, the taken-for-granted, parts of our lives that we should celebrate. In Santana, the expected behaviors of an 8-year-old girl sparkled with enough new light to remind me that, in fact, the acts of reading, and of hugging and talking, are gifts to all of us. In this case they were gifts of greater portion because they were filling in what had been absent for so long. They were the very gifts I had hoped for her to have.

Nickole

Just this morning, I saw that tall shadow of a girl at the doorway of my classroom, her eyes asking the question, Will you still want to see me? She reads the answer in my move toward her, and she opens her arms wide to hug me and wants to stay wrapped in a hug, or holding my hands, facing me during the whole conversation. I notice that she has been pulling her hair out again; I see one spot the size of a 50¢ piece, the same place she kept bald most of the first-grade year. I ask her how school is going, if she is doing what the teacher asks, and she nods, only half way listening. She is more interested to find out from me why I had rearranged the room from when she was "little." Her eyes and questions hold more than a hint of chastisement, an attitude of how dare you! "Where is Patches?" she demanded, referring to a favorite stuffed doll the children cared for and read to that year. She is relieved to spot him on the window ledge right next to a "baby doll," newly acquired, that she charged "*we* didn't have." Where is the puppet theater, the tape recorder, the clay table? She locates each, looking past me with her eyes, then she is off, following a friend to class.

Of all the children, I have had the least contact with Nickole. Much that I hear is negative and disheartening. She has become a master at using her emotional outbursts to manipulate others and has added theft to the destructive behaviors she practices. She has a quick and practiced hand. One day in second grade, she managed to return to the classroom as the class walked in line to lunch, remove a sizable amount of money from the student teacher's hidden purse, and get back into line without being detected. When the teacher saw her purchase ice cream with a large bill, she wondered about it. But it was not until the student teacher went back for her purse and reported money missing that Nickole was questioned. Her story that her mom gave it to her didn't check out with mom. She was suspended. It was not her first suspension; nor has it been her last.

She participated sporadically in group therapy offered by Human Resources but the kind of intense one-on-one therapy she needed just isn't available for free. Both the teacher and the mother thought the sessions exacerbated her behavior. She stopped going. Then as new behaviors surfaced, therapy would be tried again. The truth is that the intervention available through public mental health services is not intensive enough for her needs. She was able to do everything that was offered academically in her class but much of the time was unwilling to comply with assignments.

This year I learned that she has started some fires, small and contained, but with the express purpose of destruction. What scream for help do the fires represent? What heat from inside her cannot be contained and extinguished? Where is the help, the solace, the power, to give her some sense of peace from the fires that rage? I have always believed that persons who have the power to destroy also have the power to build. I pray that she can be helped to find her positive power before she destroys herself with a confirmation that she is as bad as she thinks she is.

She visits me infrequently but her visits have often carried the same mission. She brings in photographs of herself to show me. They are usually professional studio pictures of her with her foster family, or a picture that her teacher made of her at school. I remember after a trying and moody morning during her year with me, how she had turned on the charm for the school photographer on picture day. When the pictures came back, I was absolutely stunned at how beautifully he had captured her. I think I was stunned at how beautiful she really was, after seeing her face so often distorted by a tantrum. I asked her foster mother if I could have one of the wallet-sized ones. I kept it inserted in the corner of a frame on the wall by my desk. On bad days I looked at what the picture showed she could be. She knew I loved that photograph. Now she shares, on occasion, what she can share of herself with me. Even if the photograph is a false front, I think it speaks of what she hopes to convey, what she wishes we and she could see, what she dreams of sustaining. There is a sliver of hope in the twinkle of her eyes, in the confidence of her raised chin, and in the peaceful slope of her shoulders in all the photographs . . . a picture of what can be.

Yet of all the children, Nickole is the only one that I meet in those nightmares where things appear normal and then go terribly wrong. It is always just her face that I see, with the one-dimensional smile that, like all smiles in such pictures, hides all turmoil and pain. I seem to dream it when I have heard something about her that is troubling—as so much of what I hear is. The dream may be my way of expressing my hope that she continues to look for the joy and the peace that the picture captured even if they were only fleeting. I just hope she doesn't give up the search. I keep hearing the lines of a hymn I particularly like, one not unlike the Edgar Allan Poe verse reproduced at the beginning of this chapter and not unlike the song from *Carousel*. "*O joy that seekest me through pain/I cannot close my heart to thee/I chase a rainbow through the rain and feel the promise is not vain/That morn shall tearless be*" (Matheson & Peace, 1882).

Tommy

Yesterday Tommy was rewarded by the principal during our televised morning announcements. He didn't have a reading log at home over the holidays. So he kept a list of all the reading he did over winter break on his own paper. He had read close to 1,000 minutes in the month of December outside school time. I think I felt a little like a parent when he got that award. What a reader!

I have two Kodak-moment memories of Tommy, one as opposite from the other as it could possibly be. The first is of his surprised, breathless look the day he realized he had read that book by himself, and the other is, well . . .

Shortly after Tommy and I shared our elation in that unforgettable twirl around the room, we had to take the Iowa Test of Basic Skills. We did the usual things to prepare for a standardized test. I showed them how to bubble in and we practiced focusing and listening and thinking silently instead of out loud. I told them that we were going to take a reading test and I saw Tommy beam. He was pumped, ready. Of course, he had no idea that the test wasn't about reading but was about assessing one's ability to think like those in the middle-class mainstream.

Still, he zipped through the decoding and the questions for which he had to match a picture to the last word in a sentence. But when it came time to read the longer passages, in which the illustrations were key clues to the story, he became frustrated.

He had never been on an airplane, never seen his mother off on a business trip from an airport, and never been on a camping trip. Such scenarios were depicted in the illustrations for the stories that the first graders had to read. For the most part, the illustrations were not within his lived experience, leaving him and many others without the ability to draw inferences or make predictions about the text.

He became more and more frustrated. I went to him when I saw him pointing to the words as he tried to hide the tears he was flicking away from his eyes. He was looking at a picture of a family eating hot dogs. There was a tented pop-up camper in the background.

"It's OK, Tommy. Just do the best you can do," I whispered to him.

"But I can't make it say *circus*." He whispered.

I patted him on the back and said, "Don't worry about it."

I understood in that moment that whoever sought information about Tommy from that test would learn nothing about his desire to read, nothing about his excitement over his newfound skill, nothing about his determined effort on the test. They wouldn't know that a small traveling circus had come to our town that year and that many of the children, including Tommy, had experienced it. The circus people had their little trailers and campers and pop-up tents in a circle close to the big top. I had also seen them, along with the community tables set up in the middle of them. The people who will look at test scores can't see that connection, and in the context of that test I couldn't build on that connection either. It was a lost hour for him, but an hour I remember, because it holds that second Kodak moment of Tommy. I will never be able to clear my mind of the defeat I saw in his face as he tried to read in the artificial context of a test—a context that no matter how you present it translates as important.

You see, the bad thing that happens to us—and it does happen to the most enlightened of teachers at times—is that we allow ourselves to be governed by that test. It happens when test scores "drop" and we begin to talk about children as their test scores define them. We see the children as making *us* look bad when they test poorly. The public and their parents see us as making the kids look bad when they don't score well. So there builds a wild fury of teaching kids to score well on "the" test, which of course reduces the time we have to spend on more appropriate reading and writing. Everybody loses except the people who make and sell the test, and those who sell test-preparation materials.

The positives in that year far outweighed the negatives, and Tommy ended the year with a bang. Unfortunately, at the end of the year Eric moved to another state. I'll never forget the way Tommy and Eric hugged each other as school ended and Tommy boarded the bus. He looked back out the window until the bus turned the corner. Eric's mother had come to say good-bye to all of us. The family was leaving for Brazil the next morning and from there would move to their new home in Florida. As the boys waved, Eric's mother said through her tears, "This is so hard. I don't think the boys realize how permanent this is."

About 6 months after Eric moved, I asked Tommy if he'd heard from him. "No, it costs money to call where he lives now." He was matter-of-fact, tough, as always. Then he added, "I've got a game today. We haven't lost even one game yet!"

"Well, great! What team is it?"

He didn't hear me. A quick slap on the shoulder caused him to run, suddenly intent on beating his friend to the bus.

"Bye, Ms. Hankins!" he said breathlessly.

He darted expertly, climbed the bus steps, and turned to gloat just as the shoulder slapper got to the bus. They gave each other a high five and got on the bus together.

Kenny

Today I saw Kenny leaning up against the wall with the other after-school program kids, waiting to go into the gym to play basketball. Word has it that he is a talented player, but he has difficulty being coached. He bristles at direction, reprimand, forced drill and practice. He whines over fouls and has had to sit out a number of times during practice. The coach knows he's good, though, and keeps after him.

He grinned when he saw me and was ready to tell me play by play about the game he had been in last night. His excited narrative was full of gestures. The movements of his tall body were alternately childlike and adolescent, as was his voice. His eyes sparkled brighter the longer he talked and held my attention.

He has come a long way in a year from the backward emotional spiral he took in second grade, a spiral that was building when that school year ended. He had multiple screaming tantrums that could be heard in the next hallway. I hate tantrums, but they signal an immaturity that I can deal with at one level. I tell myself that I am smarter than an emotional 2-year-old who is unable to express himself properly. I just ride the tantrums out. When tantrums are replaced by more serious acting-out, I am more often at a loss. What happened next was no tantrum. In the spring of Kenny's second-grade year, his teacher saw me walking by the principal's office and motioned for me to come in. She was with the principal and Kenny was with her. She was having him show the principal what he had shown her.

He lifted the sleeve of his shirt and showed me three scars, lines about a half inch in length that had been scratched deep into his skin in an amateur hacking of pen and ink. The scars were ugly and raised, possibly as permanent as a tattoo. He said, "Some big boys did this to me if I helped them. They said I belong to them now cause I am marked. But I got scared. They said if I told anybody they would hurt my brother and find my sisters. They said they would kill me if I told. That boy named _____ already shot a bunch a people. He the one shot my cousin's hand off and got him put in jail."

I was not sure what had happened in the office up to that moment or in the classroom earlier, or if he was in some kind of trouble for behavior. I think back on it and feel embarrassed that I never stopped to consider that my only place was to listen. But I was seized with a white-hot bolt to the stomach at the same time that I began to freeze all over. I went into emergency mode, I guess, and took over, uninvited. I knelt in front of him and said, "Kenny, tell the truth. I want to hear you say it out loud why you were not afraid to tell Ms. Todd. You know why you told your teacher. You told Ms. Todd because she cares for you. You told us because you *know* that you belong to this school family. People here care about you. Nobody *here* will hurt you or your family. But Kenny, those boys you are hanging out with are dangerous. They don't play around."

"I know they dangerous. My auntie told them to never come on our street again or she'll call the police."

I asked if we had a school T-shirt. We dug around in the closet, found one, and put it on him right then.

"Now, that tells people something you belong to that you can be proud of. You were smart to tell us and your auntie was smart to tell them to stay away. You listen to what she says and if they bother you again you tell one of us at school or call the police yourself."

As he waited outside the door, we were afraid to utter the word. I think we whispered it simultaneously . . . *gang*. In our small city, the general public believes that there are no gangs. The word on the street is another matter. Children are being preyed upon to run drug money, to carry weapons, and to be "slaves" to those who are older. They are having to go through initiation rites that can include bringing a weapon to school, taking school equipment, or stealing money. I wanted to call the police immediately! My principal's more measured response, one that correctly followed protocol, was better.

She called the security officer at the district central office. He contacted the police, who confirmed what Kenny had reported to us. The boys were already being watched and this was more needed firsthand evidence. They would follow up.

I had once remarked to my husband that Kenny was a child who was likely to belong to a gang or cult someday. He would be enchanted with the idea of a "'hood," of being a "homeboy." He so desperately needed to belong to something. I just didn't think the chance would present itself so soon. I think he was surprised himself. Why else would he have told? Surely his telling was a way of checking to see if anyone else would lay claim to him.

A fortunate thing happened. A teacher in our school fell into a mentor relationship with Kenny's little brother and through that relationship began to include Kenny as well. She takes him places, brings him books and clothes. She makes sure that he attends any special school events on evenings and weekends. She sees the gifts that shine through his faults. She has stayed on top of things now for almost 2 years. He trusts her. She has been a strong link in a chain of people who have given attention to this little boy in trouble. She has shown the patience of one who absolutely will not allow the negative to overpower the positive. "A person can be whole if they have but one strong connection, one unconditional relationship" (J. Dagley, personal communication, October 3, 1998). I think of the ways that school has been a sustaining force in Kenny's life and feel a sense of pride in the quiet strength of our profession.

When the coach opened the door of the gym, Kenny was in midsentence. He stopped immediately and rushed to get in line again.

Just after he went into the gym, his mentor stopped by the room. A DFACS worker had informed her that Kenny and his little brother had been released for adoption. What a spot of hope! What could it mean to be taken into a home by a family who could remind you over and over again that they had handpicked you? For that matter, what could it mean to adopt a child who is so willing to love? It's hard to say who would be luckier.

Randel

I will always remember the second-grade play that following year, knowing that the children on stage were the same children I had become so absorbed in writing about over the summer. The play/musical was about learning to live together in peace and harmony. The finale was a song we had sung almost daily the year before and contained the message that *the world is a rainbow of people.*

Randel was in the front row of the chorus, slightly left of center stage. Alhough the "stars" of the show were front and center, it was Randel who captured the attention of many. The people next to me were talking during the song:

"Look at that kid next to Mary. He got the moves don't he."

"Um-hum. I been watchin' him too . . . Move just like a preacher."

"He's the cutest thing I ever saw!" Delighted laughter infused all their comments.

"He into it now! Look at him."

"Y'all seeing that little boy?" asked someone in front of them.

"What church he go to I wonder? He got it going!"

They had seen it too.

After the play, I spoke to the children I knew, congratulating them on a job well done. I told Randel what I'd heard the women next to me saying about him. He just smiled. I asked him if he still "preached."

"I'm not old enough to preach yet. I sing in the choir," he told me. Clearly, he was moving the idea of preaching out of the realm of playing with his sister.

"Well, I will always remember the time you preached for us in first grade."

He looked as if he were trying to remember which time I was talking about. I realized then that for him, preaching that day truly had been a natural response, not one that he had perceived as pivotal or extraordinary. It had made its way into the meshing of all school days for him.

"Well, you'll grow into it," I said.

He blushed and ducked his head. He smiled a genuine, acknowledging smile.

Just yesterday I saw him getting in line on the playground with his third-grade class. He answered my hello with a wave of the hand and little eye contact, his eyes focused instead on the ball he carried as he defended his place in line from would-be "cutters." He wore a new silver cross, a Christmas gift, I suppose. He had never been without his gold cross, even in first grade. I had asked his teacher, just before she blew her whistle, how he was doing.

She hesitated. "Well . . . all right. He works hard, tries his best. He doesn't get into trouble. But . . ."

"Not at the top of the academic ladder?"

"It's not that. Oh, I don't know. It's just that he seems sad to me."

"I saw some of that to," I remembered this sadness as I answered her.

The task of herding children into a building, helping them make the unwelcome transition from the whooping freedom of play to the decorum required in the strictly enforced "quiet zone" surrounding other classrooms, took her full attention away from our conversation. She and the class entered the building. I noticed that Randel complied with every request she made.

That conversation did nothing to help me erase the recent contact I had had with him. I had boarded a bus at the request of my principal. It was fully loaded, ready to leave. I boarded this bus with at least four other teachers to keep order while the driver gave the principal a list of children he was suspending from the bus for bad behavior. This bus is notorious; everyone knows its number and that it is usually associated with the word *bad*. It is the most crowded of our afternoon buses, with a daily load of three to a seat. It travels to a neighborhood widely considered a ghetto, and so this bus was provided with all the expected requisites. The belief that the children needed six teachers on that bus to maintain order, to keep fights from breaking out, was not without justification. A history of one or two teachers not having enough eyes to keep children from fighting on another occasion had increased the vigilance the principal employed that day.

Still, I felt guilty, with all of us behaving like wardens in this bus that was so quickly heating up from the afternoon sun and the press of so many little bodies in close contact. I smiled at the rows of children closest to me. They smiled back. One kindergartner fell asleep. Looking toward the back of the bus, farther away, I caught sight of Randel. He was sitting alone, his seat mates, who had been taken off the bus to be disciplined, standing outside with the driver and the principal. I couldn't catch his eye. He was staring out the window, seemingly deep in thought, while he fingered his cross, which glinted in the reflection in the window. That cross, I had never seen him without one, seemed to fit his 9-year-old body better than it had the tiny first-grade body that I remembered so well.

When the driver returned with the offenders and handed out several disciplinary notices, I learned that one of the infractions that had occurred had involved Randel having been taunted. The name-calling included the terms *gay boy* and *sissy*. He is only 9 years old, too young to have a smile that came less often than it had and that was full of suspicion when it did come.

He is already coming up against the shadow side of having a heightened, precocious sensitivity to the larger issues of life. I can remember the tears of sympathy he shed for others in our class. I recall the responses he had to literature; these came from a deep observation of human nature and his belief in rules to live by. Remembering his strengths helps me carry the hope that he will be able to fall eventually on the strong side of that thin line between make or break, between wounded and healer.

I search back to that second-grade play and see again the energy that came from every part of him, from his eyebrows and fingertips. There was not one ounce of him that was still or silent when he sang, *"Now you be you and I'll be me, that's the way we were meant to be . . ."*

I hope he appreciates the very special "me" he is becoming long enough to overcome the battering that comes from being bullied and taunted. I believe he has the gift to help us all someday.

NOTES FROM THE CHILDREN

I hope this present-tense writing about the children has given you some sense of where they are now, a few years away from that first-grade year. It is true that they remain within the definition of "the children I worry about most," some of them more than others. They all wear the serious face of one going into battle, of jumping hurdles that children should not be expected to deal with. They also wear the faces of academic progress, faces that project a sense of attachment and belonging to the school community. I see each of them often enough to realize that, with the exception of Clarrissa, I am simply one of their used-to-be teachers, one who is, quite appropriately, occupying less and less memory in their minds. While my writing about them made a tremendous difference in our yearlong school time, it would take a trip to the future to know what difference we made in our collective destiny. In reality, they molded me more than I could possibly have molded them.

The final shaping word or lesson I take from them, and the one I offer to you, is a word of hope. For in their particular ways they all face the future with hope. From Randel's insisting, "I'm going to be a preacher when I grow up," to Kenny's query to the visitor, "Know why they call me the professor? 'Cause I might be one someday!" to Nickole's constant reminders to me about what treat she was trying to earn, each spoke in some way of a hopeful future.

On the last day of school, I always ask the children to tell me what they will remember about me and what they want me to remember about them. It has become an exercise in allowing the memories we have made together to lend an air of grace to the present at the same time that we are depositing those memories more exactly into a treasure we all can take from in the future.

In their childlike way, they wrote; and they all included illustrations depicting happy faces, rainbows, balloons, clouds, and flowers. They told me what to remember about them. For the most part these were typical things, and only by knowing the children can you fully appreciate their statements. (I have edited their statements and corrected their spelling for ease of reading.)

Randel wrote: I will remember you. Will you remember I can sing and remember me how I build good in blocks?

Kenny wrote: I will remember when you standed on the roof and I want you to remember about me that I am smart.

Tommy wrote: I will remember you gave us chocolate pizza and blowed bubbles. I want you to remember when I didn't know how to read but now I can.

Santana wrote: I remember when we read 500 books and you was a clown. I want you to remember ME when you grow up old.

Nickole wrote: I remember when we read 500 books and about Peter Rabbit and I love you. I want you to remember that you will take me to a movie [a treat she had earned]. Do it tomorrow.

Clarrissa wrote: I remember when we walked outside and Mrs. Hankins I want you to remember that you love *me*!

I first saw those writings and heard them read aloud as we sat in our final circle before the bell rang on the last day of school. When I read them now, I can still hear and feel that whole afternoon. I can hear the pride in their voices, hear the giggles of support, and feel the almost tangible anticipation of vacation. I remember thinking that the clock would never move quickly enough and wishing at the same time that it would slow down so that I could bask a bit longer in the grace that came into that circle. I would long remember the smiles, giggles, and genuine shared friendship evident among the children as they nodded and otherwise reacted as each child read his or her "I remember" statements. As wild and stormy a ride as we'd made together, we had bonded in a strength that may not be repeated in my career. Our memories were full and our futures open.

As we filed out of the building that final day, I looked especially hard at the line of kindergarten children leaving the building with us, knowing that some of them would come through my door in the fall.

Although I felt the tiredness that one allows only when one's race is run, I also felt that familiar wave of energy for beginning again—I felt hope.

SUSTAINING HOPE

Lately, I have sensed a loss of hope among colleagues in education. The things I hear in conversations suggest a niggling though unspoken fear that the children we teach are the by-products of a world in decline. We wonder aloud how much longer we will teach and why it is that we seem to be failing. When I hear the judgments that are attached to the necessity of teaching "other people's children," I am reminded of the soldier's lament in the song "Bui Doi," from the musical *Miss Saigon* (Schonberg & Boublil, 1989). The soldier sings of the mixed-race children left behind in Vietnam after the war, shunned by both sides and *"called Bui Doi, the dust of life, conceived in hell and born in strife."* I find myself hearing those words in the context of my life and see instead the children of poverty and of the drug culture, children of abuse and neglect, children marginalized because they are not fluent speakers of English. I hear the soldier sing, and thinking of many of my students, know they too are America's *"living reminders of all the good we failed to do."*

Instead of losing hope as I focus on my own plight in a widening culture shock, it would be ethical for me to confess as the song continues that *"deep in [my] heart [I] know they are all [my] children too."* It would be ethical for all of us to rid ourselves of a dichotomous vocabulary that shuns the children of poverty and to go into legislative battle for them. It would be ethical for me to become a more informed, more enlightened voter; to let that vote be more reflective of my practice; and to become a more outspoken voice, speaking from the ranks of education to the voting public.

As we try to expand our teaching craft to meet varied ways of learning and to honor all cultures, it is easy to lose hope when the learning curve doesn't correlate overnight with the amount of energy that goes into our planning. More despair than hope comes across in conversations about standardized test scores and the unfortunate assumptions that politicians encourage the public to link to them. I refer back to the picture of defeat I carry of Tommy and the test. Teachers are currently being defined by their students' standardized test scores. We teach in the knowledge that such a correlation without a narrative context is ridiculous and serves only to undermine real progress in schools. Tests of that nature serve, in my opinion, to reify a middle-class protocol and power structure and are driven by a fear of a diverse United States. Have you noticed that the more diverse our school populations become, the more uniform the assessments? If it is true that teachers touch the future in a way that no other profession does, then it is also true that the current thrust toward uniform standardized testing is a move back into a more homogeneous past. When schools serving children of poverty and children of color are the ones most often cited as failing, without regard to non-standardized-tested curriculum and these children's progress in other areas, everyone suffers. Deciding that schools are good or bad based on one week and one test allows an ill-informed public to draw one of two conclusions: either poor children of color "can't" learn or their teachers "don't, can't, or won't" teach them. It is then that I tend to bristle, become defensive, anxious for myself and my little ones. The publication of test scores, which I rarely find surprising or enlightening in any way, does nothing to enhance my teaching. It does nothing to inspire my students or me, to build dreams, to boost confidence, or to actualize promise.

In addition, current human world events can seem crushing and do have an impact on the micro world of school. Hope is somewhat eclipsed when staff meetings focus on revising emergency-preparedness plans to cover bomb threats and mass shootings. We go in and out of school suppressing a fear of that catastrophic possibility, pushing back any thought that those skills may actually be called for at a moment's notice. But subconsciously, the possibility, that waking nightmare, we imagine shakes our hopes.

When I begin to absorb too much of the negative, begin to question a positive future for education, second-guess my ability to teach, I like to reread the I-remember letters from the end of each school year, those written words from my children. The scrawling letters and roughly representative illustrations from real little hands holding fat red pencils and worn-down crayons center me again. I am reminded of a passage I read in *Amazing Grace* (Kozol, 1995) a book about the horrors of life in the South Bronx. Kozol admittedly struggled with his own ability to walk in and out of a ghetto that seemingly held its inhabitants hostage. In the middle of the worst moments, he found himself needing a ray of light, a word of the future, a sigh of hope. To find it he visited the children—at school.

> When I look for hope these days, I tend to look less often to external signs of progress such as housing reconstruction . . . than to words and prayers of children and the spiritual resilience of so many of them. It is above all

the very young whose luminous capacity for tenderness and love and a transcendent sense of faith in human decency give me reason for hope. (Kozol, 1995, p. xiv)

In that spirit, I bolster my commitment to writing that centers my vision on the very young, for that vision reminds me that once I was a child too. In that same spirit I urge us to be vessels of hope for our students, to catch and hold the hope that brims over from them. As we walk into school each morning, it can help to remember that we don't walk in alone. We are accompanied by the hopes of the child we once were and by the dreams for us from those who, as Fred Rogers puts it, "loved us into being" (Junod, 1999). We walk in the wake of other teachers, those whom we have known, as well as those who are connected to us only by the common choice of profession. We must name, among those who continue to bring us into being, teachers who act on the hope they have for humanity, the promise they see in people that gives sustenance to their hope. We must also name the children who call us into being every morning. Surely, if we walk with hope, we will deliver hope as well.

Indeed, the cornerstone of education is hope. Teachers pull from a wellspring of hope on a minute-by-minute basis. We confess, if only in action, to a strong narrative of hope. We act on the assurance that by teaching, we protect the future. We are, after all, the future that was once hoped for and imagined by those who taught *us*.

The need for hope is not new to our generation. While we walk in the shadow of the events of September 11, 2001, our own teachers walked through the shadows of the Cold War. We are living through the dark fear of terrorism, of drive-by shootings and a rising climate of hate crimes, but our teachers lived through the constant talk of a nuclear arms race that threatened to annihilate us all. Still, they came to teach, to act out their hope of easing the present in order to build a future. From those classrooms in which we sat came presidents and prisoners, givers and takers, artists and corporate heads. There emerged rock stars and rabbis, inventors of personal computers and cell phones, doctors and drug lords, and, of course, teachers—they will be born in our classrooms as well.

There was a time when research meant hard science, things one could see. There was no room in the discussion for ideas as nebulous as hope or faith or dreams. Even when research turned to the interpretive nature of ethnographic method, we were quick to add disclaimers on ambiguity or double meanings. Perhaps it was when research took writers such as Jonathan Kozol into very near though still "foreign" places in our own country (places we ignore at best and hide from view at worst) that we began to look less suspiciously at concepts such as despair, resilience, and hope and to recognize in a very real way how varying degrees of these are attached to performance.

Hope need not be relegated to a purely contemplative idea. I put the word *hope* into the computer's thesaurus. More than 20 synonyms and links came up. Some I expected, such as *belief*, *dreams*, or *inspiration*. Others are more likely to be associated with action and are more freely used in research: *expectations*, *aspiration*, *ambition*, *encouragement*, *confidence*, *prospect*, *aptitude*, *capability*, *endeavor*, *goal*, *motivation*, *promise*, *possibility*, *potential*, *purpose*, *reassurance*, *anticipation*, and *support*. These words all define what education is all about: the boldness of being human and the possibilities that exist in our interactions with one another and with the world.

In a place as defined by humanness as school, there can be no serious learning without all the synonyms for *hope*; and without them, there is certainly no reason to teach.

RAISING THE TEACHER'S VOICE

The world needs to be reminded from inside the ranks who we are who call ourselves *teacher*. People who read newspapers and magazines and academic journals need to have a more thorough picture of the myriad faces, the profusion of brain power, and the gift of varied points of view that we offer.

It is imperative that we write and speak our teacher voices in whatever ways we can, explaining who we are and what we do, what we see and hear, what we know to be true of children (Dewey, 1904; Greene, 1995). My way was to sing songs of hope despite the storms and to speak in the way in which clarity finally came to me—slowly, recursively, in and out of confusion—by writing narratives. Then I tried to explain by example what had happened to me because of the writing. Telling my own story, my way, convinces me that the real hope of education lies in the connecting points teachers make between our own stories and the stories of those we teach. Being accepted as a writer, despite the nonlinear construction of my writing, teaches me to be open to varied, unexpected narrative styles offered by my students and their parents. To become more open I begin by listening more to the message than to its construction. For certainly as we look for a firm footing in the realness of the worlds merging in our classrooms, "the central concern is not how the narrative text is constructed, but rather how it operates as an instrument of mind in the construction of [that] reality" (Bruner, 1995). Beginning with the very young, our classrooms must vibrate with wider definitions of narrative "that include talking, writing, dancing, drawing, painting, and singing an understanding of the world" (Gallas, 1994). Then the narratives of teachers must surge into the world of research with an equally wide definition of ways of communicating our own impressions of the world, specifically the reality of life in classrooms.

My narrative construction of the world is admittedly shaped by the songs that run though my head; I will never ignore them in the future.

"You'll Never Walk Alone" had played in my head long and strong enough to be included in my writing, especially after I attended to the words, which for me, represented a powerful serendipity. Just as when I write the classroom narratives, reflecting on the song made me curious about its larger context, a deeper look into its history.

I called my dad. He is the resident repository of all Broadway musicals past and present. A playbill's synopsis of the storyline may read differently than Daddy's narrative on it, because the main character for him was the one he remembered longest. He informed me of the context of the song immediately and it was easy for me to understand why this scene had not left his memory, one-time principal that he was. The setting for this song from *Carousel* (Rodgers & Hammerstein, 1945) was a graduation ceremony. The principal of the school took the podium and delivered a message of encouragement to a student body still grappling with a tough and tragic year. She urged them to walk into life's storms with hope and the sure knowledge that golden skies would follow. Daddy remembered that a girl in the class encountered a life-changing "visit" from her dead father, who came in the form of a ghost to stand beside her during the principal's speech. In what Dad termed a "classic Broadway moment," the crescendo of music pulled all the students into the song, and as the girl's father receded into the spirit world, she stood and joined in the singing as well, with its soaring injunction to walk on with hope in your heart.

Even as he talked, I was impressed with the connections to the final narratives the song held for me: the context of the last day of school; the memory of a father and the strength it gave the daughter; the obvious play on levels of time, past, present, and future, held in that scene; and the strong reference to carrying "hope" as a traveling companion into the classroom each day. In the end, of course, it was the educator's taking the challenging role of holding hope up to her students as boldly as she knew how in the face of all she knew they had experienced and were facing.

As the dreams embodied in the ideal of a quality education for all are being "tossed and blown" about as so much confetti in a spring wind, it becomes apparent that those dreams depend on today's educators modeling and reinforcing hope, walking into school carrying all those synonymns I listed earlier. We must exude *confidence, ambition,* and *aspiration,* regardless of pejorative misrepresentations of teachers in the popular press or in the minds of legislators. We must provide *encouragement, motivation,* and *support,* regardless of the ways that standardized tests falsely define our students. We are the harbingers of *faith, reassurance,* and *inspiration,* in the face of the violence that threatens the peace in our schools. Our demeanor must project *goals, high expectations,* and *purpose* in the midst of the standard chaos inherent in classroom profiles and management. Our vocabulary must acknowledge the *promise, possibility,* and *potential* inherent in every student, despite the growing number of bridges we are compelled to create between ourselves and complicated, diverse classrooms.

Personally, I hold on to the dream by writing, largely for myself, in quiet streams of journaled thoughts. It is there where I confront the possibility that I am both problem and possibility for children; where I understand that I am ripe with the ability to undermine or to resurrect ideas that sprout from the minds of the very young; where I acknowledge that I am the standard bearer of an attitude that offers either despair to those who sense their sojourn outside of my expectations or hope in the common ground we share. It is into the written confrontation of those realities that I add the songs and poetry that offer me hope. I add them in the margins of my own words and wonder at the ability of lyricists to have penned the words of so many unsuspecting hearts.

Melodies, lyrics, and stories replay themselves when once they penetrate one's psyche in the same way that smells evoke memories. It is hard at times to know whether an event brought me back to the song or whether the song led me to the event. It is sometimes difficult to ascertain exactly how many times I've "heard" the song before I realized I was singing it. And yet it plays from start to finish, beginning over and over again, much like the recursive nature of our narratives. We replay often the narratives we attach to ourselves and to those we know, traveling back and forth between present and past. We act on them without realizing we are replaying them. Just as often, we tell the old family stories over and over, to connect our past to the present and to the future. It is appropriate to let Charles's story, like the songs and the narratives of our lives, bring us full circle to the place in which we began.

Charles

That frightening first visit and the haunting words from Charles about guns in the pocketbook—which caused me immediately to remember his mother's clinch-pat-release, clinch-pat-release—are small memories now in comparison to those of the rest of the year and the multitude of other contacts we had together. I try to guess when the relationship turned around for us.

Was it the night I visited Charles's home and watched three little brown children, fresh from the bathtub, in white thermal pajamas tussle with one another and their white fluffy puppy? I had laughed so hard, admitting I couldn't tell where one kid ended and another began; they were all arms, legs, and little round bellies. Charles's mother had responded then, "Now, you see, at home they mostly just kids, just three kids. One don't get treated different from the others."

Was it when he had the first of three eye surgeries and she called me nightly to report his progress and to express concern over his coming back to school?

Was it when, shortly after surgery, he became ill at school and was afraid to stay in the clinic with the nurse until Mom picked him up? When she came for him, he was asleep in my lap. Was it then that she began to decide I was not the enemy she had first thought me to be?

Perhaps it was when she came to me saying, "Charles wants to learn some spelling words but you know he just can't remember them. He really doesn't even know the letters from one day to the next." I nodded, holding my breath, as she slowly formed the question, "What's going to happen to him, really, Ms. Hankins, tell me what will happen? He can't just keep showing up to school now that he *knows* the others do things he can't do."

I knew, from years of experience, that she had come to the other side of a huge internal battle. That was the day she asked that he be tested for what she termed "special help." I moved slowly, removing myself from as much of the process as possible, remembering my promise to her in the beginning.

She had two surgeries herself at the end of the year, requiring a lengthy hospital stay. I had to take some documents by for her to sign. Was it during the time she signed the papers in that hospital bed that we developed a firmer trust in ourselves? when surrounded by the faces one always meets in hospital corridors we sensed our mutual vulnerability and felt no need of asserting our power? We spoke easily, the signatures anticlimactic.

Or was it in her honesty with me, her refusal to play games or to use rhetoric that I could not wade through, or to ever say anything she did not mean, that taught me to trust what she said?

It's hard to know when the fingers of hope begin to untangle the knots of distrust between people, allowing the links between them to stretch out in chainlike strength to do the work it is meant to do.

School had been out for just a week when she phoned me for the last time.

"You know they are holding Charles's report card till I pay for the library book he lost," she began. "So I haven't seen it yet and what I wondered is, what did you put about next year? I noticed it has a place for the next grade promoted to here on the other two kids' cards."

I told her it stated what we agreed on, second-grade classroom with special education pull-out sessions. She didn't say much in response, just "OK, then."

We exchanged some back-and-forth small-talk comments before she added, above the noise of children running and tussling in the background, "My kids are going to relatives in Virginia for the summer, they are already driving me crazy! I'm going to go back to school."

I congratulated her but made a joke about different ways to drive yourself crazy—such as going to school. She said that Charles had told her she might get a "way-to-go sticker if she did good for the teacher."

"Tell him you plan to be a star student!" I responded. It was a phrase I often used with Charles.

"I don't know about that but I do know one thing," she said, seriously now, "I know I enjoy you Ms. Hankins. I am really going to miss you. By the way . . . you are one *fine* teacher."

"So are you," I said, thankful for that unexpected gift of grace. "The feeling is mutual."

We were quiet for a minute before she ended with her trademark sign-off, "All-l-lright then . . . I hope I see you soon."

"Hoping makes it so," I answered back.

I smiled as I pressed the red button on the telephone marked "end."

Epilogue

As this book goes to press, my children are graduating to middle school, which begins in sixth grade in our community.

On graduation/honors day, I watched this group of children with more emotion than I have ever watched a graduating group. They marched in, tall, self-assured, and dressed up. Randel in a just-right-for-preaching solid white suit, tie, and shoes led them in. I was thrilled with the many awards the children from the year of El Niño received. I was especially proud of the reading achievement award that several received. Tommy, Clarrissa, and Randel also received awards honoring their perfect assignment records, all assignments (homework, class work, and projects) completed and in on time for the entire year. Nickole received a math award for excellent achievement. Charles was noted as an exceptional citizen in the school and was commended for outstanding reading improvement.

Santana and Kenny moved to another school last year, but their teachers report that each has made good academic progress.

Kenny's mother admirably worked to bring herself and her children back together. Kenny is happy with his whole family now. I understand that he is quite the basketball star as well.

Eric and his family have now moved to another mission field and he is, I'm sure, lighting up the fifth grade wherever he is.

Clarrissa has been writing her narrative to include our family since she was seven years old. Over the years she has spent weekends and holidays with us and she has asked me more than once point blank, "why can't you adopt me?" I am too old to have another small child I told her and did not go into the legal difficulties I imagined.

However, a sad and somewhat alarming phone call from her this Christmas Eve sent us to get her. Our intention was to treat her to a wonderful Christmas for several days.

But over the course of those few days she gave us a clearer picture of her plight. Our investigation began an unfolding of the oddest set of circumstances. Then, just like a surprise ending to a movie, she was placed with us.

When the social worker asked her if she wanted to stay at our house Clarrissa asked us two questions. First, she wanted to know if the whole family would vote that she could belong. So we all raised our hands in a big "aye."

Then she asked, "Will I have a picture on the wall . . . like the other kids?" Once I absorbed her meaning, I assured her that her picture would definitely go up on the wall. She sighed deeply, resolutely, and said, "I've always wanted to be a kid with a picture on the wall." Now, she is proving again the power of narrative to create our place in the world.

References

Adler, A. (1980). *What life should mean to you.* (A. Porter, Trans. & Ed.). New York: Putnam's Sons. (Original work published 1931)

Agar, M. (1980). *The professional stranger.* New York: Academic Press.

Allen, J. B., Shockley, B., & Michaelove, B. (1993). *Engaging children.* Portsmouth, NH: Heinemann.

Angelou, M. (1969). *I know why the caged bird sings.* New York: Bantam Books.

Apple, M. (1990). *Ideology and curriculm* (2nd ed.). New York: Routledge.

Ashton-Warner, S. (1963). *Teacher.* New York: Simon & Schuster.

Bakhtin, M. (1981). *The dialogic imagination: Four essays by M. M. Bakhtin.* Austin, TX: University of Texas Press.

Bateson, M. C. (1990). *Composing a life.* New York: Penguin Books.

Bell-Scott, P. (1994). *Life notes.* New York: Norton.

Berger, A. (1997). *Narratives in popular culture, media, and everyday life.* Thousand Oaks, CA: Sage.

Beuchner, F. (1982). *The sacred journey.* San Francisco: Harper.

Beuchner, F. (1991). *Telling secrets: A memoir.* San Francisco: Harper.

Beuchner, F. (1992). *Listening to your life.* San Francisco: Harper.

Britton, B., & Pellegrini, A. (Eds.). (1990). *Narrative thought and narrative language.* Hillsdale, NJ: Erlbaum.

Britton, J. (1978). The third area where we are more ourselves. In M. Meek, A. Warlow, & G. Barton (Eds.), *The cool web: The pattern of children's reading* (pp. 40–47). New York: Atheneum.

Britton, J. (1993). *Language and learning: The importance of speech in children's development* (2nd ed.). Portsmouth, NH: Heinemann.

Bruner, J. (1986). *Actual minds, possible worlds.* Cambridge, MA: Harvard University Press.

Bruner, J. (1994). Life as narrative. In A. Dyson & C. Genishi (Eds.), *The need for story: Cultural diversity in classroom and community* (pp. 28–37). Urbana, IL: National Council of Teachers of English.

Bruner, J. (1995). *The culture of education.* Cambridge, MA: Harvard University Press.

Buber, M. (1957). *Between man and man.* (R. G. Smits, Trans.). Boston: Beacon Press.

Burnette, F. (1987). *A little princess.* New York: Scholastic Books. (Original work published 1893)

Calkins, L. (1986). *The art of teaching writing.* Portsmouth, NH: Heinemann.

Cassirer, E. (1944). *An essay on man.* New Haven, CT: Yale University Press.

Childs, M. (1999). Helping teachers to act early in childhood education. *Research Reporter, 2*(1), 5–9.

Climo, S. (1989). *Egyptian Cinderella*. New York: Crowell.

Cochran-Smith, M. (1984). *The making of a reader*. Norwood, NJ: Ablex.

Cooley, C. (1956). *Human nature and social order*. Glencoe, IL: Free Press. (Original work published in 1902)

Cronon, W. (1992). A place for stories: Nature, history, and narrative. *Journal of American History, 78*(4), 1347–1376.

Cusick, P. (1973). *Inside high school: The student's world*. New York: Holt, Reinhart, and Winston.

Dagley, J. (1999). Adlerian family therapy. In A. M. Horne (Ed.), *Family counseling and therapy* (3rd ed.). Itasca, IL: F. E. Peacock.

Dandy, E. (1991). *Black communications: Breaking down the barriers*. Chicago: African American Images.

Delpit, L. (1995). *Other people's children: Cultural conflict in the classroom*. New York: New Press.

Denzin, N. (1989). *Interpretive biography*. Newbury Park, CA: Sage.

Dewey, J. (1904). The relation of theory to practice in education. In M. L. Borrowman (Ed.), (1965), *Teacher education in America: A documentary history*. New York: Teachers College Press.

Dewey, J. (1916). *Democracy and education: An introduction to the philosophy of education*. New York: Free Press.

Dorris, M. (1994). *Paper trail*. New York: HarperCollins.

Douglass, F. (1962). *Life and times of Frederick Douglass: Written by himself*. New York: Collier Books. (Original work published 1892)

Dyson, A., & Genishi, C. (1994). Introduction: The need for story. In A. H. Dyson & C. Genishi (Eds.), *The need for story: Cultural diversity in classroom and community* (p. 2). Urbana, IL: National Council of Teachers of English.

Emerson, R., Fretz, R., & Shaw, L. (1995). *Writing ethnographic fieldnotes*. Chicago, IL: University of Chicago Press.

Eusden, J., & Westerhoff, J. (1998). *Sensing beauty: Aesthetics, the human spirit, and the church*. Cleveland, OH: United Church Press.

Feinberg, W., & Soltis, J. (1992). *School and society*. New York: Teachers College Press.

Foster, M. (1997). *Black teachers on teaching*. New York: New Press.

Fountas, I., & Pinnell, G. (1996). *Guided reading: Good first teaching for all children*. Portsmouth, NH: Heinemann.

Freire, P. (1985). *The politics of education*. Granby, MA: Bergin & Garvey.

Friedman, W. (1990). *About time*. Cambridge, MA: MIT Press.

Gallas, K. (1994). *The languages of learning: How children talk, write, dance, draw, and sing their understanding of the world*. New York: Teachers College Press.

Gambrill, J. M. (Ed.). (1907). *Selections from Poe*. Boston: Ginn and Company.

Gates, D. (1968). *The blue willow*. New York: Scholastic. (Originial work published 1940)

Giroux, H., & McLauren, P. (Eds.). (1994). *Between borders.* New York: Routledge.

Greene, M. (1985). A philosophic look at merit and mastery in teaching. *Elementary School Journal, 86,* 17–26.

Greene, M. (1994). Multiculturalism, community, and the arts. In A. Dyson & C. Genishi (Eds.), *Need for story: Cultural diversity in classroom and community* (pp. 11–27). Urbana, IL: National Council of Teachers of English.

Greene, M. (1995). *Releasing the imagination: Essays on education, the arts, and social change.* San Francisco: Jossey-Bass.

Hamilton, V. (1985). *The people could fly: American Black folktales.* New York: Knopf.

Hankins, K. (1996). One moment in two times. *Teacher Research, 4*(1), 24–28.

Hankins, K. (1998). Cachophony to symphony: Memoirs in teacher research. *Harvard Educational Review, 68,* 80–85.

Hankins, K. (1999). Silencing the lambs. In J. B. Allen (Ed.), *Class action: Teaching for social justice in elementary and high school.* New York: Teachers College Press.

Hardy, B. (1978). Narrative as a primary act of mind. In M. Meek, A. Warlow, & G. Barton (Eds.), *The cool web: The pattern of children's reading* (pp. 12–23). New York: Atheneum.

Hatch, J., & Wisniewski, R. (1995). *Life history and narrative.* Washington, DC: Falmer Press.

Heath, S. (1996). *Ways with words: Language, life, and work in communities and classrooms.* New York: Cambridge University Press.

Heidegger, M. (1962). *Being and time.* (J. Macquarrie & E. Robinson, Trans.). New York: Harper & Row. (Original work published 1927)

Holt, J. (1983, 1967). *How children learn.* New York: Delacorte Press.

Hubbard, R., & Power, B. (1993). *The art of classroom inquiry.* Portsmouth, NH: Heinemann.

Hughes, L. (1940, 1964, 1994). *The big sea.* New York: Hill & Wang.

Humphreys, L. (1990). Hermeneutics. In W. E. Mills (Ed.), *The Mercer dictionary of the bible.* Macon, GA: Mercer University Press.

Hurston, Z. (1991). *Dust tracks on a road.* New York: HarperCollins. (Original work published 1942)

Jackson, P. (1968). *Life in classrooms.* New York: Holt, Reinhart, and Winston.

Josselson, R., & Lieblich, A. (1993). (Eds.) *The narrative study of lives.* Newbury Park, CA: Sage.

Junod, T. (1999). Can you say . . . "hero"? In P. Zaleski (Ed), *The best spiritual writing, 1999.* San Francisco: Harper.

Kamphouse, R. W., Huberty, C. J., DiStephano, C. D., & Petosky, M. D. (1997). A typology of teacher-rated child behavior for a national U.S. sample. *Journal of abnormal child psychology, 25*(6), pp. 453–463.

Kozol, J. (1991). *Savage inequalities.* New York: Crown.

Kozol, J. (1995). *Amazing grace.* New York: Crown.

Kreikemeier, S. (1993). *Come with me to Africa: A photographic journey.* New York: Western.

Labov, W. (1972). The transformation of experience in narrative syntax. In W. Labov (Ed.), *Language in the inner city: Studies in the Black English vernacular* (pp. 354–396). Newbury Park, CA: Sage.

LaRossa, R., & Reitzes, D. (1993). Symboblic interactionism and family studies. In P. Boss, W. Doherty, R. LaRossa, W. Schumm, & S. Steinmetz. (Eds.), *Sourcebook of family theories and methods: A contextual approach* (pp. 135–163). New York: Plenum Press.

LeCompte, M., & Preissle, J. (1993). *Ethnography and qualitative design in educational research* (2nd ed.). San Diego, CA: Academic Press.

MacIntyre, A. (1981). *After virtue.* Notre Dame, IN: Notre Dame University Press.

McInerney, P. (1991). *Time and experience.* Philadelphia: Temple University Press.

Marshall, J., Smagorinsky, P., & Smith, M. (1995). *The language of interpretation: Patterns of discourse in discussion of literature.* Urbana, IL: National Council of Teachers of English.

Martin, B. (1993). *Brown bear, brown bear, what do you see?* New York: Holt. (Original work published 1967)

Merleau-Ponty, M. (1964). *The primacy of perception.* Evanston, IL: Northwestern University Press.

Michaels, S. (1981). Listening and responding: Hearing the logic in children's classroom narratives. *Theory into Practice, 33*(3), 218–224.

Miller, P., & Mehler, R. (1994). The power of personal story telling in families and kindergartens. In A. Dyson and C. Genishi (Eds.), *Need for story: Cultural diversity in classroom and community.* Urbana, IL: National Council of Teachers of English.

Missildine, W. H. (1963). *Your inner child of the past.* New York: Simon & Schuster.

Murray, P. (1984). *Proud shoes.* New York: Harper & Row. (Original work published in 1956)

Nodleman, P. (1996). *The pleasures of children's literature* (2nd ed.). New York: Longman.

Ochberg, R. (1994). Life stories and storied lives. In A. Lieblich & R. Josselson (Eds.), *The narrative study of lives: Exploring idenity and gender* (Vol. 2) (pp. 113–144). Thousand Oaks, CA: Sage.

Paley, V. (1979, 1989). *White teacher.* Cambridge, MA: Harvard University Press.

Peshkin, A. (1978). *Growing up American.* Chicago: University of Chicago Press.

Piantanida, M., & Garman, N. (1999). *The qualitative dissertation: A guide for students and faculty.* Thousand Oaks, CA: Corwin Press.

Poe, E. (1907). Hymn. In J. M. Gambrill (Ed.), *Selections from Poe* (p. 16). Boston: Ginn and Company.

Polacco, P. (1989). *Uncle Vova's tree.* New York: Philomel.

Polacco, P. (1996). *The tree of the dancing goats.* New York: Simon & Schuster.

Polanyi, L. (1985). *Telling the American story: A structural and cultural analysis of conversational storytelling.* Norwood, NJ: Ablex.

Polkinghorne, D. (1988). *Narrative knowing and the human sciences.* Albany, NY: State University of New York Press.

Quinton, A. (1993). Spaces and times. In R. LePoidevin & M. MacBeth (Eds.), *The philosophy of time.* Oxford, Eng.: Oxford University Press.

Ricour, P. (1981). Narrative time. In W. Mitchell (Ed.), *On narrative* (pp. 165–186). Chicago: University of Chicago Press.

Ricour, P. (1984). *Time and narrative.* (K. McLaughlin & D. Pellauer, Trans.). Chicago: University of Chicago Press.

Riessman, C. (1993). *Narrative analysis.* Newbury Park, CA: Sage.

Ringgold, F. (1991). *Tar beach.* New York: Crown.

Romano, T. (1995). *Writing with passion: Life stories, multiple genres.* Portsmouth, NH: Boynton/Cook.

Rylant, C. (1982). *When I was young in the mountains.* New York: Dutton.

Schön, D. (1983). *The reflective practitioner: How professionals think in action.* New York: Basic Books.

Slife, B. (1993). *Time and psychological explanation.* Albany, NY: State University of New York Press.

Smith, D. (1991). Hermeneutic inquiry: The hermemeutic imagination and the pedagogic text. In E. C. Short (Ed.), *Forms of curriculum inquiry* (pp. 187–209). Albany, NY: State University of New York Press.

Smitherman, G. (1977). *Talkin' and testifyin': The language of Black America.* Boston: Houghton Mifflin.

Smitherman, G. (1981). "What go round come round": King in perspective. *Harvard Educational Review, 51*(1), 40–55.

Smitherman, G. (1994). "The blacker the berry, the sweeter the juice": African American student writers. In A. Dyson & C. Genishi (Eds.), *The need for story: Cultural diversity in classroom and community* (pp. 80–101). Urbana, IL: National Council of Teachers of English.

Sperling, M. (1994). Moments remembered, moments displayed: Narratization, metaphor, and the experience of teaching. *English Education, 26*(3), 142–155.

Swadner, B., & Lubeck, S. (Eds.). (1995). *Children and families "at promise."* Albany, NY: State University of New York Press.

Taxel, J. (1988). Children's literature: Ideology and response. *Curriculum Inquiry, 18*(2), 32–40.

Taylor, M. (1976). *Roll of thunder, hear my cry.* New York: Puffin.

Traubough, A. (1997). *Praise Jerusalem.* Grand Rapids, MI: Baker Books.

Vygotsky, L. (1986). *Thought and language.* (A. Kozulin, Ed. & Trans.). Cambridge, MA: MIT Press.

Ward, L. (1978). *I am eyes: Ni macho.* New York: Greenwillow Books.

Weatherhead, L. (1965). *The Christian agnostic.* New York: Abingdon Press.

Wells, R. (1997). *Divine secrets of the Ya-Ya-Sisterhood.* New York: HarperPerennial.

Wertsch, J. (1991). *Voices of the mind: A sociological approach to mediated action.* Cambridge, MA: Harvard University Press.

Widdershoven, G. (1993). The story of life: Hermeneutic perspectives on the relationship between narrative and life history. In A. Lieblich & R. Josselson (Eds.), *The narrative study of lives: Exploring idenity and gender* (Vol. 2) (pp. 113–144). Thousand Oaks, CA: Sage.

Williams, C. (1990). *Golimoto.* New York: Trumpet Book Club.

Williams, V. (1990). *"More more more," said the baby.* New York: Greenwillow.

Willis, G. (1999). [Review of the book *The new Augustine*]. *New York Review of Books, 44*(11), 44.

Wolcott, H. (1990). *Writing up qualitative research.* Newbury Park, CA: Sage.

Wright, R. (1944). *Black boy.* New York: Harper Collins.

SONGS AND RECORDINGS

Miller, S., & Scelsa, G. (1978). The world is a rainbow. On *We all live together* (Vol. 2) [Record]. Los Angeles: Little House Music.

Rodgers, R., & Hammerstein, O. (1945). You'll never walk alone. [Broadway play *Carousel*].

Schonberg, C. M., & Boublil, A. (1989). Bui Doi. On *Miss Saigon* [CD]. London: Geffen Records.

Valenti, D., & Cullen, B. (1967). Get together [performed by Jesse Colin Young]. On *Earth music* [Record]. Valenti, CA: RCA.

HYMNS

Matheson, G., & Peace, A. (1882). Oh love that wilt not let me go.

Scott, C. H. (1895). Open my eyes that I may see.

FOLKSONG

Loch Lomond. [Traditional Scottish folksong].

Index

ABOUT THE AUTHOR

Karen Hankins is a first-grade teacher in Athens, Georgia. She has taught for twenty-five years in primary and elementary grades in inner-city, rural, and urban schools.

In addition to her first graders she enjoys occasional college level teaching at both the University of Georgia and Piedmont College. Even more than writing, she enjoys public speaking, especially as it affords the opportunity to talk about schools and children.

She received her PhD in Language Education from the University of Georgia in 2000. Her research interest in narrative allows her to view all of life as research and all research as life. She and her husband live with varying influxes of children and pets within walking distance of relatives, church, school, and her writing mentor.

DATE DUE

DEMCO 38-296